# Contents

*Khm*

# Health

...cial
...nes

## Dr Anne Roberts

**ACE
BOOKS**

© 1995 Dr Anne Roberts MB, BS, MRCP
**Published by Age Concern England**
1268 London Road
London SW16 4ER

Editor Gillian Clarke
Design and typesetting Eugenie Dodd Typographics
Production Andrew Clifford
Copy preparation Vinnette Marshall
Printed and bound in Great Britain by Bell and Bain Ltd, Glasgow

A catalogue record for this book is available from the British Library.

ISBN 0–86242–156–X

# Foreword

This book was written as a result of an agreement between Age Concern England and the Department of Health about the need to provide sound, professionally based advice on the health care and social needs of older people in residential accommodation.

The last decade has witnessed enormous changes in the delivery of social care services. In particular we have seen the continuing growth of independent sector providers, both voluntary and private, alongside local authority homes, resulting in far greater diversity and choice of residential care being offered to users.

More recently, the implementation of the community care changes has provided the catalyst to open up a range of opportunities for older people. Older people are the largest group of users of residential accommodation and the new arrangements have given local authorities greater flexibility to tailor services to individuals, and to help ensure that users and their families are fully involved in the process. Where residential care is appropriate, local authorities can now offer a full range of homes from which the individual can choose.

It is very important that those involved in the running of homes, whether local authority or independent sector, have a sound basic knowledge and awareness of the health care needs and illnesses that most commonly occur during old age, and of the positive benefits of promoting health for older people. This book provides a comprehensive guide for managers of residential care homes and care staff on how to care for older people in residential settings, and includes a wealth of relevant information on health promotion, common illnesses, confusion, dementia and frailty, medicines, emergencies, terminal illness and bereavement, and help from other agencies. Each chapter and section are summarised in a helpful set of key points, making the contents more accessible.

I believe this book will prove to be a valuable resource for everyone involved in caring for older people.

**John Bowis**
*Parliamentary Under Secretary of State for the Department of Health*

# About the Author

Anne Roberts is a doctor specialising in geriatric medicine. Her main current interest is in teaching those who look after older people, especially wardens of sheltered housing, staff of residential homes, home care assistants and control centre operators. Her previous books include *A Warden's Guide to Health Care in Sheltered Housing* (Age Concern England), *Keeping Well – A Guide to Health in Retirement* (Faber & Faber), *Health and Illness in Sheltered Housing – A Case Study Approach* (Centre for Sheltered Housing Studies) and the health section in *The Time of Your Life* for Help the Aged. She has also written numerous articles on health-related topics, and produces a regular feature for *Nursing Times*.

Anne is on the Board of Management of Anchor Housing Association, is an almshouse trustee and advises many organisations connected with health and housing for older people. She lives in London with her child-psychiatrist husband and two sons.

## Acknowledgements

The author would like to thank:

- Gillian Clarke, Vinnette Marshall and the Publishing Department at Age Concern England for their continued help and patience
- Evelyn McEwen of Age Concern and staff at the Department of Health, who were kind enough to read the typescript
- her family, Eric, Thomas and Paul Taylor, for their understanding and support.

# How to Use the Book

Without bossiness or interference, it is possible for heads of Homes and their staff to influence residents' health. This book is designed to help you do this. For instance you can:

- Encourage a healthy lifestyle. Older people benefit from keeping physically and mentally active, from a sensible diet, from taking alcohol only in moderation, from giving up smoking, from taking care of their eyes, teeth and feet, and from using health checks sensibly. You will find information on all these topics in Chapter 2, on Good Health Promotion, and Chapter 3, on Essential Body Maintenance.

- Give basic information about illness and disability, as found in Chapter 4, on Common Illnesses. However, do not be afraid to admit ignorance, and refer the resident to a doctor or nurse when you are out of your depth.

- Make sure that frailer residents are as comfortable as they can be and enjoy the best possible quality of life. Physical disability is discussed in Chapter 5, and confusion, dementia and mental frailty in Chapter 6.

- Help residents to use their medicines to best effect, or administer their drugs safely when they are unable to take charge of these for themselves. Information to help you do this is in Chapters 7 and 8.

- Be competent in emergencies, and able to give truthful and calming reassurance when things look worse than they are. See Chapter 9 for further information on this topic.

- Support dying residents and their families, helping the residents to end their lives with dignity and minimal distress; you will find useful information in Chapter 10.

- Help your residents to use health and social services and mobilise these on their behalf when necessary (Chapter 11). Older people are often well able to put their own case forward, but some who are frail, unwell or less assertive by nature may find this difficult to do. They may then be glad of an advocate (see pp 19–21).

- Keep yourself up to date by attending training courses, and encourage your staff to do the same. You will also find regular background reading helpful and stimulating. The Further Reading and Useful Addresses sections are useful resources to draw on.

Every Home is unique; as you read the book and think about the topics discussed, you will need to modify the suggestions for action to fit in with the needs of your Home and its individual residents.

# 1 Introduction

Good health is not an end in itself, in old age or at any other time of life; it is the means of enjoying life in one's own way, for as long as possible. In promoting health and reducing the effects of illness among your residents, you and your staff can improve their lives in a way they well deserve.

## AGEING – NORMAL AND ABNORMAL

Bodies and minds change throughout life. Everyone can recognise the more obvious signs of ageing – grey or thinning hair, wrinkled skin, the need for reading glasses. These changes happen at different rates in different people: almost every 70 year old has grey hair, but so do some people of 40, and some men have less hair at 25 than others do at 75. Different parts of the body age at different rates: one person may have grey hair but be able to read the smallest print unaided, whereas someone else of the same age may still have brown hair but have needed reading glasses for some time.

How people look matters to them whatever their age, and the appearance of an older person affects the behaviour of those around them. However, other less noticeable ageing changes in the body have greater consequences. These, too, happen at different rates in different people; 'chronological age', how long a person has lived, is often a poor guide to their 'biological age', how well they function.

# IMPORTANT PHYSICAL AGEING CHANGES

## Difficulties with homoeostasis

'Homoeostasis' is the technical word for keeping the body physically and chemically the same. An older body is more difficult to keep warm and may become cold (hypothermic); water balance is more uncertain, with the risk of dehydration. The balance of body chemicals becomes shakier, so stomach upsets that disturb this balance can make an older person very ill.

## Poorer function of the body's control systems

In a healthy younger person who trips up a step, the brain rapidly registers that the body is tipping over and about to fall. It then alerts the right muscles to contract, so the person stumblingly regains their balance and does not hit the ground. In an older person this process takes longer, and this fault in 'postural control' makes it more likely that, having tripped, they will hit the ground and perhaps break a bone.

The immune system, an important body defence, also becomes less efficient with age. The body becomes less able to recognise and deal with hostile, 'non-self' threats such as bacteria and viruses, so older people are more likely to catch infections and become sicker from them. In the same way, malignant cells are less easily destroyed; this is why cancer becomes more common in later life. The body can also mistake its own 'friendly' tissues for hostile substances and react against them, leading to a so-called 'autoimmune disease'. Pernicious anaemia and some forms of thyroid disease happen in this way.

## Slowing down of basal metabolism

'Basal metabolism' is the rate at which the body burns up food at rest. This means that, as we get older, we need to reduce our food intake or we will put on weight.

## Changes in the make-up of the body

A larger proportion of body tissues is fat, and there is less 'lean body mass' (ie organs, bone and muscles). This has important effects.

As the body's organs shrink, they work less well. When an older person takes a medicine, it takes longer for the body's ageing liver and kidneys to get rid of it, and this is one reason why older people often suffer unwanted effects from drugs.

Osteoporosis makes older bones more fragile and easily broken than younger ones. This happens much faster in women than in men because the female hormone oestrogen is suddenly lacking after the menopause, whereas male hormone levels fall much more slowly as the years pass. Fractured hips are therefore seven or eight times more common in older women than in older men.

Muscles shrink from the age of 40 onwards, with a parallel decline in strength and stamina. This is not inevitable; though older athletes perform less well than younger ones, keeping active and mobile still strengthens older muscles and helps maintain independence. On the whole, disease and disuse are much greater threats to the quality of life than the effects of ageing.

# MENTAL AGEING CHANGES

Staff of residential homes often regard mental frailty as more disabling than physical frailty, and they are probably right. However, the great threats to mental function are illnesses such as dementia, depressive disorder and the effects of physical disease – not normal ageing; true ageing changes in psychological and mental function are comparatively unimportant. They are listed below.

## Lengthening of reaction time

From the 50s onwards, it takes the body longer to react to new events. This can be important in activities such as driving.

## Deterioration of recent memory

'Retrieval' – pulling out information from memory (such as a friend's name) – when under pressure is especially affected. Long-term memory – recall of events in the distant past – is less affected, but does not improve.

## Changes in problem-solving abilities

The ability to solve problems can vary widely between one older person and another. Repeated testing improves their performance because they still have the ability to learn. However, on the whole, older people may be easily distracted. They also tend to be more cautious, and being anxious not to make mistakes tends to slow them down.

## Improved conservation of time and energy

Older people tend to set sensible priorities and do not waste effort on inessentials.

## Continued ability to learn and use artistic talents

Both these can enrich the retirement years.

## Personality shows 'stable variability'

Older people tend to become exaggerated versions of their younger selves. Chronic worriers can become almost crippled by anxiety, constant complainers drain dry the sympathies of their family and friends, while warm and loving people reap the reward of their outward-looking and unselfish lives.

# AGEING IS NATURAL; ILLNESS ISN'T

Ill health and disability are very common among older people, but are not due to the effects of ageing alone. They happen because something has gone wrong, so there is a chance of putting things right. Physical, mental and social factors often act together to produce disability; someone's reluctance to go out, for instance, may result from a combination of problems such as arthritis, depression and lack of money.

Though sick older people can and do get better, they need prompt treatment to do so. This may be difficult if a serious illness seems undramatic; a heart attack, for instance, may be painless.

# AGEISM AND HEALTH

This section discusses why older people sometimes receive poorer health care than other groups.

## Too old for treatment?

Older people encounter 'ageism' in health care whenever they are discriminated against just because of the length of their lives. This is especially likely to happen when resources are short and when measures such as the 'QALY' are used. This 'quality adjusted life year' attempts to measure the benefits to health of different forms of treatment by calculating the length of 'good quality life' they give the patient, and such calculations inevitably put older people at a disadvantage.

It would not be sensible or kind to suggest that every form of treatment that is available to an old person should always be given. Older people are more likely to have complications after surgical operations, and more likely to suffer unwanted effects of medicines than are younger people. However, the test of whether a treatment is suitable for a patient of any age is whether its benefits outweigh its risks and unpleasant consequences; the balance often comes down in favour of treatment, even in very old people.

# How you can help

What can the manager and staff of a residential establishment do to counteract 'age discrimination' in health care? Mainly, you should make sure that residents are fully informed about the treatment options available and that, as far as they are able, they make their own choices as to what treatment they should have. Quality of life is as important as quantity at any age, and may become more so in later life. It is very difficult to decide whether somebody else's life has quality for them, however; whenever possible, the older person should be consulted and their views taken into account. When this is not practicable – perhaps because the person is too confused – past opinions and attitudes may give useful clues to what they would like done.

Sadly, there is often a good deal of 'ageism' in older people's own attitudes, though this is hardly surprising. Surrounded on all sides by media glorification of youth and by negative stereotypes of old age, it is a strong-minded older person who can retain enough self-esteem to be adequately assertive. Older people sometimes fall between the twin stools of 'not wanting to be a trouble', and over-compensating by being aggressive; either way they ruin their case. The philosophy of a residential home and the behaviour of its staff can do a great deal to build up the morale and self-esteem of its residents, and thus give them the confidence to voice their needs and be assertive in getting them satisfied.

Professionals such as doctors sometimes behave in an ageist way, and some are poorly informed about geriatric medicine. Though residents have every right to choose their own GP, those who need to choose a new one on entering a Home often ask staff for advice. It is obviously sensible for you to have done sufficient 'homework' to be able to recommend a doctor who is both knowledgeable about health and illness in old age and is sympathetic to the needs of older patients.

It is worth remembering that the exaggerated respect many older people show to doctors has its roots in experiences long ago. Many modern doctors do not crave god-like respect, and would much prefer an equal and honest relationship with their patients. Seemingly crass remarks like 'What do you expect at your age?' may sometimes be a cover for the doctor's all-too-human feelings of inadequacy in the face of rising numbers of older people and limited resources to help them. This is not to say that older people should allow themselves to be fobbed off with 'it's your age, dear'. It is a useful rule of thumb that the passage of years makes you old but not ill. In any case, even 'ageing changes' can sometimes be treated. A sensible and non-threatening response to 'What do you expect?' would be on the lines of 'I expect you to listen to my story, to try to find out what has gone wrong with me, to explain it to me as best you can and then do whatever you can to help, please. I don't expect to be 21 again, but I shall be most grateful for anything you can do to help.'

# THE ROLE OF STAFF IN HEALTH CARE

Older people in residential homes, like the rest of us, have a right to 'personal autonomy'. In other words, as far as their mental state permits, they should make their own decisions about their lives, as long as their behaviour does not interfere with other people's rights. Residents have a right to decide what sort of health care they want and how they want to receive it, though in practice shortage of resources may limit this right.

## Confidentiality

Health and illness are private matters, and people have a perfect right to keep these intimate details of their lives to themselves. However, it is good practice to ask new residents about their health, explaining that the information will help you care for them. It may be that, in order to get advice and help, they have to share this important information with someone else, such as a doctor or nurse. When they do this, the shared information still remains the private property of the individual concerned. Doctors and nurses get into serious trouble – and rightly so – if they fail to keep their patients' affairs strictly confidential.

As health care has become complex, more people need to know a patient's medical history. For instance, an elderly woman resident who goes into hospital to have her broken hip pinned will meet radiographers, physiotherapists, a social worker and possibly a dietician or pharmacist, as well as an assortment of doctors and nurses.

In the normal run of your daily work, you will often be unable to avoid learning some of your residents' medical secrets. You, too, will of course be expected to keep this information strictly confidential.

Some breaches of confidence are obvious and easily avoided: you are not likely to astonish the residents grouped in the lounge by blurting out, 'You'll never guess what the doctor says about Mrs Smith!' However, it is dangerously easy to break a confidence by accident, for instance by:

- Discussing a resident's health or medical problems within the hearing of others, whether in the Home or outside it; 'debriefing' to colleagues can be very therapeutic, but must be done discreetly.
- Forgetting to shut the door when making a private phone call concerning a resident.
- Leaving a memo on a pad where it can be read by a casual eye.
- Omitting to make sure that medical articles such as parcels of incontinence pads are given to their recipients in private.

## Health records

GPs sometimes like to keep residents' NHS health records at the Home. These are confidential documents, and should not be made available to staff. The doctor and the head of the Home should arrange for these records to be kept safely locked away.

Residents, or someone acting on their behalf if they are mentally impaired, have a right to see these records and to ask for any mistakes in them to be corrected. If someone asks to do this, you should refer them to the GP. This is because it will help to have someone on hand to explain any puzzling or potentially worrying entries. Indeed, access to medical records can legally be denied if it is thought that the information in them could harm the patient's physical or mental health.

You will also want to keep your own health records. Residents who are physically and mentally fit have every right to keep their entire health history to themselves. They can look after their own medicines and see their doctors or attend hospital clinics without telling you the outcome or even letting you know that the visit has taken place. If they do this, however, they must take the consequences: you and your staff would not be held responsible for taking a wrong course of action in an emergency when your mistake was a result of inadequate information. If you are in doubt about a reticent resident's mental competence, check with the GP and make sure you have noted your misgivings in writing.

It can sometimes be in a resident's best interests for you to have current and relevant information about their health. For instance, if you know that a resident with diabetes is prone to 'hypo' attacks (see p 224), you can give sugar quickly and prevent the risk of serious complications that could occur if precious time were lost. One way to gather a few important health facts is to say to the new resident, 'Is there anything I ought to know about your health so I can help you if you are taken ill? Anything you tell me stays strictly confidential, of course.' The same question can be asked of the relatives, and the answers noted. Records should be compiled in consultation with the resident, who should know that they can see their file and read the contents at any time. These records, too, should be kept safely locked away.

## Respecting health choices

Caring for people often involves striking a precarious balance. On the one hand, people have a right to run their lives as they wish within certain limits, and to take risks if by doing so they will improve their quality of life. On the other hand, people who are unable to make sensible decisions for themselves have a right to be protected from the results of their ill-judged actions. A further problem is that no one lives in isolation, and in the close quarters of a residential home one resident's choice – to smoke, for instance – can affect other people's lives. Whilst residents may choose to take risks on their own account, they cannot be allowed to endanger other people. In this area of work there are no set rules or easy answers, but it can help to explore the difficulties and discuss possible approaches to them.

Age alone does not destroy judgement skills. Older people who are mentally intact have a right to be wrong and to take the consequences of their unwise decisions just as other adults do. For instance, you do not and should not have the power to stop residents from drinking more than is good for them; older people should not have to suffer interference from other people who think they know best just because they are younger.

## When to intervene

However, illness may cloud thought and judgement. When a woman with dementia wants to go out into a freezing winter night wearing only her nightdress to meet imaginary children from school, it would obviously be foolish to do nothing about it. This does not mean that mentally frail people have no rights over their own lives. Many are capable of expressing preferences as to where and how they live. Every effort should be made to find out what they want and to respect their wishes as far as possible.

## Use of advocacy

When residents, especially mentally frail ones, find it difficult to make their choices clear and to speak up for themselves, they may need someone to do this for them. A staff member who knows the resident well may be able to do this, but sometimes will be too close to the situation to think clearly. An outsider may be most helpful here, and it is worth finding out from the Citizens Advice Bureau or local branch of Age Concern whether an advocacy scheme operates locally.

# When a resident refuses help

It can be very difficult to decide at what point concerned help becomes interference. You may find this especially worrying when a resident who appears to be unwell refuses to see the doctor. This often seems to happen at night, when you have little but your own judgement to depend on.

## Finding the reason for refusal

It is often useful to try to find out why the resident is refusing medical help. Some such people do not like doctors or the medicine they practise, and prefer to rely on their own resources, whatever the consequences; this is obviously a choice they are entitled to make. Others have not had adequate explanations of their illnesses and treatment in the past. Some are depressed, and because of their illness feel unworthy to receive any sort of treatment, whilst some have a physical illness causing mental confusion that will disappear once the illness is treated. Others fear that, if they admit to a need for any sort of help, their lives will be taken over by well-meaning bullies who will force them to do things they do not want to 'for their own good'.

A staff member who is trusted enough to act on the resident's behalf can be very useful, often in places or at times when no other sort of advocacy is available. For instance, you can politely persist in asking questions of doctors until the resident has enough information to make a decision, and you can support the resident in resisting undue pressure to accept unwanted treatment or to go into hospital.

## Too sick to decide?

Deciding what to do when the resident who is refusing help seems confused or mentally ill is especially worrying. It can be difficult for an experienced specialist in old age psychiatry to diagnose depression or to discover the cause of a confusional state, so it is obviously unreasonable to expect someone to do this without the benefit of training or the back-up of hospital facilities. Also, a head of Home whose sick or confused resident got worse and died without seeing a doctor would be likely to find it difficult to defend the failure to summon help. The best – or perhaps the least bad – course is to call the doctor so as to get an expert opinion on the resident's mental state. Once this is done, you can still act as resident's advocate when decisions have to be made as to what happens next.

# RESIDENTS FROM ETHNIC MINORITY GROUPS

Your advocacy role is especially important if in your Home there are residents from ethnic minority groups: here a staff member may have to act as a translator and also explain the special cultural requirements of the residents to those who provide their health care. You may well know more about the way of life of your ethnic minority residents than do visiting professionals such as doctors and nurses. People from all groups vary in how strictly they follow cultural customs or religious practices, so you may need to make tactful enquiries as to what foods a particular person finds unacceptable, for instance. Older people from ethnic minority communities, especially those with language difficulties, may agree with what a doctor or other 'authority figure' says, out of politeness and respect. They may do this even when the advice is culturally unacceptable or when they do not understand what is said. It will be very helpful if you can clarify matters in these sensitive circumstances.

Older people from ethnic minorities prefer to consult doctors and pharmacists who share their language and culture, but may not know how to go about finding them; you may be able to help with this. Careful spoken instructions that the older listener can understand are particularly important for the resident who cannot read.

# OLD AGE ABUSE

Sadly, vulnerable people like your residents can be abused in Homes just as they can be in other places. The most obvious forms are physical violence or verbal abuse but other types include financial exploitation, sexual activity without consent, tying someone to a bed, chair or commode or restraining them with drugs that have not been prescribed for them or that are used inappropriately. You should always encourage doctors and district nurses to see residents alone if they ask for this: a private interview can give an opportunity for a frightened resident to disclose abuse to an 'outsider' without the fear of retribution. On the other hand, be aware that a resident who is frightened of an abusing relative may ask you or a member of staff to stay with them when the relative visits.

## Some points to remember

- Make sure that you and your staff talk to your residents as equals worthy of respect. For instance, do not presume you are on first name terms with a new resident but ask them how they wish to be addressed.
- Be on the lookout for signs of physical abuse such as bruises, cuts or burns that are said to be the result of repeated accidents

or to be self-inflicted; unconvincing explanations should arouse your suspicions.

■ Train yourself to notice how your residents react to different members of staff; abused residents are likely to be nervous or even fearful when the abuser comes near, or to strike out to forestall an anticipated attack.

■ Note your residents' appearance and reactions upon returning from visits or outings. An old and frail 'fallen tyrant' who has been abusive and violent themselves is especially vulnerable to retaliation from previous victims.

■ Be aware of the possibility of sexual abuse: look for signs such as pain or injury in the genital area, blood stains or a discharge on underclothes or discomfort on walking or sitting. Whilst older people have a right to fulfilling personal and sexual relationships, they should also be protected from exploitation.

■ When someone else manages a resident's money, you should note whether this is spent on their day-to-day needs or perhaps is being fraudulently taken for another purpose.

■ If you suspect that a resident is being abused, you should get in touch with the GP or the social services department, who should have a procedure for dealing with such situations. The abused person should be encouraged to make a complaint if they are able to do so; if not, it may be possible to appoint an advocate to act on their behalf.

## KEY POINTS

■ Ageing is natural; illness isn't.

■ Ageing makes older people more likely to get infections, to fall over and to become dehydrated or cold in bad conditions.

■ Despite some mental slowing, older people should still be able to enjoy running their own lives.

- Older people who seem unwell or are mentally confused or low in spirit may need medical help.

- You should respect residents' rights to make their own choices (autonomy) and to keep their own secrets (confidentiality).

- An advocacy scheme may be valuable.

- Remember that people from different cultures may have different customs and needs.

- Be aware that the unthinkable can happen, and be alert for signs of physical or emotional abuse.

# 2 Good Health Promotion

How healthy we are depends on two factors: heredity, the qualities our parents have handed on to us, and environment, our life circumstances. Though we cannot change our parentage, the lifestyle we adopt can improve our health, even in later life. This chapter describes some ways that may be appropriate for your residents.

## KEEPING ACTIVE – USE IT OR LOSE IT

### Walking for choice

Walking without help is important for residents, as it gives them independence: they can choose when they want to go to the lavatory, into the garden or back to their room. Try to encourage your residents to get up and walk without assistance, even when you are busy and it is tempting to use a wheelchair. In the long run, staff time is saved if residents stay as independent as possible.

Anyone who is fit enough to go out alone should be encouraged to do so, even when there is a small element of danger. Residents who need help to get about may still be able to visit their church, the concert hall, meeting or theatre if they are taken by car. Willing relatives and friends do not always volunteer; they sometimes have a vague feeling that outings are frowned on or not allowed. This usually has nothing to do with you or the Home, but dates back to times in which institutions such as hospitals had strictly enforced visiting times for the convenience of staff. If you think a resident would like to go out in this way, you could try mentioning it to the family. Where there are no willing relatives, you may like to explore the possibility of finding a local volunteer.

## Encouraging activities in the Home

It is often possible for residents to continue with their previous interests after moving into a Home. Raised flower beds bring outdoor gardening within the reach of someone in a wheelchair, and a housebound gardener can care for indoor plants. Grouped living gives opportunities for independent kitchen work such as preparing breakfast and hot drinks. Craft work should be encouraged even when it leads to clutter and mess.

Even frail people benefit in strength, suppleness and stamina from performing suitable exercises. EXTEND (Exercise Training for the Elderly and Disabled) is an organisation whose classes are done to music and are so designed that even chairbound people can join in. If you do not already have exercise sessions in your Home, you or one of your staff might consider becoming an instructor; find out more from the address on page 269.

Commercial firms such as Winslow (address on p 271) produce equipment for indoor activities like carpet bowls and indoor skittles which have social as well as physical benefit. Various books, videos and audio tapes on this subject might make a stimulating addition to your library.

## An active brain

Mental stimulation is especially important for mentally unimpaired residents, who can feel very lonely if most of their companions are less alert. If prospective residents enjoy arts and crafts, encourage them to bring their equipment with them; they may otherwise dispose of it, thinking wrongly that such activities are 'not allowed'.

What else to try? Among much resource material, Winslow produce a practical guide to developing an activities programme. Large-print playing cards and crosswords are especially useful for people with poor sight, and extra-large dominoes, jigsaws and noughts and crosses enable people who have difficulty using their hands to rediscover a favourite game.

Faith Gibson's book *Reminiscence and Recall* and the organisation Age Exchange are two valuable resources (see pp 279 and 267).

Many people with dementing illnesses will enjoy activities that improve their self-esteem and alertness while relieving boredom and frustration. The secret of success is to find interesting occupations within existing abilities, avoiding the risk of failure. People with dementia find it difficult to make choices or decisions, to learn new material or to concentrate for any length of time, so activities that need these abilities are best avoided.

Success is most likely with a simplified version of a long-familiar task. For instance, a lifelong cook may be able to prepare a simple recipe with supervision, or to cream fat and sugar for a cake. Social visits from children and pets can give great pleasure, but a discreet eye should be kept to ensure no participant becomes over-tired or distressed. Outdoor exercise such as walking in a park relieves monotony and may also promote a good night's sleep. Music is often popular, and it is worth experimenting with different sorts, not just endless 'singalongs' of old favourites. Specially designed articles such as adult colouring books may be popular. Many other ideas can be found in Carmel Sheridan's book, *Failure-free Activities for the Alzheimer's Patient* (see Further Reading).

It is important not to let residents from other backgrounds feel left out of an activities programme. Do not feel embarrassed at asking for ideas – from residents themselves, from their relatives or from the appropriate community leaders. Food may break down barriers: ethnic food evenings or meals can provide a welcome diversion. Ethnic elders may also have a lot to contribute to reminiscence sessions, or be prepared to demonstrate skills such as the use of chopsticks or how to put on a sari. Remember that in some groups men and women separate for social activities, and be prepared to accommodate this.

Activities should not be confined within the Home; not only should residents continue with outside interests where possible, but also people from outside should come into the Home. In some areas, volunteers from schools visit Homes regularly, and from time to time escort residents to school plays or concerts. Teenagers and older people tend to have stereotyped attitudes to each other; these can often be broken down by closer contact, with mutual benefit.

Residents must of course be allowed to choose whether or not to participate in what is going on. The suggestion of 'coming along to watch' may be a way of encouraging a previously reluctant bystander to join in. However, no one should be harried or unduly pressured if they prefer solitude and quiet.

Hard-pressed staff are often defensive, and in this state it is easy to see suggestions for new activities as implied criticism. Try to relax and listen carefully before turning down a new idea, and if necessary allow yourself time to think about it.

Tolerance of apparent 'failure' is also necessary; it is natural that some new activities will be of little interest, whereas others will be popular for a time before enthusiasm wanes. Trying new things livens a Home's atmosphere, providing interest and a talking point, and this is worthwhile in itself.

# SAFETY IN THE HOME

It is important to remember that older people are not hell-bent on self-destruction: in fact, with age we tend to slow down and become more cautious in our ways. People who have been making decisions for themselves and others all their lives should, as far as possible, go on doing so when they enter residential homes. The risks of over-protection are sometimes under-estimated, while those of normal life are over-emphasised: accident forms are filled in whenever someone falls, while gross and dangerous restrictions such as over-sedation and physical restraint go unnoticed. Well meant over-control by kindly but mistaken staff can make it more likely that the resident will develop the common, dangerous and life-poisoning illness of depression.

Staff can 'cover themselves' against criticism by making sure relatives know the Home's policy. When thinking about the design and running of the Home, the important thing is to distinguish the risks that are life-enhancing from the ones that are simply dangerous. For instance, keeping a cat provides interest, comfort and an outlet for love that are well worth the small risk of a resident tripping over it. On the other hand, a rucked-up carpet is a trip hazard that does no one any good.

## Safety regulations

The environmental health department will have inspected your Home, and regular checks will be made on working equipment such as lifts and on food handling practices. The Home will also need to comply with electricity and fire regulations. See ACE's publication, *Good Care Management* for further details.

## Designing for secure independence

The design of a Home and its fixtures and fittings should encourage independence; the practical advice of a physiotherapist and/or occupational therapist may be very useful here, as with residents' individual difficulties; residents of Homes are entitled to these NHS services. When someone seems to need help from a carer, try to think of ways of enabling them to manage for themselves – for instance, an appropriate, correctly used walking aid can replace a supporting arm. The rubber tips (ferrules) of walking sticks, tripods and frames are unsafe when worn down; find out where you can get new ones, and, if possible, keep a small stock so that worn ones can be replaced promptly.

Passages should have handrails down both sides, as of course should steps and staircases. Help residents to keep their dignity and privacy in personal hygiene by modifying baths and lavatories for independence; consider both correctly placed, easy to grip rails and handholds, and special equipment such as hoists and Parker baths. Raised lavatory seats are very useful for people who have arthritic hips or knees. Rails that hinge down from the wall give security during use to people who feel unsteady; they can then be folded up out of the way of residents in wheelchairs who need extra room for transferring. Do not forget the need to reach the toilet paper: people with only one useful hand (after a stroke, for instance) may need a supply on their accessible side; both they and people with a weak grip may find interleaved sheets easier to manage than a roll.

Floors should be non-slip, and should also look as if they are or residents will be nervous of walking on them. Changes in floor texture, indoors and out, can be a helpful guide to people with a visual handicap that a change of level or similar hazard is imminent. A ramp with a rail is always safer than steps; unavoidable steps should be made clearly visible, with a vivid contrast strip. Good lighting without glare reduces danger for partially sighted people and sharp contrast between light and dark features can help orientation: use this to distinguish between doors and their handles and to tell apart doors, walls and floors. Loop systems help hearing-impaired people (see p 143).

If grouped living allows residents a chance to do some of their own kitchen work, provide necessary equipment such as safe step stools, kitchen gadgetry that is easy to use and plenty of materials to mop up spilt liquids; then allow residents freedom of action.

Suitable chairs improve safety and help independence if residents can rise from them unaided. Both dining and sitting room chairs should have arms. The best height from ground to seat is 18–20 inches, with a few at 22 inches for the stiff hipped or tall, and at 16 inches for shorter residents. Low chairs with backward-sloping seats are difficult to get out of and should not be bought.

## Safe transferring

Residents can be taught safe techniques for sitting down and rising from a chair; a session with a physiotherapist can be useful here.

**Sitting down:** Approach the chair and turn round so that the backs of your legs are against the seat; then feel behind you for the chair arms and grasp them with both hands. Lean forward, still holding the arms, and gradually lower your bottom to sit gently on the chair.

**Getting up:** Wriggle to the edge of the chair and bring your feet back beneath it as far as possible. (The knees should be bent to an acute angle.) Place both hands on the chair arms and lean well forward. Then push down on the chair arms and, still leaning forward, stand up.

You could teach these skills to care staff, so that they can encourage residents to use them all the time. Try to discourage anyone from routinely 'helping' people out of their chairs and moving them about in wheelchairs 'to save time'; independence is best for the resident and, in the long run, saves staff time too.

Beds should be firm and about 18–20 inches off the floor, slightly higher than modern divans. If there are rugs beside them, make sure they are fixed and cannot skate away on a smooth floor, taking the resident with them. Again, safe ways of changing position can be learned.

**Sitting on a bed:** Approach the bed around its middle, turn round with your back to it and get up against it until you can feel its edge behind your knees. Lean forward and feel for the edges with both hands, then gently lower yourself to sit on it.

**Getting into bed:** Sit halfway along it and turn on your bottom so that you face the foot of the bed. Then swing your legs up on to the bed while swinging your body backwards as a counterpoise. (This needs to be done quickly and requires confidence; until this is acquired, it may help to have a non-interfering carer standing beside the bed.)

**Getting out of bed:** Roll on to your side towards the edge, swing your legs over the side and use your hands to push yourself up and away, just as if you were getting out of a chair.

## Safe shoes

Footwear can help safety: slippers and soft shoes are unstable in walking, give no support and encourage a shuffling gait. Residents of course have a right of choice here, but try to encourage the wearing of good, well-fitting shoes, perhaps by providing opportunities to buy them. The best shoes are high cut and fasten firmly with laces, Velcro or a buckle. They are made of leather and have a low, wide stacked heel. A good fit is important: in general, feet broaden as the years pass. Some irreversibly incontinent people may need washable shoes, but in general such soft shoes are inappropriate. People with swollen feet should be advised to see the doctor, and those with overgrown toenails or painful corns and callouses may be more mobile after chiropody. Surgical shoes or special 'space shoes', fitting the feet in three dimensions, are available for those with special needs.

## Smoking and fire safety

As part of your fire precautions you may want to keep a check on residents who smoke. Make sure there are plenty of ashtrays in smoking areas, and check that all smoking materials are quenched at night. People who smoke in bed, who over-indulge in alcohol or are mentally confused may need someone with them when they smoke.

Having taken sensible precautions, try not to become so obsessed by safety that you forget that a life with any quality or enjoyment to it must have some risks attached. Our lives are much safer now than when the residents were born, grew up and raised families; many of them have faced far more danger in their lives than we ever will.

# FOOD AND NUTRITION

Residents of Homes may look forward to meal times as landmarks in the day. Any change in menu or working methods is likely to prove a talking point, with strong opinions being expressed. Food and eating are of great symbolic importance, and can often evoke feelings out of all proportion to the plain facts of the case.

A good diet is important for health and well-being in later life as at other times. Such a diet contains sufficient energy and adequate nutrients. Energy requirements decrease with age, until by 80 years old a person requires less than three-quarters of what they needed at the age of 30; often appetite decreases in proportion. However, nutrient requirements are unaltered through the years, and this means that the same amount of nourishment must be contained in a smaller volume of food. There is thus less space to waste on foods that contain 'empty' calories but no nutrients; these include the refined carbohydrates in biscuits, cakes and sweets.

Although residents should be allowed as much choice as possible in what they eat, it is usually feasible to evolve a nutritionally adequate diet that will suit most tastes. The basic knowledge of nutrition you need for this is set out below.

## Proteins

**Found in** red meat, chicken, fish, milk, cheese, eggs, vegetable pulses such as peas, beans and lentils.

**Needed for** body growth, maintenance and repair.

**Daily amount** two portions; more after an operation, illness or poor nutrition.

## Carbohydrates – unrefined

**Found in** wholemeal bread, wholegrain cereals, brown rice and pasta and jacket potatoes.

**Needed for** energy, warmth, fibre and vegetable protein.

**Daily amount** should form the basis of the diet, eaten at every meal.

## Carbohydrates – refined

**Found in** sugar and white flour.

**Needed** occasionally as an energy source (eg glucose drinks in convalescence); contain only 'empty calories'.

**Daily amount** usually small; eat sparingly to avoid weight gain.

## Fats

**Found in:** oily fish, butter, margarine and cheese.

**Needed for** fat-soluble vitamins D, A and K.

**Daily amount** variable but usually small. Large amounts cause weight gain, and animal ('saturated') fats are linked with heart disease. However, frail older people may need fat to provide adequate calories (see pp 35 and 37).

## Vitamins

These are widely found in food and, though essential, only very small amounts are needed. Healthy people eating a balanced, varied diet do not require supplements, though some sick people may do so. Excess vitamins in tablets or unusual diets are usually unnecessary, and may be harmful; people who are unsure should ask their doctor.

### Vitamin A

**Found in** liver, carrots, other vegetables and dairy produce.

**Extra needed by** people with some stomach and bowel diseases. It is dangerous in excess.

## Vitamin B group

**Found in**  most foods.

**Extra needed**  vitamin $B_1$ (thiamine) by people who abuse alcohol or eat little unprocessed food. Vitamin $B_{12}$ is needed by people with pernicious anaemia; they cannot absorb $B_{12}$ taken by mouth and need injections of it instead, as do strict vegetarians (vegans) whose diet lacks $B_{12}$. Excess vitamin $B_6$ (pyridoxine) can cause nerve damage and can interfere with treatment for Parkinson's disease.

## Vitamin C

**Found in**  fresh fruit and vegetables; cannot be stored in the body.

**Extra needed by**  people with iron-deficiency anaemia – vitamin C helps the body to absorb iron; people recovering from injuries or operations – helps healing; smokers. Large doses cause diarrhoea and kidney stones.

## Vitamin D

**Found in**  oily fish (eg sardines and pilchards), fortified margarine, eggs and liver; manufactured in human skin in sunlight.

**Needed to**  prevent ageing bones from becoming brittle and breaking easily.

**Extra needed by**  housebound people, and those who absorb it poorly or are taking some drugs for epilepsy. Older people from the Indian subcontinent lack vitamin D because of a combination of genetic factors, lack of sunlight and dietary factors. Your advice should respect dietary customs: seek help from an Asian community leader if necessary.

## Vitamin K

**Found in**  most food.

**Needed for**  normal blood clotting.

**Extra needed by**  people with some stomach or bowel diseases or who have been taking some anti-coagulant drugs, especially before surgery.

## Minerals

### Iron

**Found in**  meat, especially offal, eggs and dairy foods.

**Needed for**  red blood cells.

**Extra needed**  after blood loss or if the diet is poor.

### Calcium

**Found in**  dairy produce.

**Needed to**  prevent the bones from becoming brittle.

**Required**  half a pint of milk a day and half a pound of cheese a week. Low-fat products contain as much calcium as full-fat varieties. People who cannot take dairy products may be prescribed calcium tablets by the doctor; excess may damage the kidneys.

## Emphasising the essentials

These are easy to remember as they all begin with the letter F.

### Fruit and vegetables

These are important sources of vitamin C, one of the vitamins that people in long-term care sometimes lack. It is extremely difficult to prepare, cook and serve vegetables on a large scale without losing vitamin C. Fresh fruit is a good source, especially citrus fruits (eg oranges) and blackcurrants. Rose hip and blackcurrant syrups are sweeter sources.

### Fluids

These are very important for older people, who should drink at least 3 pints (1.7 litres) daily and more if possible. In hot weather when water loss as perspiration is increased, 5 pints (3 litres) may be nearer the mark. It may help to measure this amount into cups and glasses to make the quantity obvious. The best simple guide as to whether a person is drinking enough is the colour of urine. Except for first thing in the morning, urine should be pale; perhaps the best way to explain this is 'more like a glass of ready-to-drink lime juice than a glass of orangeade'.

Frail or convalescent residents may become dehydrated, with poor kidney function and a tendency to clotting disorders. Such people should be encouraged to drink more. It helps to explain the health reasons behind your concern, to find out what cold drink they prefer and to ask exactly how they like their tea; fluids to their normal taste are more likely to be drunk. No one who fears a urinary 'accident' will be persuaded to drink more; incontinence must be investigated and treated first (see pp 124–134).

## Fibre

This helps to prevent constipation, and perhaps 'western world' diseases such as diverticular disease, bowel cancer and heart and blood vessel diseases. Also, the increased bulk of the high-fibre diet produces a feeling of fullness, and makes it easier to avoid over-eating. Fibre-rich foods include cereals, pasta and vegetables – especially pulses and potatoes. Wholemeal bread contains more fibre than white bread, but some older people do not enjoy it; these can eat the white bread they prefer and get sufficient fibre from other sources.

## Fat – a commonsense approach

Foods such as butter and margarine, fatty meat, chicken skin, sausages, whole milk and full-fat dairy produce all contain many calories. People who are watching their weight would be wise to eat them sparingly.

It is worth remembering that we all need *some* fat in our diet, as a few people eat so little fat that they run short of fat-soluble vitamins A, D and K. Very frail older people with tiny appetites may need fatty food rich in calories to give them sufficient food energy in a small volume. Not everyone, therefore, should 'eat less fat'.

## Fractures – eating to avoid them

Adequate calcium and vitamin D help to keep bones strong in later life. Half a pint of milk a day, skimmed or semi-skimmed if preferred, and half a pound of cheese a week or the equivalent in other dairy produce give enough calcium. Some vitamin D can be made in skin exposed to sunlight during the summer months, but a dietary boost is often needed. A weekly or twice weekly portion of oily fish such as herring, mackerel, pilchards, sardines, tuna or tinned salmon will provide this. However, people who are housebound or who have difficulty in absorbing fats may need a supplement. The doctor should be asked to prescribe this if necessary, as too much vitamin D can be harmful.

## Fun – what food should be

It is important not to get too earnest about the 'correct' diet, as in fact there is no such thing. There are no compulsory foods, and it is almost always possible to find an eating pattern that fulfils dietary requirements and is still enjoyable in the long term. It is also important to remember that it is the regular eating pattern that counts; the occasional cream tea or fried breakfast will not affect health, and may make it easier to eat sensibly for the rest of the time.

# Essentials of food safety

The environmental health department will make sure that the food handling in your Home conforms to the requirements of the 1990 Food Safety Act. The important principles of food hygiene are listed below.

- Before preparing food, wash hands thoroughly – especially after using the lavatory.

- Cool hot food quickly, and store it in the cold. Remember that low temperatures prevent bacteria from multiplying, as all organisms, whether human or bacterial, are more likely to reproduce when comfortably warm.

- Buy food that will be eaten cold, such as pork pie or cooked ham, from a reliable shop where food is properly stored.

- Keep raw food that may contain salmonella germs (eg raw meat and poultry) separate from cooked food, to prevent contamination. Put raw meat on the lowest shelf of the refrigerator, so it cannot drip on to other food.

- Cook food such as poultry well, as this kills salmonella germs. Large turkeys must be cooked thoroughly, and frozen ones must thaw completely before cooking.

- Store leftovers in the cold, and reheat them rapidly to boiling temperature to kill any germs – just 'warming up' will multiply bacteria.

- Do not eat food that is past its best because you want to save money, and keep to the 'use by' dates on food packaging. Food that makes a person ill is a waste of money.

# Making food interesting

Try to ensure that the menu has variety and that meal times are appropriate. Consult your residents and take note of their views as far as possible. They may, for instance, prefer to serve themselves a simple breakfast of cereal and toast, rather than to be restricted to a single time for a cooked English breakfast. The evening meal should not be too early, and snack foods should be available during the evening for people who get hungry.

A reminiscence session can be a good opportunity to gather new ideas for the menu; a favourite recipe can be named for its contributor.

# Special cases and difficulties with eating

## Elders from ethnic minorities

Whatever a resident's religious or cultural requirements, it is usually possible to plan an acceptable but still healthy diet. When in doubt, you may wish to consult the dietician and the appropriate community leaders.

Some groups are especially likely to develop nutritional deficiencies. Strict vegetarians (vegans), who eat no animal produce, need vitamin $B_{12}$ supplements and extra calcium. Older people from the Indian subcontinent may require vitamin D tablets (see p 33).

## The resident who won't eat or is losing weight

Small fluctuations in weight are common: most of us expect to put on a few pounds over Christmas or a holiday, or to lose a little if we have 'flu or go through an anxious time. Normally the situation rights itself as things get back to normal. However, an unexplained weight loss, whether sudden or gradual, is not normal and should not be ignored. It can be a sign of an illness such as cancer, thyroid disease, heart disease, an infection, depressive illness or dementia, or occur as the unwanted effect of some medicines. Prompt medical attention is needed to identify the cause; try to persuade the resident to see their doctor so this may be done.

If no illness is found, or when everything possible has been put right, a poor appetite may need tempting. It may be difficult to cram the necessary nutrients into a small enough volume for the frail resident to eat. A small amount of a favourite alcoholic drink before a meal may stimulate appetite, and will also provide a few extra calories. Small portions of favourite foods should then be served attractively in an easy to eat form. The doctor, nurse or dietician will be able to suggest useful calorie-rich food supplements, or to provide further advice.

## Residents who are overweight

Being overweight in later life not only worsens health but also reduces the quality of life. People who are too heavy have difficulty getting about; this threatens their independence and increases their risk of incontinence. Intertrigo is another common complaint, with soreness and rashes beneath the breasts and in the groin.

When overweight residents are willing to lose weight, they should be encouraged to do so in the following ways.

- Reducing food intake: a person loses weight only if they burn up more energy than they take in.
- Avoiding 'empty' calories in the refined carbohydrate of cakes, biscuits and sweets and in alcohol. Fat intake should be reduced, while fruit and vegetables can be eaten freely. Wholemeal bread and jacket potatoes without large amounts of sugary or fatty toppings are filling without being fattening. A hot, unsweetened cup of tea or coffee with skimmed milk will often quieten a complaining stomach.
- Getting support from family and friends; for instance, they could be encouraged to bring fruit rather than chocolates as presents.
- Keeping to a long-term healthy eating programme; crash diets are ineffective and may be unsafe.
- Remembering that permanent weight loss is slow: 2–4 lb in the first week and 1–2 lb thereafter is grounds for satisfaction. It may be particularly helpful if a nurse or health visitor is available to weigh, advise and motivate the resident.

## Residents who eat unhealthily

It is sometimes difficult to find a balance between respecting residents' personal choice and caring for them responsibly. When someone is eating unhealthily, the best guide to action is the severity of the problem. A resident who scoffs at 'healthy eating' while washing down their dripping toast with heavily sweetened tea can be left to do so provided they seem in good health. Things are more difficult when the person ignoring advice is seriously overweight or has diabetes, when unwise eating can lead to severe health problems. In these circumstances you should not keep the problem to yourself. Discuss it with the doctor in the first instance, after telling the resident you mean to do so. You may also want to consider talking with the relatives so you can agree on a course of action. It is especially difficult to decide what to do when a resident asks staff or visitors to bring in 'forbidden' foods. This has to be decided in each case on its merits.

## Residents who find eating difficult

Many modified utensils are available to help people whose disabilities make eating and drinking difficult. The occupational therapist can advise about this, or you could visit a Disabled Living Centre or send for a catalogue of useful equipment. Useful articles include cutlery with fat, easily grasped handles, 'Nelson' knives for one-handed use, easily grasped or extra-stable cups, clip-on rims for plates, and plates with a reservoir for hot water to keep a slow eater's meal warm enough to be palatable. It is also worth making sure that a poor eater's dentures are a good fit and that their mouth is not sore: a visit to the dentist may be a good idea.

## People with unpleasant eating habits

Residents with physical disabilities and those whose social skills have been destroyed by dementia may eat in a way that other residents find distressing. It is very difficult to balance everyone's rights with sensitivity and understanding, but it is foolish to pretend the problem is not there, or to ignore it in the hope it will go away.

One approach is to give residents with distressing habits a table to themselves, or to serve their meals in their own rooms. However, this reduces social contact and should be regarded as a last resort. Alternatively, they can eat their main course and pudding in the dining room before the rest of the residents arrive; they can then feel part of the company for the rest of meal time by joining in with a biscuit or drink.

# CHANGING SLEEP PATTERNS

The pattern of normal sleep becomes more restless and broken with increasing age. Older people may wake several times during the night, perhaps fully enough to remember afterwards that they have done so, and may wrongly believe that they never closed their eyes all night. At all ages there is a great variation in the amount of sleep that people require; it is a mistake to think that eight hours are necessary for health or that mild sleep loss is in any way harmful.

The changed sleep pattern in later life includes a tendency to sleep more in the day time. Many fit older people cope with this by taking an after-lunch siesta; together with night naps, this often adds up to a respectable sleep quota over each 24-hour period.

## Some causes of insomnia

Sometimes physical problems such as pain from arthritic joints, breathlessness from heart failure, indigestion or leg cramps keep older people awake, and treatment of these conditions will enable them to sleep well again. Elderly confused people may be unable to describe what is making them uncomfortable and restless. Likely causes of their distress could be a full bladder or constipation. It is obviously sensible to offer the opportunity to visit the lavatory before retiring to bed to anyone who needs help in getting there, and to remind forgetful people of a need they may not recognise for what it is.

People differ a great deal in their preferences for bedroom temperature, softness of bed and type and weight of bedclothes. One's own bed is a particularly desirable piece of furniture to bring into residential care. It is worth remembering that cold air may aggravate a tendency to cough. While respecting their choice, you may want to point this out to a resident if you think their open window may be making them cough and disturbing their sleep.

Mental factors may also interfere with sleep. The early morning waking of depression may not be recognised for what it is, and if sedatives are prescribed without proper investigation, the patient's mental state may be made worse. Anxiety commonly prevents people from falling asleep. Counselling and suggesting some relaxation techniques or a change of routine can be more helpful than prescribed drugs in helping people to deal with anxiety; a community psychiatric nurse may be able to help with this.

## Sleep promotion in residential homes

It is difficult to make a residential home a restful, sleep-promoting place at night, and the greatest enemy to this is noise. Staff members who are still 'at work' may not fully realise that around them are people trying to sleep; they may learn a lot by spending a few night hours in an empty resident's room, listening to their colleagues' behaviour.

Talking in loud voices is very disturbing, so conversation by night should be kept to a quiet-voiced minimum. Shoes can irritate with tapping heels or squeaking leather; it is sensible for staff to wear soft but stable shoes like trainers at night. The crashing of utensils in the sluice or kitchen can also disrupt sleep, so essential tasks should be done as quietly as possible. It may be possible for working staff to concentrate on quiet jobs such as ironing, mending and vegetable preparation at night. Noisy machinery may be quieter after servicing, and staff might use the stairs rather than the lift. When everything possible has been done to eliminate unnecessary noise, it may be sensible to offer the residents wax earplugs; these are easily and cheaply available at chemists (pharmacists).

Other residents' behaviour can cause disturbance and disagreements. Those who wish to enjoy late programmes on television or radio should be encouraged to use earphones. Late retirers and early risers will be more likely to respect other residents' rest if staff obviously do this themselves. Perhaps a residents' committee can agree times between which quiet is expected. Confused residents who make a noise at night can be gently led by staff to somewhere as soundproof as possible.

Older people who have been burgled or suffered intruders in their previous homes may be fearful at night. Talking out these experiences to an accepting, sympathetic ear can be very therapeutic. Residents should be reassured that the Home is secure, and features such as window locks can be demonstrated to them. Residents' room doors should be lockable from the inside with the sort of locks that can be opened from the outside in an emergency. A locked door can prevent a confused resident from entering some else's room in mistake for their own; though the muddled person means no harm, it can be very alarming to wake to find a stranger climbing into bed with you.

The level of lighting that suits the resident best varies from one individual to another. Many adults dislike the dark: town dwellers used to street lights may find the blackness of a suburban or country night worryingly unfamiliar. Subdued lighting may help such people to sleep – either a low wattage bulb in the room or a light outside it, seen dimly through a slightly open door or partially uncovered fanlight. On the other hand, some residents may be used to waking with the sun, and if confused may rouse the house at 5am in summer. They may sleep longer if their windows are blacked out with thicker curtains.

## Self-help for poor sleepers

Residents can help themselves to sleep better. A first step is to establish a regular bed time, as bodies are sensitive to 'programming' of this sort. Day-time activity, ideally exercise in the fresh air, can help to produce a healthy tiredness by evening. Undemanding activity for the half hour before bed, such as reading, knitting or watching television, can help people to settle down.

A milky drink taken at bed time seems to make sleep less restless for some people. Coffee and tea should be avoided, as both contain caffeine which keeps people awake.

Some older people like an alcoholic nightcap, and *small* amounts are not harmful, though they may not work very well. Though alcohol decreases restlessness early in the night, wakefulness will usually follow later on. Larger amounts can have more dangerous unwanted effects than small doses of a suitable sleep-inducing medicine. It is a mistake to regard alcohol as safe because it is familiar.

## Avoiding sleeping tablets

Sleeping pills are certainly not the answer in all cases of insomnia. Most doctors would think it unkind never to give a sedative to an older person, despite the risk of unwanted effects. However, this should be regarded as something exceptional to tide someone over a difficult patch and help re-establish a normal sleep pattern.

Many people are first prescribed a sedative in hospital, when anxiety, discomfort and noise may interfere with normal sleep. If after recovery they are given a supply of the tablets to take home, they may wrongly conclude that these form part of their treatment and should not be omitted. In fact, the comfort of familiar surroundings often restores the normal sleep pattern, and people should in these circumstances try to manage without drugs.

Whatever the circumstances of the original prescription, it is obviously sensible for only a small quantity of a sedative to be dispensed. After finishing the tablets, the patient should then see the prescribing doctor again, and the prescription should certainly not be renewed indefinitely.

Taking someone off sleeping tablets is usually done gradually. A period of wakefulness and sometimes a little agitation is common in the withdrawal period. Residents and their carers should both be told to expect this, as otherwise they may take it as evidence of an ongoing 'need' for sleeping tablets. In fact, if wakefulness is tolerated for a few nights, it will pass, and a natural sleeping pattern will soon be restored.

The Over-75s check is a good occasion for discussing sleeping patterns and the need for sleeping tablets (see p 61).

# SEX IN LATER LIFE

Sex seems to be the least discussed and accepted activity of older people, sometimes by themselves and often by those who help to care for them. Because of their upbringing, many older people are reticent about the subject and may give the false impression of a lack of interest in sex. In fact, sexual interest and activity often continue into extreme old age, especially when a long-standing relationship continues or there are opportunities to form new ones.

Why, then, is it so difficult to accept older people as sexual beings? It may partly stem from the childlike difficulty we all have in accepting the sexuality of our parents and their friends. In addition, there is the wrong image fostered by advertising, television and films that physical love is dependent on youth and beauty. Some of us with sexual difficulties ourselves find it difficult to accept that older people, or people with a disability, are more successful than we are in their sex lives. Reluctance to accept the sexuality of an elderly parent is sometimes due to relatives' unwillingness to permit a 'replacement' for a dead father or mother. They may also fear the loss of their inheritance if a parent remarries.

## Sexual performance over 60

The effect of ageing on sexual function is, in fact, much less than is generally supposed. In men there is some decline in erectile capacity, but generally erections remain sufficiently firm for intercourse to be satisfactory for both parties. There may also be some delay in ejaculation, and orgasm may occur without ejaculation taking place at all. When a man expresses concern that this represents the beginning of the end of his prowess, he should be reassured that this is not so. Impotence (the inability to achieve an erection) is abnormal and may be treatable, especially if the cause is the unwanted effect of a medicine.

In women, sexual problems may develop with the menopause. As the levels of female hormones fall, lubrication of the vagina and adjacent areas becomes less efficient and takes longer to achieve, while the lining membrane becomes thinner and less elastic. Urinary problems resembling attacks of cystitis can occur for the same reason. The sexual problem can sometimes be solved by the use of a simple water-soluble lubricating jelly (eg KY Jelly); doctors and nurses use lubricating jelly for internal examinations and it is easily available from pharmacists without prescription. It is occasionally necessary to use replacement oestrogens (female hormones), either as a locally applied cream or as tablets. These hormones make the vaginal lining thicker, softer and more elastic, as it was during the child-bearing years.

When sexual performance declines, the loss of a source of pleasure and expression of love in a relationship of many years' standing adds yet another bereavement to those that commonly pile up as the years pass. More importantly, the sexual aspects of a relationship always affect its general quality. If a woman rejects her partner's sexual advances because sex has become painful for her, he will feel rejected as a person, particularly if difficulties in communication prevent her from explaining the situation fully. The whole relationship is then liable to deteriorate, and it may be sadly difficult for the affected people to find help.

## Homosexuality

Do not presume that a resident's sexual preference is for a partner of the opposite sex; at least one in 20 of the population, and possibly considerably more, is exclusively homosexual.

Older people are less likely than younger ones to 'come out' and admit their gayness, and it is not necessary to delve into the sexual intimacies of a relationship or to force confidences. A long-standing homosexual relationship should be accepted as corresponding to a marriage, and you should be able to provide appropriate sympathy and support in severe illness or following a partner's death; the Lesbian and Gay Bereavement Project may be able to provide further help.

Some residents may find others' gay relationships distasteful and make their disapproval felt. Staff should make it clear that, while everyone is entitled to their own views on sexual morality, discrimination on grounds of sexual preference is not acceptable. They should also make sure they understand enough about HIV and AIDS to counter any wrong views that gay people are a health hazard to those around them.

## Helping residents express their sexuality

You can help ensure that your residents do not accept a decline in their personal lives as a consequence of old age. You could, for instance, give them the opportunity to become better informed by adding books on relationships and sexuality to the Home library (see Further Reading, p 273).

People with an illness or disability often find this affects their sex lives. Sometimes there is a direct effect: a stroke or Parkinson's disease may affect the body's control of the sexual process. Pelvic operations such as a hysterectomy or an open (retropubic) prostatectomy can damage the nerves supplying the genitals, or they can be affected by the complications of diabetes. This can cause impotence (failure of erection) in men, or poor arousal and lubrication in women. The more commonly used prostate operation is the 'TUR' (Trans-Urethral Resection). This leaves no visible scar, as the surgery is done with operating instruments passed up the penis. It does not affect potency, but causes retrograde ejaculation. This makes orgasm feel different for both partners, as the semen does not gush out of the end of the man's penis, but flows into the bladder and is passed mixed with urine next time he visits the lavatory.

Many medicines can affect sexual function, usually by reducing sexual drive or affecting potency. Any drug with a sedative effect can do this, as can some medicines used to treat high blood pressure. Other common culprits are the male hormone opposers used to treat prostate cancer, and too much alcohol, sometimes mistakenly taken as 'Dutch courage'. In addition, there is always a psychological aspect: once a man has 'failed' to achieve a satisfactory erection, subsequent performance may be interfered with, regardless of the physical effects of disease or of the medicines used to treat it.

Pain and discomfort are other indirect effects of illness and disability. For instance, a woman with arthritis of the hips may find that the traditional 'face to face, man above' missionary position has become uncomfortable. She will need guidance in adopting new positions for intercourse that will hurt less. Body image is also important: someone who has had a mastectomy or an amputation or has acquired a stoma may feel much less attractive than they were, and may fear that their partner will find them repulsive. Sadly, in a few cases this is so, but more often, if the people concerned can discuss their feelings, the disabled one will find their partner's love for the person inside the altered body has not changed.

People with sexual problems arising from an illness or disability should be advised to contact their GP in the first instance. Telephone advice, counselling and a wide range of literature are available from SPOD, the Association to Aid the Sexual and Personal Relationships of People with a Disability. Your residents may want to get in touch with SPOD themselves, or you may wish to do so, either to gather information on a resident's behalf or to improve your own knowledge.

Sometimes practical advice about a change of position or technique can solve the problem, or reassurance can put the person's mind at rest. It is, for instance, perfectly safe to have intercourse after a hysterectomy, usually after the post-operative check-up has established that all is well. Sex can be resumed after a heart attack once the sufferer is well enough to climb two flights of stairs without breathlessness; sudden death during intercourse is in fact very rare, and almost unheard of in familiar circumstances with a long-standing partner.

When impotence is permanent, or when full intercourse with penetration is otherwise impossible for health reasons, sexual partners can give each other great pleasure in other ways – stroking, caressing the genital area or other erogenous zones, mouth to genital contact – whatever both enjoy and which hurts neither. Obviously, older people are able to work this out for themselves, but sometimes they find it helpful to receive medical 'permission' for such activities, and to be reassured there is nothing 'kinky' about them.

## Relationships old and new

It is most unwise to jump to conclusions about existing relationships. Although many loving husbands and wives will want to stay together when they move into a Home, not every married couple will want to share a room, far less a bed. It seems that in the generation that is now elderly, people whose marriages have broken down often do not separate in the community, but jump at the chance to do so when this is offered on entering a Home. On the other hand, two residents may form a new relationship and want to move in together, or to have intimate visits. Staff must resist the temptation to interfere. They should not act as clumsy cupids, trying to bring people together, as this can blight rewarding sources of companionship. It is also improper to try to sabotage burgeoning friendships, whether on the staff's own initiative or at the request of shocked relatives. It is very sad to hear of Homes where residents are not 'allowed' so much as to hold hands, and where those expressing affection more obviously are promptly separated.

Try not to be over-protective in dealings with your residents, as this diminishes them as individuals. When it may seem that an older person is 'making a fool of themselves', remember that older people, like the rest of us, are entitled to decide on their own fate; their choice of partner is no one's business but their own.

# Residents without a partner

People, whether elderly or not, miss the human warmth, comfort and physical well-being they had from a sexual relationship if they are separated from their partner by death or circumstances. They will need to express their feelings and mourn their loss. Some will find masturbation helps to relieve tension, and they need to be able to do this in private without any fear of interruption. Staff must get into the habit of knocking on bedroom and bathroom doors and waiting until told to enter. Older people sometimes fear that masturbation is harmful, as when they were young it was blamed for all sorts of afflictions from blindness to insanity. It hardly needs saying that it is quite harmless, and is the only alternative to celibacy for someone who lacks a partner.

# Staff feelings and attitudes

Few of us are entirely comfortable in our sexuality and many of us have sex-related problems or secrets. Unfortunate experiences and harsh teachers or parents encountered in childhood may have set up patterns that prove difficult to discard. All of these factors affect our attitudes to our own, and others', sexuality.

In daily life we may have our own opinions about the sexual behaviour of family, friends and neighbours, but we are not normally called upon to get involved. A very different situation faces staff of residential homes. A disabled couple may ask a staff member to help them into the same room or the same bed; the partners may not necessarily be married to each other, and may be of the same sex. A resident might ask to be taken on an outing to visit a sex shop or prostitute, or even ask for help in achieving orgasm. New, young or inexperienced staff may be surprised to find that older people have sexual feelings at all, and be shocked and upset if a resident has an erection during a bath. Another difficult and recurring problem springs from the tension between allowing residents their freedom but protecting them from injury if they cannot look after themselves. If, for instance, Mrs Y has a dementing illness, this does not disqualify her from having a sex life, but may make it more difficult to decide whether she fully understands and consents to the physical side of her relationship with Mr X.

Staff need opportunities to give vent to their feelings and to discuss their practical problems. Written material may help, such as SPOD's publications or ACE's book, *Living, Loving and Ageing* (see Further Reading). When a staff member has difficulty with a particular resident, it may be possible to find a carefully matched key worker to undertake that person's care. In general it is wise to explain the Home's philosophy regarding sexual matters at the first employment interview; then those whose moral or religious views are out of keeping can avoid coming to work in the Home.

## Inappropriate sexual activity

People with a dementing illness are especially likely to expose themselves (show off their genital organs) or to masturbate in public. It is important to remember that a mentally frail person who behaves in this way has normal sexual feelings; they have merely forgotten how to express them acceptably. The technical word for this sort of behaviour is 'disinhibition'.

Whilst masturbation is a normal human activity, it should not be done in front of other people. It is worth explaining this gently to someone who is behaving inappropriately in a public place, while leading them to somewhere more suitable and leaving them in private with a supply of tissues. You could consider asking the doctor to check that the resident's physical health is as good as possible, and to review drug treatment, as illness or the medicines used to treat it can worsen the mental state. It can also help to make sure that discomfort or itching are not directing undue attention to the genital area: a common cause of this is thrush infection in older women. It is also useful to think about the resident's daily round – whether they have control of their life and have opportunities for enjoyment other than masturbation; where care is poor, an orgasm can be the only nice thing residents can make happen for themselves.

Sedation is not the answer in this situation; it will not help and may make things worse by removing more curbs on behaviour. It can also cause extra problems such as incontinence and a tendency to fall. Anti-androgen drugs are occasionally suggested for men who masturbate publicly or expose themselves. These work by 'chemical castration': they abolish libido, so that the man loses interest in sex altogether. Other effects include impotence, shrinking of the genitals and enlargement of the breasts, and these can be very distressing. There are also important ethical issues. On the one hand, it is a very serious step to castrate someone in this way, and by doing so to take away one of their few pleasures. On the other hand, the rights of others deserve to be considered; if this sort of behaviour continues, the resident may need to move. There are no easy answers to problems of this sort, and a decision has to be made on the merits of each case.

## Unwelcome sexual overtures to staff

Though these may come from mentally impaired people, others may misinterpret kindly behaviour from staff as invitations to intimacy; this is especially likely from people with little sexual experience. Staff members of course have rights of their own, and are not expected to put up with sexual harassment. However, they should remember that people of all ages and all degrees of mental function need to love and be loved. Clumsy overtures stemming from physical or mental incapacity should be treated with compassion.

When a resident makes gentle verbal overtures to a staff member – for instance by asking them out – it is important to say 'No, thank you' as firmly but as pleasantly as possible. The object is to establish a firm refusal without crushing the would-be suitor's self-respect. Useful phrases might be, 'I like you a lot, Mr Jones, but I can't think of you in that way', or 'I've been married for 15 years now, and I think I'm suited'. Afterwards it is a good idea to be slightly more formal and distant than before, without neglecting the resident. Make sure that careful, confidential, written notes of the incident are kept; this is because the occasional person in the pain of rejection makes counter-accusations that the staff member made improper advances to the resident.

The situation is more serious when a resident uses suggestive language persistently, or touches a staff member in a way they do not like – stroking women's breasts or putting hands up their skirts, or groping at men's flies. Again the staff member should make it clear they find this sort of behaviour unwelcome and unacceptable, and a senior staff member should voice their own disapproval in support.

It is sometimes possible to change circumstances so that the situation is less likely to arise. Staff members may be able to stay out of reach for much of the time if the resident can attend to their own personal hygiene, and bathing or shower aids may make this possible. Also, it sometimes helps to change the key worker to someone the resident finds less attractive or who is less distressed by this sort of problem.

The doctor may be able to help by making sure the resident's mental state is no worse than it needs to be: for instance, withdrawing sedation can have a good effect on both mental state and behaviour. The doctor can also arrange referral to an old age psychiatrist (psycho-geriatrician). In addition, a community psychiatric nurse or clinical psychologist may be able to suggest ways in which staff can modify the resident's behaviour. For instance, if the resident is behaving inappropriately, only necessary care should be given, with little extra social contact; on the other hand, the resident gets extra attention and conversation when they are behaving acceptably.

Behaviour of this sort is not, of course, a subject for giggling or gossip. Great care must be taken about confidentiality; it is important to make sure that records are not left where unauthorised persons can see them or the problem discussed where others can overhear.

It is essential to remember that sexual activity between people is psychological as well as physical. Older people, like the rest of us, fall in love, court each other, kiss and cuddle, and suffer the agonies of sexual jealousy. Regarding sex purely as a matter of anatomy and physiology and its difficulties as 'plumbing faults' is a mistake. People need to give and receive love all their lives, and residents of Homes should be given every opportunity to achieve fulfilment and happiness in this way as in others.

# SMOKING

There is no good word to be said for smoking tobacco – the habit kills perhaps as many as 100,000 people every year in Britain, smokers dying on average ten years before their time. Smoking causes lung cancer, chronic bronchitis and emphysema, coronary artery disease and the disease of the limb arteries that makes amputation necessary. It worsens other illnesses such as peptic ulcers, and makes it more difficult and dangerous for an anaesthetic to be given for any surgical procedure. What is more, smokers hurt others besides themselves; they injure both the passive smokers who are forced to inhale the fumes they produce and children who learn to take up the habit.

These risks are reduced as soon as smoking is stopped, and continue to fall thereafter.

Though cigarettes are the most dangerous, cigars and pipes also carry their own hazards. Changing the way tobacco is smoked is not an alternative to giving up the habit altogether.

# Giving up smoking

It is never too late to stop smoking: there are benefits to health even in extreme old age. The most important of these is a reduction in the number and severity of chest infections. Because the body fights germs less well as the years pass, mild respiratory infections that younger people would fight off tend to 'go to the chest', and smoking undermines the body's defences even further. Non-smokers and ex-smokers also have fewer strokes and heart attacks, and if surgery is needed the anaesthetic carries less risk in a non-smoker.

## Helping residents to break the habit

Wanting to stop smoking is what really matters. However, advice and support are useful; you may want to find out whether the health centre or GP surgery can help here. The organisation ASH (Action on Smoking and Health) produces good free literature, including a 'Give Up' pack.

The nicotine in cigarettes produces dependence, and this accounts for the withdrawal symptoms some people experience when they stop smoking. Nicotine taken in other ways (chewing gum, skin patches, mouth sprays) helps to reduce these symptoms. The quantity used is gradually cut down and then stopped altogether. Both gum and patches can be bought over the counter in pharmacists' shops. People who have peptic ulcers or suffer from angina may want to check with the doctor before using these preparations.

People trying to stop smoking can be reassured that the worst of the withdrawal period is usually over within a month; they should be encouraged to think instead of ways to spend the money saved on something less dangerous. A weight gain of about half a stone (3kg) is quite common after smoking is stopped but does not always happen. It can usually be lost without too much difficulty, and, even if retained, it poses much less of a danger to health than continued smoking.

## Respecting choices

Your residents are entitled to choose their lifestyle, as long as they respect other people's rights. In your Home there are likely to be older people who choose to smoke and others who prefer not to. Some of these will be distressed or made ill if exposed to other people's smoke. These preferences should be respected, and suitable 'smoking' and 'non-smoking' areas provided.

Difficulties may arise when a smoker behaves dangerously, setting themselves or their surroundings alight. It is not possible to make rules in this situation; after careful thought, the most appropriate course of action must be decided in each case. It may be possible to show the resident how to smoke more safely – for instance, to put the cigarette down in an ashtray between puffs. A staff member sitting with the resident when they are smoking will also reduce danger.

A fire or health and safety officer may be able to suggest a good solution that would be acceptable to the resident. They may also be able to advise on the use of non-inflammable clothes or furniture.

Of course, staff members can choose whether or not to smoke. However, it is important to remember that you are in a position of power in relation to the resident. For instance, it would be very difficult for one of them to ask you not to smoke or to refuse you permission to do so. You must be sensitive to this difficulty and take care not to abuse your position.

You should also recognise the fact that smoking is genuinely bad for health, even if you choose to continue to do so. It would be improper for you to undermine health care advice, or to sabotage a resident's efforts to give up smoking, by offering them cigarettes.

# ALCOHOL – USE AND ABUSE

## Older people are more vulnerable

Drinking alcohol differs from smoking in that light and occasional drinking seem to do little harm. Nevertheless, there has been a great increase in problems of excessive alcohol consumption since the 1960s, and older people have followed this trend. Unfortunately, even habitual drinkers become more vulnerable to the effects of excessive alcohol as they get older, because of the bodily changes of ageing. This effect is worsened in people who have other ailments or who are taking medication.

Older people who abuse alcohol often fall and may bang their heads, causing brain damage. Malnutrition is common, and any tendency to incontinence or mental confusion is worsened. Heavy drinkers who smoke in bed or drive cars put themselves and other people at risk of injury. Residents who behave unpleasantly when drunk are often ostracised; they then drink more to relieve their loneliness and thus aggravate the problem.

Older men may have drunk heavily all their lives, and do not trouble to hide the fact. Older women may conceal their drinking, as alcohol was not considered a respectable indulgence for 'ladies' in their young days. Some of these 'take to drink' in later life, having previously drunk little or no alcohol. This often seems to be a response to bereavement, loneliness, poor health or other stress and distresses. Unlike life-long drinkers, this group may respond well to kind and competent help with their problems, and become able to enjoy life without abusing alcohol.

## Sensible drinking

The risks from drinking alcohol become greater as the intake rises. Men can drink more alcohol safely than women can because of their different body composition. Safe upper limits are: 3–4 units two or three times a week for an older man (6–12 units per week) and 2–3 units two or three times a week for an older woman (4–9 units per week).

A unit of alcohol is the amount of alcohol found in:

    half a pint of beer, *or*

    one pub single of spirits, *or*

    one glass of wine, or

    one small glass of sherry, vermouth or port.

Strong beers, large glasses and unmeasured drinks poured at home contain extra units. People with balance problems may find it wise to space their intake well, and it is sensible to remember that some medicines do not mix with alcohol at all.

## Caring for heavy drinkers

Staff in Homes often feel a conflict between their duty to allow residents to make their own choices and their responsibility to protect vulnerable people from the consequences of their unwise actions. They respect residents' rights but worry that alcohol abusers are ruining their health and putting themselves and others at risk. They may also fear criticism from managers and relatives if something goes wrong. What is more, other residents may be distressed by the drinker's noisy or unruly behaviour and demand that 'something must be done'. There are no easy answers to problems like these, but a few guidelines on how to act are set out below.

First, try to take an objective view: how bad are things, and how much worry is appropriate? This depends on how much the resident is drinking, whether there are any complicating factors such as poor health or incompatible medicines, and whether the resident is behaving in a dangerous or seriously disruptive way.

Next try to decide whether the resident is able to make a free choice. Life-long heavy drinkers without mental health problems can be presumed to be able to make their own decisions and to take the consequences. The chances of such a person deciding to change their drinking habits are slim. However, some of the people who start drinking late in life may be clinically depressed or developing a dementing illness. Such people are unable to look after themselves, and have a right to the protection and care of others. Again, those who have 'taken to drink' to escape from the stresses and distresses of later life may welcome kindly help to find less self-destructive ways of coping with their problems.

Lastly, think about confidentiality. In some cases the problem is out in the open, but in others the resident is trying to hide it. You should not then mention the subject to relatives or even the doctor without careful thought. A resident who thinks you have abused the trust they placed in you may never tell you anything 'private' again, and may suffer because of this.

Let us consider some examples of the sort of situations you may meet. If a mentally unimpaired resident drinks heavily and seems to be little the worse at the moment, your role is only to give advice if asked for it.

If a resident's drinking seems to be affecting their health, you should discuss the situation with them and ask if they would like you to call the doctor on their behalf. If you are seriously concerned about their physical or mental health, you should say so, and try to persuade them to agree to medical help. You may sometimes need to speak to the doctor even without their consent. This breach of confidence may be a lesser evil in some circumstances than allowing a resident to suffer harm when too ill to make sensible decisions for themselves. If you do speak to the doctor, you should explain the grounds for your suspicions, the reasons for your serious concern and the resident's wish for secrecy.

Suppose one of your residents is in real danger – perhaps through starting fires by dropping off to sleep when smoking while fuddled. Things are usually out in the open by the time this stage is reached. In any case, the risks may be grave enough to outweigh your duty of confidentiality: you should discuss the situation with any concerned relatives or friends and inform your managers in writing if appropriate.

Some people who seek help for an alcohol problem aim for controlled drinking. Others are advised to abstain from all alcohol permanently. However, an alcohol-dependent person may become acutely confused when drink is suddenly withdrawn. You should be aware of this as a possible cause of unexplained confusion. It requires urgent medical treatment, or it can progress to the frightening and dangerous condition of delirium tremens (DTs). Alcohol Concern (see Useful Addresses) have details of organisations providing advice and help with alcohol problems.

Some specialists believe that older alcohol abusers are easier to treat and do better than younger ones – as a group of 'survivors', they may have tougher personalities and bodies than the average person.

After all this, it is important to remember that most people enjoy alcohol sensibly; the older man who spends a sociable hour nursing a half pint in the local every day and the older woman who enjoys a glass of sherry occasionally are deriving good rather than harm from their little indulgence.

## KEY POINTS

■ Try to encourage and maintain the independence of your residents.

■ It is sometimes right to tolerate risk-taking if this improves a resident's quality of life.

■ A good diet should be both nutritious and enjoyable.

■ Promote residents' sleep by:

encouraging day-time exercise, evening relaxation and a regular bed time;

combating pain and discomfort, mental distress, noise, bright lights and the routine use of sleeping tablets.

■ Older people may enjoy sexual relationships as much as younger people do.

■ It is never too late to stop smoking.

■ An occasional alcoholic drink may be a harmless pleasure, but too much alcohol is harmful.

# 3 Essential Body Maintenance

Just as a car requires regular servicing, people's eyes, teeth and feet need regular maintenance, no matter how old they are.

## SAVING SIGHT

All older people should have a regular eye examination every two years. They should do this even if they have no eye problems, and should go more often if they have difficulties. Some eye symptoms require immediate attention, and these are listed on page 225.

An eye test is free for older people who:

- have glaucoma or are closely related to a glaucoma sufferer;
- have diabetes;
- are on low incomes (see Social Security leaflet G11, from the Benefits Agency office or Post Office);
- are registered blind or partially sighted;
- need certain sorts of complex lenses.

Older people outside these groups may be charged a fee, though not all opticians do this.

You can obtain a list of opticians who will make home visits from the Family Health Services Authority (FHSA).

The eye examination will detect treatable conditions such as glaucoma that may threaten sight without causing obvious symptoms. It is also a chance for spectacle lenses to be checked, to ensure that vision is as good as possible.

You may be able to help your residents to look after their spectacles properly. To be useful they must be kept clean, and may need a gentle wash in mild detergent, with careful drying of metal parts. They should be stored lenses downwards in the case provided, so as not to scratch the lenses or distort the frame. Attaching a chain or cord to be worn around the neck may prevent loss. Even though they are an expensive item, it is a false economy for residents to wear a pair of glasses originally prescribed for a friend or relative, or to make do with a pair of their own that are no longer satisfactory. You could remind them that cheaper spectacles are available to people on low incomes (leaflet G11, as above).

Suitable lighting is very important in making the most of whatever sight a person has, and also for safety in the Home. Adjustable angled lights are very useful for close work and should be directed over the shoulder directly on to a book or handwork. Prevent glare by proper shading. People with cataracts may find over-bright light makes vision difficult; tinted spectacle lenses also help with this. Occasionally, using a more powerful light bulb may be enough to solve someone's visual problems. If you advise this, you should make sure that the recommended wattage for the lamp-shade is not exceeded, or the excess heat may start a fire.

# AVOIDING DENTAL PROBLEMS

The major dental problem of middle and old age is the build-up of plaque, sometimes called tartar, on and between the teeth. The bacteria in plaque produce substances that cause gum inflammation and disease, an early sign of which is bleeding. If the gum disease is not treated, the teeth may become loose and eventually fall out. Plaque can be removed from teeth by regular brushing and by the conscientious use of dental floss every other day to reach the spaces between teeth. Frequent visits to the dentist are important both for thorough cleaning and for advice about care. Even people who have full dentures should go at least once a year to ensure that the dentures remain well fitting and that the mouth is healthy. Age Concern England's Factsheet 5 'Dental Care in Retirement' includes advice on finding a dentist and how to arrange treatment. It also explains how the charging system operates and how to get help with these costs.

The local FHSA keeps a list of local NHS dentists, which can be consulted at the FHSA office or in main post offices and libraries. Residents can ask the chosen dentist to accept them as NHS patients. If this proves difficult, residents should get in touch with the Community Health Council, the FHSA, their local branch of Age Concern or Citizens Advice Bureau or the District Dental Officer of the Community Dental Services (addresses and telephone numbers in directories or at the library).

In some areas the Community Dental Service will visit and treat patients at home; a GP referral is required. You can find out more about this from the District Dental Officer at the Health Authority, or from the FHSA.

Dental problems can have more far-reaching effects on health than might at first be expected. For instance, many older people avoid fibre-rich foods and take only a soft diet because they have problems with their teeth, and it is not uncommon to meet people who take out their dentures at meal times because they do not fit properly. Speech may also become indistinct. It is usually wise to remove dentures only for cleaning and at night, unless advised otherwise by the dentist.

# HEALTHY, COMFORTABLE FEET

Contrary to the popular image as 'plates of meat', the feet are beautifully engineered and precision built. Just as buildings deteriorate when subjected to excessive loads and stresses, our feet often complain under the pressure of increased weight after middle age. Losing weight can often help not only a person's feet but also the weight-bearing joints above them.

Foot problems are often caused by ill-fitting shoes. You may need to help arrange a shopping expedition so a resident can replace outworn or unsatisfactory footwear. A chiropodist or a Disabled Living Centre should be able to suggest where to buy shoes for people with problems.

Try to encourage residents to wear shoes rather than bedroom slippers around the Home, as shoes are more stable, help to prevent feet from swelling and preserve morale and self-respect. Daily careful washing and drying of feet are important; toe nails will be easiest to cut when they are soft after bathing or washing. Many older people need help with this; try to make sure that anyone who is involved has been shown how by a chiropodist.

It is unwise for elderly people or the Home staff to attempt to deal with corns and callouses themselves; these should be left to a qualified chiropodist. Only state registered chiropodists, who can use the letters 'SRCh' after their names, may work in health authorities and trusts. Non-registered chiropodists have various forms of qualifications and training. Chiropody is vital for diabetes, because lack of sensation, poor healing abilities and a tendency to acquire infections may mean that serious septic foot wounds can develop unnoticed.

Older people are entitled to free chiropody under the NHS, but in some parts of the country the service is sparse. This can result in long delays before being seen in the first place, and in some areas a long wait between appointments thereafter. Because of this, many older people may decide to obtain private treatment; the local NHS chiropody service may keep a list of registered chiropodists who do private practice.

Information about NHS costs and benefits to help with them can be found in the current edition of *Your Rights* (see p 280).

# SENSIBLE USE OF HEALTH CHECKS

## The Over-75 examination

Under the 1990 NHS contract, GPs have to offer every patient over 75 years old on their list an annual consultation, either at the surgery or at home. This is designed to identify unreported or unnoticed illness, and also to make it easier for older people to get any help they need. The check may be performed by the doctor, or by a practice nurse, health visitor or another staff member, who can then refer the older person to the doctor if this seems necessary.

The examination takes special note of the older person's daily living abilities. It also checks on sight and hearing and on general physical and mental health. Medicines can be reviewed and altered if necessary, and appropriate equipment and help arranged if the older person wants and needs it.

Residents over 75 do of course have the right to refuse this examination if they so wish. Some may do this because they are failing in health and are fearful of what may be found. If, however, they do decide to see the doctor, their worries often prove to be groundless, and early treatment ensures a good outcome to the illness. In this situation, you may sometimes think it right to encourage a reluctant resident to have their check. It may help to offer support in making their wishes clear to the doctor or nurse. However, you should not use undue pressure.

# Other screening tests

Medical examination of people who have no obvious signs of disease is called 'screening'. It is useful only when it detects a potentially serious condition at a stage when the sufferer would not otherwise know it was there. There is no point in finding out about an illness unless it can be treated, and no value in an early diagnosis unless it gives a better result than waiting until the condition becomes obvious. The benefits of screening have to be set against the drawbacks – the discomfort or inconvenience of the test procedure, the needless anxiety over the 'false positive' result that turns out to have been wrong and the financial costs. It is still not certain whether, or to what extent, the tests described below are useful, and experts differ strongly in their views about them.

## The cervical smear

This detects changes in the cells of the cervix that could later progress to cancer. The cells are scraped off the cervix during the internal, vaginal examination. This tends to be more uncomfortable in older women than in younger ones, and bleeding afterwards is more likely. On the other hand, more than 40 per cent of deaths from cancer of the cervix in England occur in women over 65, so older women are still at risk of the disease.

Balancing factors for and against, the most sensible course for a woman over 65 who has been or still is sexually active is to have a cervical smear if she has never had one before. Older people who have had smears in the past should ask for advice from the doctor or clinic they usually attend. Many women whose smears have been normal up to the age of 65 are at very low risk from then onwards, so further smears may not be necessary.

The Women's National Cancer Control Campaign is a good source of advice about this aspect of women's health.

## Mammography (breast screening)

This is a special form of X-ray which can detect breast cancer while the lump is still too small to feel with a hand. Mammography may be uncomfortable but this soon passes off. As with some other sorts of screening, its benefits in women over 65 are still unclear. It is offered free to women between the ages of 50 and 64, and older women can get it on request. Women with a family history of breast cancer are the most likely to want to do this, and they may also want to persevere with breast self-examination. Again, useful information is available from the Women's National Cancer Control Campaign.

## Blood pressure (BP)

People with higher than normal blood pressure have a higher than usual risk of suffering a stroke or a heart attack than those whose BP is within normal limits; men are at greater risk than women. Adults up to 75 years old should have their BP taken at least every five years; people over 75 should have this done at their annual check. The benefits of lowering the BP have to be balanced against the drawbacks of the unwanted effects of medicines, which can be disabling in some older people. An individual decision about what is best to do must be made in each case.

## KEY POINTS

- Eyes should be tested at least every two years, and more often if an abnormality is noticed.

- Older people with their own teeth should have a dental check-up every six months.

- Older people with full dentures need a dental check-up once a year.

- Foot problems may reduce mobility, but chiropody can help.

- Everyone over 75 years old is entitled to an annual health check.

- Cervical smears are more difficult and uncomfortable in older women but mammography remains useful; both tests may be available on request.

- People with high blood pressure run an increased risk of stroke and heart disease, but in older people the treatment can sometimes be more dangerous still.

Old age need not be spoiled by poor health; the aim is 'to die young as late as possible'.

# 4 Common Illnesses in Later Life

Many of the disabilities that older people – and their carers – put up with because they wrongly attribute them to 'ageing' are, in fact, due to medical conditions that can be treated. By reading about these, you will be better able to help your residents get appropriate medical attention or other help when they need it.

The illnesses described in this chapter are grouped according to the body system they affect, except for cancers which are explained together, and HIV and AIDS:

| | |
|---|---|
| **Heart and blood vessels** | **The blood** |
| **Lungs and airways** | **Bones and joints** |
| **Digestive system** | **The glands** |
| **Nervous system** | **Cancer** |
| **The eyes** | **HIV and AIDS** |
| **The ears** | |

## HEART AND BLOOD VESSELS

The heart is a muscular pump which circulates the blood round the body through the blood vessels (arteries and veins). Because the heart works hard and continuously, it needs a good blood supply to give it oxygen.

# Common problems

## Angina

The chest pain of angina occurs when the blood supply to the heart muscle is insufficient because the coronary arteries are partially blocked. Angina is often brought on by exercise, such as hurrying up a hill, or by emotion that makes the heart beat faster. It is relieved by rest, when the heart needs less oxygen.

Angina is very frightening; people experiencing it should not be left alone. Help them to take their prescribed medicines (see p 201). Increasingly frequent angina attacks may lead up to a coronary, so anyone with this problem should see the doctor.

## Heart attack or coronary

This happens when part of the heart muscle dies because the coronary blood supply is too poor to keep it alive. In young people a coronary is accompanied by very severe, crushing chest pain, often radiating up into the neck and down the arms, with breathlessness and distress. Sometimes the patient collapses, becomes unconscious, and may die. An older person may not experience pain, but instead may faint, fall, vomit or become confused or breathless. Unexplained collapse or confusion may therefore be a sign that a heart attack has occurred.

The doctor will arrange for treatment either in the Home or in hospital. One new treatment involves the injection of a substance that dissolves the clot blocking the coronary artery and thus restores the blood supply to the heart muscle. This has to be given soon after the block has formed if it is to work properly. Some people who have suffered a heart attack, as well as those with severe angina, may be offered coronary artery bypass surgery. This aims to re-route blood around an arterial blockage by grafting in a piece of blood vessel from elsewhere. Alternatively, a narrowed artery can be stretched during the procedure of angioplasty. These newer treatments work just as well in older people as in younger ones. Medicines called beta-blockers seem to reduce the chances of suffering a further heart attack, and a small dose of aspirin may be prescribed for the same purpose.

Residents who are not admitted to hospital are not usually confined to bed; moderate activity such as walking short distances to the lavatory is better for the general health.

A heart attack is not a trivial event, but should not lead the sufferer to despair. In general, normal activity can be resumed afterwards.

It is sensible for even the oldest smoker to stop if further heart attacks are not to follow. However, a little alcohol is usually harmless, so long as it does not lead to weight problems; people who have had a coronary should avoid becoming overweight. Cholesterol-lowering diets are rarely suggested to elderly people, as they do not seem to be very helpful. Moderate exercise is excellent; try to encourage residents who have had heart attacks to keep as active as possible. As well as reducing the risk of further attacks, this enhances well-being and reduces the risk of depression.

Both angina and heart attacks are twice as common in people from the Indian subcontinent as in native Britons. However, they are only half as common in Afro-Caribbeans.

## Disturbances of heart rhythm (cardiac arrhythmias)

These can cause a number of symptoms such as palpitations (an uncomfortable awareness of the heart beat), breathlessness, falls and attacks of unconsciousness. Severe problems can be fatal. Treatment may involve the use of drugs or the implantation of a pacemaker.

A pacemaker is a simple electrical device consisting of a battery with a wire to conduct an electrical impulse to the heart and thus stimulate it to beat. Pacemakers are not only life-saving but can also improve the quality of life even in very elderly people. Problems with pacemakers are rare, but if they do occur the person should be sent immediately by ambulance to the hospital unit that supplied the device. Someone with a pacemaker should check with the clinic about whether it is affected by equipment such as a microwave oven or electronic security checks at airports and some libraries.

## Heart failure

This happens when the heart cannot provide adequate blood circulation because the muscle has been weakened by a heart attack, or strained by high blood pressure. After a chest infection, someone whose heart failure was well controlled before it may become breathless, develop a bluish colour around the lips, and their ankles may swell. Urgent treatment with appropriate drugs is needed.

## Ankle swelling

This is often not a sign of heart failure or of other serious illness. When it occurs without breathlessness or other symptoms, the usual cause is sitting too much.

Diuretic tablets with their occasional ill-effects are therefore not needed. To help reduce the swelling, patients should prop their feet up above the level of their bottom when seated. Moderate exercise such as walking also helps to disperse the fluid, and residents should be encouraged to do this as much as possible.

Elastic stockings or support hose are helpful. They should be kept on the bedside table overnight and put on in the morning before putting a foot to the floor. Residents with poor finger function may need help in doing this. Stockings and hose must be washed according to the instructions supplied with them, or they will lose their elasticity.

## High blood pressure (hypertension)

Because blood pressure (BP) depends on the strength of the heart beat and the condition of the blood vessels, it can vary considerably in the same person under different conditions. It has, however, been shown that a higher than average resting blood pressure can go with an increased tendency to suffer from heart attacks, stroke or kidney failure. High blood pressure is thus a risk factor for these conditions. Afro-Caribbeans, who are especially likely to suffer from high blood pressure, are also more likely to have strokes.

People up to and including those in their late 70s benefit from taking medicines to lower high blood pressure, but for someone past the age of 80 the situation becomes less clear. Though people in their 80s and 90s with high blood pressure still appear more likely to have a stroke or heart attack than someone of the same age whose blood pressure is normal, unwanted effects from BP-lowering medicines seem to be more likely to occur than in younger people, and cause more disability when they do happen. Confusion, incontinence and a tendency to fall brought on by the medicines may be too high a price to pay for reducing the risks of future illness. Until more research is available, an individual decision needs to be made in each case, balancing the benefits and drawbacks of treatment.

## Low blood pressure (hypotension)

Some older people have a decreased ability to control their BP when rising suddenly from a sitting or lying position. They feel faint and may fall. This is especially likely to happen first thing in the morning when BP tends to be lowest.

The doctor's advice should be sought, as it may help to stop medicines such as sleeping pills, diuretics or unnecessary BP-lowering tablets. Alternatively, new tablets to raise BP may be prescribed. In any case, many older people find it helpful to sit on the edge of the bed for a few minutes and get up slowly.

## Arterial disease

This is more common in smokers and in people with diabetes, and the leg arteries are the ones usually affected. They become narrowed, and therefore supply insufficient blood to the muscles and other tissues. The affected person's symptoms depend on how bad the disease is. In the mildest form there is pain only during exercise, when most blood is needed, and this gets better with rest. In more severe cases the muscles get painfully short of blood even at rest. In the worst situation there is not enough blood to keep the tissues alive. Minor injuries to the feet may easily progress to ulcers or even gangrene.

Someone with arterial disease may need help to take special care of their feet. After daily washing and drying, the feet should be carefully inspected; prompt, skilled nursing care should be arranged for any breaks in the skin. Rough areas in new shoes should be smoothed out before wearing. It is unwise for people with arterial disease to go barefoot.

Various forms of treatment are available to improve the blood supply. Heart failure, anaemia and dehydration make things worse, so the resident should keep their general health as good as possible. Surgery is sometimes used to relax arteries, to remove blockages or to bypass them with grafts. A few patients need an amputation to rid them of a dangerous infection or of a painfully useless limb.

Amputation is especially likely to be needed in people who have diabetes as well as arterial disease. The need for the operation will be discussed carefully with the patient beforehand. It will be particularly helpful if they can talk to someone who has had an amputation already and adjusted well. After the operation, discharge from hospital should be planned early so that equipment can be ordered and necessary alterations to the building or fittings made in good time.

How independent the resident will be after the amputation depends on several factors. Strong motivation always helps, but the level of amputation makes a big difference. Someone who has lost their leg below the knee is much more likely to walk again than someone operated on above it. Here wheelchair independence may be a more realistic aim. Walking will also be hindered if the 'good' leg is weakened by arthritis, a stroke or arterial disease.

Potential walkers will be fitted with a 'prosthesis' (artificial leg) by expert staff at a limb fitting centre or equivalent. Sockets may need to be adjusted several times to ensure a good fit with a changing stump. A new prosthesis is supplied when appropriate. During wear, the stump is covered with a fabric 'sock' that needs regular changing. Alteration of sock thickness can affect the fit of the limb on the stump.

If the resident does not know how to look after the artificial leg, they should ask for advice from the limb fitting centre. Do not be tempted to oil the leg, or to adjust it yourself, as this may cause severe damage, or make the limb unsafe.

Phantom limb pain is pain that seems to come from the part of the limb that has been removed. It may be continuous or intermittent, and the cause is not fully understood. Pain-killing tablets should be tried first; if these do not help, the resident should be referred to a pain clinic for possible transcutaneous nerve stimulation or other forms of therapy.

## Varicose veins and ulcers

A vein that becomes varicose is wider and longer than a normal one. It looks unsightly, and it works poorly because the valves that normally prevent blood from flowing backward cannot work properly when they are stretched. Aching and swelling of the leg follow, and in the worst cases the swollen tissues break down to form an ulcer, often just above the ankle on the inner side of the leg. Other complications include itchy varicose eczema and phlebitis, which is infection of a vein. Bleeding may be severe if a varicose vein is injured (see p 217).

Elastic stockings help varicose veins to empty, and reduce backward flow and swelling. They should be put on in bed before the person stands up and the veins distend with blood. Walking helps blood flow, but sufferers should not stand still for long, as the blood pools in the veins. The feet should be raised when sitting down (see 'Ankle swelling', p 68).

Varicose ulcers are usually treated with pressure bandaging applied by the district nurse. Occasionally the sufferer needs to be admitted to hospital for bed rest to heal the ulcer, and sometimes a skin graft is applied.

You can find out more about heart and blood vessel disease from the British Heart Foundation.

### KEY POINTS

- Angina and heart attacks are caused by narrowed or blocked coronary arteries; treatment can help.
- Pacemakers can much improve the quality of life of people with disturbances of heart rhythm.
- Older people with swollen ankles do not always need diuretics ('water tablets').
- Elastic stockings may help people with varicose veins and/or swollen ankles.
- Varicose ulcers can heal, with good nursing care.

# LUNGS AND AIRWAYS

These are responsible for getting oxygen into the body, where it is needed to burn up food for heat and energy. As the chest expands when breathing in, air rushes down the airways into the lungs. Here oxygen from it crosses a thin membrane to reach the blood and the red blood cells which carry it around the body. At the same time the waste product, carbon dioxide, passes back from the blood into the lungs, and, as the chest returns to its resting state, is breathed out.

# Common problems

## Chest infections

Many older people, especially men, have chest trouble (bronchitis or emphysema) which gets worse in the winter months. Some may have a hereditary tendency, but this is worsened by smoking and air pollution. A 'chesty' person who has a cold may cough up mucus (spit) that changes from its usual clear or whitish appearance to yellow, showing that the cold has developed into bronchitis. In acute attacks the person may become severely short of breath, and when really ill may become drowsy or confused. In these cases medical help is needed urgently. However, all people with chest infections should be seen by a doctor so that an antibiotic may, if necessary, be prescribed.

## Colds

People with a cold may take a paracetamol or aspirin preparation as necessary for discomfort. Aspirin should be taken with or just after food; paracetamol is better for someone with peptic ulcers, indigestion or asthma. Sufferers should also drink plenty of fluids and keep warm.

The doctor should be called if the cold develops into a chest infection or heart failure, or if the person does not recover as rapidly as would be expected.

## 'Flu

True influenza is a viral illness which occurs in epidemics. In the early stages the temperature is higher than with a simple cold; headache and muscle aches may be severe and the sufferer may become very unwell. After recovery, a period of depression is quite common.

Because colds and 'flu are caused by viruses rather than by bacteria, antibiotics are not helpful in combating the original infection. They may, however, be useful if secondary infections attack the person who has already been weakened by the virus.

People with diabetes or heart, lung or kidney disease should ask their doctor about an annual 'flu injection. Some people have a mild 'flu-like illness for a day or two after the injection, but this is much less severe than 'flu itself.

## Pneumonia

This is an inflammation of the lungs themselves. It may happen because an upper respiratory tract infection has spread downwards into the chest, but it can occur on its own, or it may develop as a complication of another illness.

When pneumonia occurs in someone who has previously been unwell and 'chesty', it is usually quite easy for the doctor to diagnose by listening to the patient's chest. However, pneumonia in an older person can cause other symptoms such as mental confusion or a tendency to fall. If this happens in someone with few signs of chest illness, their mental state may be wrongly attributed to 'senility' and the pneumonia missed. You can prevent this mistake by telling the doctor that the resident's confusion is of recent onset and apparently related to the physical illness.

### KEY POINTS

- Residents who cough up green or yellow spit need to see the doctor.
- A chest infection can make an older person confused.
- Older people with diabetes or heart, lung or kidney disease should ask the doctor for an annual 'flu injection.
- Heart and lung diseases are more common in smokers; it is never too late for quitting the habit to help health.

# DIGESTIVE SYSTEM

This consists of a long tube running from the mouth to the opening of the back passage, together with various glands that open into the tube. It processes food into a form that can be absorbed into the blood and used in the body for energy, maintenance and growth. Undigested food, bacteria, bile and intestinal juices are passed out as stools (faeces).

# Common problems

## Diverticular disease

This is a very common condition, especially in people who over a long period have not taken sufficient fibre in their diet, so the bowel muscle does not have enough to squeeze against. The pressure inside the bowel then becomes high, and pockets of the lining tend to be forced outwards, rather like portions of an inner tube ballooning through weak places in a bicycle tyre. These soft pouches are called 'diverticula'.

Many people with diverticular disease have no symptoms at all. Others have pain on the left side of the abdomen and suffer from constipation or diarrhoea. A few develop complications such as infection, abscesses or bowel blockage. These complications make the person seriously ill, with abdominal pain and sickness, and urgent medical help will be required.

However, such problems are rare. A high-fibre diet will help, and the doctor will be able to prescribe medicines to relieve bowel muscle spasm if this proves necessary.

## Peptic ulcers

These occur when acid gastric juice attacks and starts to digest an unprotected part of the stomach or duodenal lining. The commonest complaint of ulcer sufferers is of abdominal pain, which usually occurs before meals or during the night when the stomach and duodenum are empty of food. The ulcer may go on giving trouble in this way for a few days or even weeks before it gets better, and the person then may be well for some time before symptoms recur. People with uncomplicated ulcers do not usually vomit or lose weight.

The GP will usually refer a person with a suspected ulcer to the hospital for diagnostic tests. Common ones include gastroscopy, when the stomach lining is inspected through a slim telescope passed down the gullet. An alternative is the barium meal, when the ulcer is made visible on an X-ray when it is coated with a special liquid drunk by the patient. You should help the resident to follow the hospital's instructions as to how to prepare for the tests. Once a diagnosis has been made, the ulcer can usually be healed by a course of tablets or medicine. Most patients are able to eat a normal diet and drink a little alcohol, but smoking slows ulcer healing. Surgical treatment is now rarely necessary to treat uncomplicated peptic ulcers, but may be needed occasionally to stop bleeding or to close a perforation, if the ulcer eats right through the gut wall. These complications are serious, but uncommon.

## Hernias

A hernia happens when a part of the gut slips into the wrong position. Two sorts of hernia are especially common in older people: inguinal hernia and hiatus hernia.

### *Inguinal hernia*

Commonly called a rupture, this happens when a piece of bowel pushes out of the abdominal cavity into the groin or into the scrotum in men or the labium in women. The swelling enlarges when the person strains or coughs and may become uncomfortable by the end of the day. By lying down, the sufferer may be able to push the swelling back into the abdomen and thereby 'reduce' the hernia.

A neglected hernia may sometimes become stuck (irreducible), and the bowel loop that cannot return to the abdominal cavity is at risk from losing its blood supply. This is a serious condition ('strangulated hernia'), causing abdominal pain and vomiting, and it requires urgent treatment.

The best treatment for an inguinal hernia is surgery. The usual operation 'reduces' the hernia and repairs the tunnel, so that the exit route of the bowel loop is blocked.

Sometimes a truss is supplied instead when a person is unwilling to have an operation or is unfit to undergo surgery. This is put on before getting out of bed, so that the pressure pad blocks the exit tunnel and keeps the bowel loop from emerging. The truss should be kept on until bed time. Not all hernias are suitable for control by a truss, and an operation often makes the patient much more comfortable. Also, emergency surgery for a strangulated hernia is much more risky than the routine procedure. Because of this, doctors usually advise a hernia operation for anyone who is fit for it.

### *Hiatus hernia*

This happens entirely out of sight within the body when a part of the stomach slips upwards through the diaphragm. Several symptoms can follow: the person may have pain because stomach acid irritates the gullet, food may stick at the bottom of the gullet, and an ulcerated or compressed area may bleed. However, someone with a hiatus hernia may have none of these symptoms.

Hiatus hernia sufferers may be advised by the doctor to sleep with the head of the bed raised, to lose weight and to avoid bending which pushes stomach acid into the gullet. Alternatively, the amount of acid in the stomach may be reduced by tablets or the sore area coated by a protective liquid taken after meals.

## Stomas

A *colostomy* is an opening made in the abdominal wall through which the bowel empties into a stoma bag. An *ileostomy* is an opening made higher up the bowel, and a *urostomy* drains urine to the outside via the bowel loop. A colostomy is the likeliest sort of stoma for an elderly resident to have.

Stomas are formed for several reasons. Sometimes they are temporary, but a permanent one is inevitably an upset to the individual. However, normal life is still possible with a stoma, and equipment and know-how are improving all the time.

The need for a stoma is bound to come as a shock, and counselling before the operation is helpful when possible. The stoma nurse is the expert on stoma care. She or he will usually visit the patient after discharge from hospital, and can be called on for help if problems arise.

The stoma site is chosen carefully, to be away from bones and the scars of previous operations. It should not interfere with clothing, and should be placed where the resident can see it clearly. You may be able to help a diffident resident to express their preferences to medical staff, and can also pass on useful information about their capabilities – for instance, that they see poorly or have limited finger movement.

After the operation, some patients know so well when the stoma will function that they only need a gauze dressing between times. A few can empty the bowel by irrigation – flushing it out with water. However, most people with a stoma need an appliance to collect the stools reliably without leakage or smell. Bag-changing kit should be kept together, ideally in a bathroom cupboard. Used bags may be collected by the local authority's dirty dressings service, or a germicide-impregnated container may be collected by the supplying company when full. As a last resort, used bags may be emptied, rinsed, wrapped in newspaper and sealed in a plastic bag before being put in the dustbin.

People with stomas commonly complain of smell, change in function or soreness round the bowel opening. Deodorant drops in the bag or a charcoal filter will reduce odour. Particular foods may cause liquid stools or excessive wind; once identified, they can be avoided. Sore areas of skin usually get better with a barrier cream to protect them from stools or from appliance materials. The stoma nurse can advise further.

Any new doctor (eg a locum) should be told about the resident's stoma. This is because the effects of medicines prescribed for other conditions may be altered by it, or they may affect the function of the stoma itself.

People with a long-established stoma who move into the Home should have a check to make sure all is well, and to see whether new appliances might be useful to them.

Despite these difficulties, many older people adjust well to coping with a stoma; further information can be obtained from the British Colostomy Association.

## Haemorrhoids (commonly called 'piles')

In this condition, part of the lining of the back passage slips down, swells and bleeds. The blood is usually bright red, comes just after a stool is passed and stains the lavatory paper. In between times, piles hurt and cause itching round the back passage opening.

Most bleeding from the back passage is caused by piles. However, there is a small chance that the blood is coming from a bowel cancer, and therefore anyone who notices this sort of bleeding should see the doctor for an examination to rule out the possibility of a cancer. The doctor can also help the symptoms of piles by prescribing creams or suppositories; surgical treatment is occasionally needed.

## Gall bladder disease

The gall bladder concentrates the bile ('gall') produced by the liver; bile helps to digest fat in food. Bile may solidify, forming gallstones; these cause severe pain, vomiting and jaundice if they block the bile passages.

The gall bladder may sometimes become infected – the condition of 'cholecystitis'. However, many people with gallstones have no trouble from them.

Because neglected gallstones sometimes cause complications, people with gallstones producing symptoms are usually advised to have treatment for them – usually removal of the gall bladder, called 'cholecystectomy'. People waiting for this are more comfortable if they take a high-fibre, low-fat diet. Occasionally, gallstones can be dissolved by bile acids taken by mouth, and new techniques for breaking them up inside the body are being tried.

## Malabsorption

Some older people become malnourished because they cannot absorb the nutrients from their food; this is called malabsorption. One common cause of this is coeliac disease. Malabsorption also follows when digestive juices are not produced properly by a diseased liver or pancreas, and when the bowel has been damaged by injury, operation or poor blood supply.

People with malabsorption often lose weight and usually show signs of nutrient lack, such as anaemia or bone disease from vitamin D deficiency. They may have fatty diarrhoea, and if this is severe they may become incontinent of stools.

The treatment is to correct the cause whenever possible; people with coeliac disease need to avoid wheat and rye flour in their diet and possibly oats and barley, too. Even a small lapse can cause symptoms to recur. Fresh milk and meat, fish and eggs, fruit and vegetables, rice and maize, tea, coffee and sugar are all safe, but many processed foods contain gluten and must be avoided. Special gluten-free bread will also be needed. A dietician's advice may help the resident to enjoy their meals while keeping to their diet.

When the cause of malabsorption cannot be removed, affected people need extra nutrients such as vitamins.

**KEY POINTS**

- Diverticular disease is common but rarely serious.
- Peptic ulcers can usually be healed by medicines; surgery is only needed for bleeding and perforation.
- An inguinal hernia is best treated surgically.
- A hiatus hernia can cause pain, heart-burn and internal bleeding; treatment helps.
- A stoma is an artificial opening through which the bowel empties. Stoma nurses help with care.
- Haemorrhoids (piles) often bleed, but serious causes such as cancer of the bowel should be ruled out.
- Gallstones causing symptoms should be removed surgically.
- Some older people lose weight because they cannot absorb the goodness from food. Treating the cause helps.

# NERVOUS SYSTEM

The brain, the spinal cord running down from it within the backbone and the network of nerves carrying information through the body make up the nervous system. It is responsible for communications within the body, and also processes information reaching it from the outside world via the senses. This it compares with information stored in the memory and then organises the body's response.

## Common problems

### Stroke

A stroke (called a 'cerebrovascular accident' by doctors) happens when a brain blood vessel blocks or bursts. Strokes are especially common in Afro-Caribbeans because of a tendency to high blood pressure. In a major or 'completed' stroke, the section of the brain normally supplied by the damaged vessel loses its blood supply and dies, while the surrounding sections swell and work less well than before. The part of the body controlled by the dead area of brain loses its function. The person may become gradually or suddenly unconscious, or in a milder case may be confused and may vomit. When examined by the doctor, evidence of damage to the brain may be found.

The most common pattern is one of paralysis of movement and loss of sensation down one side of the body. Speech may be interfered with – either the ability to understand or to speak, or both. Vision may also be disturbed, and the person may also become incontinent. In a completed stroke the symptoms last longer than 24 hours.

In a transient ischaemic attack (TIA) the symptoms and signs disappear within 24 hours. They may include confusion, a fall, weakness of one limb or half of the body, drooping of the eyelid or one half of the face, or speech disturbance. Symptoms of a TIA should always be reported to the doctor, as treatment with a small dose of aspirin, or other measures, may prevent a later stroke.

The recovery of a person who has suffered a stroke depends on the severity of the damage to the brain and on the quality of rehabilitation received from professionals and from family and friends. Someone who is paralysed may be rehabilitated in hospital, a day hospital or a specialist centre. Here physiotherapists, occupational therapists, speech therapists and others help the stroke sufferer to strengthen muscles, improve co-ordination and balance, and make the best use of remaining abilities. Rehabilitation may be carried out in the person's home by a visiting therapist, and special equipment may be provided.

It can be difficult to diagnose a stroke in the early stages. Headache, confusion, nausea and vomiting may precede obvious weakness. Some stroke patients become gradually or suddenly unconscious, and may die without coming round. On the whole, the longer and deeper the period of unconsciousness, the worse the outlook is.

If a resident with a stroke goes into hospital, you should keep in touch and make sure a Home visit by an occupational therapist or physiotherapist is organised long before discharge is planned: then any equipment or adaptations needed to keep the resident independent can be arranged in good time. The simplest aids are often the most useful: non-slip mats to go beneath cups and plates, rocking knives and clip-on plate edges for one-handed eating are examples.

If the stroke sufferer stays in the Home, you should call on the community nursing service for help with care. If domiciliary physiotherapy is not on offer, you may need to help the resident press for out-patient rehabilitation. Make sure you and your staff know how to position the person in bed and chair so as to preserve maximum function in joints and muscles. The physiotherapist may advise on this, and a useful booklet, *Home Care for the Stroke Patient in the Early Days*, is available from the Stroke Association.

Many older people have other disabilities that interfere with their rehabilitation; these include poor heart and lung function, muscle wasting and joint disease. They may need a lot of emotional support from staff to stop them becoming disheartened. It is important to continue to encourage stroke sufferers to become more independent, as improvement remains possible indefinitely.

Speech impairment after a stroke may be of several different types. The stroke sufferer may have difficulty in understanding what is said, difficulty in speaking, or both. Speech and language therapy is very useful, but is sometimes scarce. Try to arrange for at least a speech therapy assessment, as the therapist can then advise family, friends and carers how best to help. There may also be a local Volunteer Stroke Scheme, whose members will work on speech skills; the Stroke Association will be able to tell you what is available in your area.

When talking with a stroke sufferer, make sure you stand where they can see you: their vision may be restricted on the paralysed side. Get their attention by touching their 'good' hand: the weak one may have no feeling. Speak slightly slower than usual, in short, simple sentences. Closed questions which can be answered with 'yes' or 'no' may be useful if the person has little or no speech. If necessary, a code can be used; for example, one hand-squeeze for 'yes', two for 'no'. You may also find a word and picture chart useful; the person can then point to what is wanted – toilet, drink, spectacles – without the need for speech. These charts can be obtained from the Stroke Association.

Remember that a speechless stroke sufferer may still have full understanding, so avoid 'talking down' to them.

Some stroke patients are troubled by 'emotional incontinence', a tendency to laugh or cry very easily. This is best dealt with by matter-of-fact kindness while distracting the sufferer with conversation on neutral topics. Depression is common after a stroke, and you should watch for signs such as persisting lowness of spirits, failure to progress with rehabilitation and unexplained pain. All of these may be helped by treatment.

## Parkinson's disease

This is a disorder of the ability to move, often associated with tremor, and was originally called 'the shaking palsy'. It may start with difficulty in using one arm or with performing complex movements such as climbing out of a car. Because the facial muscles are stiffened, people with Parkinson's disease lack expression and may drool saliva. Despite this appearance, they may be mentally normal and merely imprisoned in an unco-operative body, though mental decline may be noticeable in the later stages of the disease. Walking may be difficult, and they will shuffle their feet and adopt a hunched posture.

Correctly prescribed and used medication can make a great difference to the independence and comfort of the person with Parkinson's disease. Your resident may benefit from reassessment of their condition by a neurologist. This can be arranged through the GP. Medicines for Parkinson's disease must be given exactly as prescribed, and must never be stopped suddenly.

People with Parkinson's disease commonly have speech difficulties, and the lack of clues from facial expression mean that it can sometimes be difficult to tell whether the person understands you. If necessary, encourage the use of gestures, or show the person a communication chart with pictures and letters to point to. Speech therapy is useful, and a single assessment for the guidance of carers and family is better than nothing.

If you do not understand someone with Parkinson's, ask them to repeat what they have said, more slowly if necessary. Give them time to respond, and do not shout; raise your voice only if you know they are deaf. Do not finish sentences for them but, after several failed attempts, try 'Do you mean ... ?' A 'twenty questions' approach, each answerable by 'yes' or 'no', may reveal what the person wants. Above all, remember how frustrated the resident feels, and try to be as patient as possible.

People with Parkinson's disease should be encouraged to remain active. They may be helped considerably by physiotherapy, speech therapy and by the provision of aids to help with eating, dressing and other daily activities. They sometimes have 'tricks' for keeping themselves moving; it can help to aim for a mark on the floor slightly beyond the natural length of the stride. Other people attach a small prong to the side of the walking stick, and aim to step over it. The physiotherapist's advice may be useful here.

People with Parkinson's disease who find eating difficult may need a swallowing assessment, done by a speech therapist, plus the dietician's help: foods of a porridge-like consistency may be the easiest to cope with. Posture is important, an upright position making swallowing easier; sips of iced water may help the food down. Dietary advice may also minimise weight loss and relieve constipation.

Medicines are available to help with dribbling. It also helps to keep the head upright and the lips tightly closed: sufferers can help keep their mouth closed by holding a wooden spatula or lolly stick between their lips when relaxing to read or watch television.

Depression can be difficult to notice in someone with Parkinson's, but should be watched for all the same. Drug treatment is possible, but requires extra care in a person taking levodopa.

The Parkinson's Disease Society is a good source of further information for the affected resident, for their family and for you.

## Depression

Studies suggest that as many as one-third of the residents of Homes may have a depressive illness. One reason this is not identified is that younger people wrongly imagine old age to be inevitably a miserable time. Depression can also be difficult to notice in people from other cultures, especially if they do not speak English.

Depressed people may be obviously sad, though some keep up a front of apparent cheerfulness. They usually have a disturbed sleep rhythm, waking in the small hours of the morning when they feel worst. Some sufferers become mentally and physically slow, with loss of interest in life, concentration and memory. They may be wrongly thought to be suffering from dementia. Other people become agitated, demanding of attention and fearful of being left alone. Depressed older people may complain of physical symptoms that have no obvious cause. If they have a genuine illness, they may seem to lose the will to recover, and chronic problems may seem to be 'getting on top of them' more than usual.

Depression poisons the lives of sufferers and those around them. It can be fatal: sufferers can neglect themselves so much that they become dangerously ill, or they can kill themselves. If a resident threatens suicide, you should notify the doctor without delay.

Two sorts of treatment are available for depression. These are the various sorts of psychotherapy, and 'medical' treatment with medicines or, less commonly, electroconvulsive therapy (ECT). Psychotherapy may be enough for less severely ill people, whilst sicker ones may need to respond a little to medical treatment before they can usefully have psychotherapy.

The pattern of daily life in a Home can reduce depressive illness in residents. You can help to prevent it by:

- Trying to ensure that your residents' physical health is as good as possible.

- Helping them to make the most of impaired sight or hearing.

- Encouraging your residents to take charge of their own lives and make their own choices whenever possible. 'Risky' behaviour that improves a resident's quality of life without endangering anyone else should not only be tolerated but actively encouraged.

- Acting as confidant for any resident who lacks one among their family and friends. Be aware that they will need to express 'unacceptable' feelings as well as the expected ones: as well as mourning a dead partner, they may want to tell of their anger and sexual longing.

- Helping residents to compensate for the losses in their lives by finding new interests and new friends. It may be possible to use an old skill to boost present self-esteem: a disabled gardener can still provide expert care for pot plants.

- Making sure residents' social circumstances are as good as possible. Help them to claim benefit entitlements, or any charitable grants that will pay for life-enhancing items. Provide information about local services such as Dial-a-Ride schemes, clubs, social opportunities and adult education that can relieve isolation and add zest to life.

Useful literature about depressive illness can be obtained free from the Royal College of Psychiatrists.

## Normal and abnormal anxiety

It is normal to be anxious some of the time, and slight anxiety can even make us perform better. However, high levels of anxiety are both distressing and disabling. Some anxious older people have a dementia or a depressive illness, while in others anxiety is the main problem. The person may be anxious most of the time – 'anxiety state' – or only in response to a particular situation – 'phobia'. Agoraphobia is an example, when the affected person avoids going outdoors into open spaces because of the anxiety this induces; this aggravates the problem, as phobias get worse when sufferers avoid triggering events. In 'panic attacks' the feelings are so intense as to be overwhelming. 'Post-traumatic stress disorder', the long-term consequences of particularly unpleasant events such as rape, serious accidents or disasters, has recently been recognised in older people, especially those with civilian or military war service.

### Symptoms and signs

In an anxiety state, people have feelings of foreboding and dread, and they are unable to concentrate because they are preoccupied by worrying thoughts. They are irritable, extra-sensitive to noise and their sleep pattern is disturbed. Physical signs of anxiety are common: they include palpitations, dry mouth, sweating, diarrhoea, urinary frequency and an aching head, neck and back because the muscles are clenched tight. Very anxious people over-breathe, which worsens palpitations and chest pain, and also causes dizziness, faintness and tingling in the hands and feet. As older people quite often have physical illness causing similar symptoms, it can be quite difficult to decide just what is going on.

### How to help: setting things in motion

Encourage the anxious resident to see the doctor. A good physical examination and tests if necessary will enable the doctor to diagnose and treat any physical problems or, alternatively, to give convincing reassurance that all is physically well. A busy GP may need help in diagnosing and managing the psychological aspects of the person's problems: depending on local services, an old age psychiatrist (psycho-geriatrician), clinical psychologist or community psychiatric nurse may be available for this, and you may like to suggest that they are called in. It is especially important to make sure that obvious anxiety is not masking a depressive illness, as this requires different treatment.

## Psychological forms of treatment

Though this will be done by an expert, you and your staff can be shown ways of supporting and helping the resident through it.

**Relaxation therapy** involves learning how to loosen muscles. The person begins by clenching their fists and tightening all their muscles for a count of three. They then relax the tension and let themselves go loose. Once they know what this feels like, they can relax even further. Meanwhile, they take slow, regular breaths and call up a restful picture in their mind's eye – a quiet scene or a favourite activity, for instance. Once learned, relaxation needs to be practised regularly, and you and your staff can encourage this; an audiotape on a personal stereo can also help.

**Anxiety management** helps people who are sufficiently mentally alert to control their own anxiety level. They deliberately think about topics that provoke anxiety and then use imaging, relaxation techniques and opposing thoughts to make their feelings more tolerable.

**Cognitive therapy** helps people to correct false thoughts that maintain anxiety. For instance, someone with palpitations can worry that they will develop heart disease: they can be helped to see that they are thinking in circles, and can then accept alternative psychological explanations.

**Exposure to triggers** is used in treating phobias. In agoraphobia, 'flooding' works best: the person is taken to an open, public place by the therapist, who encourages them to experience the anxious feelings in a safe setting until they start to subside. For other types of phobia a graded approach can be used, working up through thinking about the object, to looking at pictures and parts of the object and finally the thing itself.

**Response prevention** is used in obsessive compulsive disorders. Instead of, for instance, returning time and again to check that the door is shut, the person resists the impulse and endures the anxiety. Whereas yielding to the checking impulse worsens the problem, resisting it in this way can break the cycle.

## Drug treatment

Medicines have only a limited place in the management of anxiety. The benzodiazepine anxiolytics or minor tranquillisers (see p 204) induce dependence, and withdrawal from them worsens anxiety. It is occasionally justified to use them over a very short, limited period for a particular reason – to induce sleep, for example.

Anti-depressants (see p 203) may be useful when anxiety is part of a depressive illness, and their sedative properties are sometimes useful to control anxiety in people who are not obviously depressed. Newer drugs may have fewer unwanted effects than older ones.

When the person is severely distressed and nothing else seems to work, 'anti-psychotic' medicines such as thioridazine (see pp 167 and 204) may help, though there is considerable risk of unwanted effects.

## Panic attacks

These are often part of a phobia or anxiety state, when they should be treated as described above. Anti-depressant drugs are also helpful. More specialised psychological treatment can help people with mainly physical symptoms.

## Post-traumatic stress disorder

This is the result of very distressing events such as disasters or personal tragedies. It has recently been noticed in older people who had terrible experiences in war time. Features of the disorder include:

- preoccupation with unpleasant memories;
- flashbacks, with sudden vivid reliving of the experience;
- nightmares and other sleep disturbance;
- general anxiety and signs of depression;
- avoidance of situations reminding the person of their bad experience;
- a tendency to abuse alcohol or other substances.

Treatment involves giving the person the opportunity to talk about their terrible experience, to relive their feelings and to 'process' their emotions in the company of someone who will be with them while they cope with their distress. Other problems such as alcohol abuse or depression may need separate treatment.

## A listening ear

In general, it seems that the more time staff and others can spend in listening with careful interest to residents talking about their worries, the easier residents will be in their minds and the less medicines will be needed.

This account is not intended to turn you and your staff into amateur psychiatrists. Instead, it may help you to understand your residents better, and to use your day-to-day encounters with them to help them cope with present and past experience, and to see a total meaning in their lives.

## Shingles

This is a localised form of chickenpox (herpes zoster). After the original attack, the virus lies dormant in the spinal cord until it is reactivated, when it causes shingles. The commonest area to be affected is one side of the trunk, but an especially unpleasant form affects the forehead and eyes (ophthalmic herpes).

Shingles starts with pain and soreness, after which the affected skin becomes red and blisters appear. The shingles patient is infectious until the blisters dry to form scabs. Someone giving personal care to a resident with shingles could catch chickenpox; pregnant women can develop a serious form and have a miscarriage.

Most people with shingles can be treated in the Home. Some forms of treatment work best if started early in the illness, so if you suspect a resident has shingles the doctor should be called without delay. People with ophthalmic herpes or severe disease elsewhere may need to go into hospital. A few people who have had shingles develop persistent, unpleasant pain called post-herpetic neuralgia.

**KEY POINTS**

- Enthusiastic rehabilitation improves the quality of life of someone who has had a stroke.
- A transient ischaemic attack may herald a stroke; call the doctor.

- People with Parkinson's disease should see a specialist to get expert treatment. Physiotherapy, occupational therapy, speech therapy and good general care also help.

- Depression in old age is common, serious, often missed but often treatable. Good care practice makes it less likely to happen.

- Excessive anxiety, phobias and panic attacks can be very distressing but are treatable.

- Shingles causes pain and soreness followed by a blistered rash. Prompt treatment works best. A few sufferers get persistent pain (post-herpetic neuralgia).

# THE EYES

The eyeball has a transparent window, the cornea, at the front for light to enter. The light is then focused by the cornea, the lens and the fluids within the eye on to the retina which lines the back of the eye. Visual information is carried from the retina along nerve pathways to the brain, where it is interpreted and stored.

In middle age, people need to hold books and objects away from their eyes in order to see clearly. This is due to ageing changes in the lens and is usually corrected by reading glasses. However, no other change in sight should be accepted as normal, but should be reported to the optician or doctor. For information about conditions needing urgent attention see 'Eye emergencies' in Chapter 9.

## Common problems

### Cataract

This happens because of irreversible changes in the protein that makes up the lens of the eye, so that it becomes opaque and light can no longer pass through it. The person notices a gradual clouding of sight, and the doctor or optician can see the opacity with an ophthalmoscope. Cataracts are six times as common in older Asian people as in native Britons. This happens because diabetes is more common in this group, and sometimes because of excess exposure to ultraviolet light in early life in the Indian subcontinent.

## Treatment for cataract

The lens has to be removed surgically so that light can reach the retina again. This operation is usually done when the person's sight has deteriorated to the point where reading or daily life becomes difficult. Although cataracts often affect both eyes, usually one eye is affected more seriously than the other, and the worse one will be operated on first.

After surgery a new lens has to be put in the line of vision to replace the cloudy one. Best results follow when an artificial lens is implanted in the eyeball where the old one used to be, but this is not always technically possible. Instead, cataract spectacles may be provided; the wearer needs to become accustomed to these gradually. Contact lenses are rarely suitable for older cataract patients.

## Macular degeneration (age-related maculopathy)

This affects the macula, the central part of the visual field. Affected people first notice distortion of their vision, straight lines appearing curved. They have difficulty in matching colours and in adjusting to changes in light intensity, as when going out from a well lit house into a dimly lit street. Later it becomes difficult to read small, faint print, to thread needles and to do similar fine work.

One form of macular degeneration, the 'wet' form, can be treated by laser therapy. Unfortunately, 85–90 per cent of older people have the 'dry' form, which cannot be helped in this way.

People with macular degeneration do not go completely blind, as the periphery of the visual field is not affected. Because of this, sufferers remain fairly independent, especially if they make the most of their remaining sight (see pp 136–141).

## Glaucoma

This happens because the pressure of the fluid inside the eye rises, causing damage to the light-sensitive retina, which is unable to repair itself. Someone with acute glaucoma feels sick and ill. The affected eye is red and painful, with little vision. Anyone with these symptoms should seek medical help urgently. The more common, chronic cases produce a gradual loss of sight, which may not be noticed by the sufferer until considerable damage has occurred. Seeing coloured haloes around lights suggests that pressure is rising, and this should be reported to the doctor promptly.

Medical treatment involves the use of drugs, as eye-drops or as tablets, or both. If this is insufficient, surgery may become necessary. This is now much less disturbing because of the development of lasers.

People with glaucoma must use their eye-drops regularly and correctly; the practice or district nurse can teach these skills. Residents may be able to manage by themselves, especially if they use inexpensive devices to help with instillation, which are available from pharmacists. If staff need to help, make sure they know how to do this.

With adequate treatment and good follow-up, sight should not deteriorate, though retinal damage that has already occurred will not get better.

## Diabetic retinopathy

In some people with diabetes, new blood vessels grow (proliferate) in the retina of the eye. These can endanger sight, gradually by replacing nervous tissue or suddenly by bleeding into the eye. This sometimes causes retinal detachment. The changes of diabetic retinopathy can be seen when the eye is examined through an ophthalmoscope.

It is now possible to clot the new blood vessels with a laser beam as they develop and thus prevent them from impairing sight. Detecting the proliferation process early is therefore important, so people with diabetes should have regular eye examinations to detect such abnormalities.

## Retinal detachment

This may happen because of a blow on the head, but it also occurs in people with diabetes. The first signs are new 'floaters' in the field of vision; these consist of blood or bits of pigment from the torn retina. The strain on the retina makes the sufferer see flashing lights in the affected eye. Eventually the retina is pulled away from the back of the eye and crumples up; as this happens, part of the visual field goes black and is lost.

A detached retina can produce partial or complete blindness, but urgent repair using a laser beam prevents further tearing and preserves sight.

Anyone who suffers a sudden loss of vision should go at once to their GP or the emergency department of the nearest eye hospital.

## Giant cell arteritis (GCA)

In this condition the arteries supplying the face, scalp and eyes become inflamed and partially blocked by the big cells that give the disease its name. The sufferer feels generally unwell and complains of pain in the side of the head; it hurts to chew food, and the face is often tender to touch. If sight deteriorates, this shows that the retina is at risk of damage because its blood supply is threatened. This can lead to permanent blindness if untreated.

Steroids are an effective treatment; if sight loss seems imminent, steroids are started before the diagnosis is clinched by tests. In less urgent cases, blood tests are performed and a sample (biopsy) of the temporal artery is taken. This can be looked at under the microscope to see if tell-tale giant cells are present. Once the condition is under control, the dose of steroids can be reduced, and they can often be stopped altogether after a year or so.

People with giant cell arteritis have an above-average risk of developing polymyalgia rheumatica (see p 100).

## Conjunctivitis

This is an infection of the outermost membrane covering the eye, which becomes red because of the dilation of tiny blood vessels: hence the name 'pink eye'. Pus may stick the eye-lids together when the person is sleeping, and it also collects during the day in the corner of the eye, which feels gritty and uncomfortable. Conjunctivitis usually gets better quickly if treated with antibiotic ointment; the resident should see the doctor so that this can be prescribed, and also to make sure that the symptoms are due to conjunctivitis and not to more serious causes of a painful red eye.

- It is normal to need reading glasses as we age; all other sight difficulties should be reported to the doctor.
- An opaque lens in the eye (cataract) must be removed surgically. An artificial lens can be implanted or worn in contact lenses or spectacles.
- People with macular degeneration benefit from making the most of remaining sight.
- Blindness resulting from retinal detachment, glaucoma or diabetes may be preventable.

# THE EARS

The outer ear canal funnels sound waves inward to the ear-drum, which in turn transmits them through the tiny linked bones of the middle ear. The sound waves then reach the inner ear, which is concerned with balance as well as hearing. The hearing organ in the inner ear transforms sound vibrations into impulses that are carried by the auditory nerve to the brain, where they are interpreted and compared with past experiences.

## Common problems

Most older people lose some hearing for high-pitched sounds, but this does not cause inconvenience or affect social life. Anyone who finds it difficult to join in group conversation or who needs the television or radio turned up abnormally loud has hearing loss (deafness) and should be encouraged to seek help. Deafness is medically described as being either conductive or perceptive (sensori-neural).

### Conductive deafness

This is due to an impairment of the transmission of sound waves from outside the body to the boundary between the middle and the inner ear. It is easier to treat than perceptive deafness.

Wax in the outer ear canal is a common and easily remedied cause of conductive deafness. Because of the fragile skin lining the canal and the risk of damage to the ear-drum, objects should never be poked into the ear in an attempt to remove wax – even cotton wool sticks can push it further into the ear and tamp it down into a solid mass. People who suspect that accumulated wax may be affecting their hearing should go to the doctor's surgery to get it removed.

Damage to the ear-drum also causes conductive deafness. This may happen because of an injury, either directly or through blast, or because of an infection and subsequent perforation of the ear-drum. It is sometimes possible to restore hearing by repairing the damaged ear-drum.

**Otosclerosis**, another form of conductive deafness which may start in middle age or before, happens when one of the tiny bones in the middle ear becomes fixed in place and can no longer conduct sound waves. Otosclerosis is treated by a delicate surgical operation which restores hearing.

## Perceptive (sensori-neural) deafness

This is due to disease or damage of the inner ear or of the auditory nerve connecting it to the brain. Because nerve tissue is unable to heal, this sort of deafness cannot usually be cured, but good care and help can make life more enjoyable for the deaf person.

**Presbyacusis** is the nerve deafness common in elderly people. It produces hearing loss, especially for high-pitched sounds such as 't's and 's's, so that speech is distorted. 'Loudness recruitment' means that a slight increase in the loudness of a sound is heard painfully loudly. Hearing abilities may vary from day to day, and deafness may be accompanied by tinnitus (see below). Because hearing aids only make sound louder, they are not always very helpful in this type of deafness.

**Menière's disease**, another cause of perceptive deafness, usually occurs in middle age, with attacks of giddiness, sickness and deafness. Gradually the attacks cease, but the deafness persists into old age. Nerve damage to the ear can also result from drug treatment, a head injury, a blast or loud noise during working life or war service.

## Tinnitus

This condition, which means 'noises heard in the ear', can be particularly bothersome at night. The noises are usually due to the malfunctioning of the inner ear, and are very rarely a sign of illness. Occasionally they are the result of aspirin taken in large quantities, and they will clear up if this is stopped.

It often helps people with tinnitus to be examined by an ENT (ear, nose and throat) specialist and be reassured that there is no underlying serious illness. Once they are no longer listening apprehensively for the noises, they may be able to ignore them, as they would the continued presence of a ticking clock. In other cases where the noises continue to be a nuisance, a tinnitus masker can be helpful. It fits behind the ear like a conventional hearing aid and produces a noise that conceals that of the tinnitus. The equipment needs to be fitted by an expert, and is unfortunately not nationally available under the NHS. Some sufferers find a personal stereo or radio with an earphone helpful in the same way. The British Tinnitus Association provides information, funds research and runs self-help groups for sufferers.

### KEY POINTS

- Conductive deafness may be curable if due to ear wax, a perforated ear-drum or otosclerosis.
- Deafness caused by nerve damage cannot be cured, but you can help people with this problem to make the most of their remaining hearing.
- The troublesome noises of tinnitus are less disturbing after expert reassurance and the provision of a 'masker' or earphones playing music.

# THE BLOOD

This is the body's transport system. It carries oxygen and nutrients to wherever they are needed and takes waste products to the kidneys for excretion in the urine. Chemicals such as hormones produced within the body or drugs introduced from outside also travel in the blood, and it also distributes heat.

# Common problems

## Anaemia

In this condition the blood contains less than normal of its red pigment, haemoglobin, which carries oxygen round the body. Anaemia is common among older people, and may be difficult to identify. Anaemic older people are often confused and apathetic, with a tendency to fall. They may also be dizzy, tired and breathless, with a sore mouth and tongue.

Anaemia is diagnosed from a blood test. Further testing can identify the sort of anaemia that is present, for there are many different causes. Some people, unknown to themselves, may be losing blood from the gut. The leakage may be from some comparatively harmless condition such as piles, or from a hiatus hernia, diverticular disease or a peptic ulcer, but anaemia can also be the first sign of cancer of the bowel. Bleeding from the gut may also follow the use of some drugs in the treatment of arthritis. A diet low in folate and iron may make things worse. Once the cause of the anaemia has been found, treatment can be started.

### Pernicious anaemia

This is due to difficulty in absorbing vitamin $B_{12}$ from food, and is serious if left untreated. The usual symptoms of anaemia may be present, and mental and nervous symptoms may be quite severe. Vitamin $B_{12}$ deficiency is, in fact, one of the reversible causes of mental confusion in older people. This sort of anaemia is treated by replacement of the deficient vitamin $B_{12}$; this has to be done by injection as these people cannot absorb it by mouth. Once pernicious anaemia has been diagnosed, injections of $B_{12}$ must continue for life.

**KEY POINT**

■ Anaemia is the commonest blood problem; it has several different causes.

# BONES AND JOINTS

The bones consist of a protein scaffolding stiffened by calcium salts, in the same way as fabric is starched. Bones meet and move on each other at the joints where the bone ends are covered in shiny cartilage, enclosed in a capsule and lubricated by synovial fluid to reduce friction. Bones tend to thin with age, especially in women after the menopause, and this osteoporosis may result in an increased tendency for bones to break.

## Common problems

### Arthritis

The commonest form of this condition is osteoarthritis, called 'OA' for short. OA is especially severe in people with injured joints or who are overweight. Women seem particularly likely to get OA in their hands, which become knobbly or gnarled, and acquire a 'squared-off' shape if the joint at the base of the thumb is affected. This impairs the ability to grip tightly, as when undoing screw tops. Other areas of the body commonly affected are the hips, the knees and the spine.

People with arthritis have dull and aching pain which often worsens in bouts and then improves. It tends to be affected by changes in the weather. Stiffness especially in the morning is also a problem. These symptoms may interfere with daily activities.

A good deal can be done to make life more pleasant for the arthritis sufferer. Someone with arthritis is helped both physically and mentally by keeping as active as their pain will allow. They may also benefit from the expert advice of a hospital rheumatologist.

Pain killers help, and the doctor should work with the sufferer to ensure that the effect of these medicines 'peaks' at the time the pain is most troublesome. In addition, painful joints should not be over-worked but moved gently between periods of rest.

Stiffness is often helped by the warmth or cold of a jelly pack (whichever the person finds gives most relief) or a warm bath. Packs can be bought from local pharmacists. If you have thermostatically controlled heat pads, be sure that they are used and maintained properly, or they could cause a burn or even a fire.

Some osteoarthritis sufferers also benefit from physiotherapy to strengthen muscles and encourage joint movement. The physiotherapist may suggest the use of a walking stick to help the person remain as mobile as possible. It should ideally be carried in the hand opposite the side of the painful hip or knee, and the arthritic leg and the stick should strike the ground at the same time. Daily activities are often made easier by the use of equipment provided by the occupational therapist.

Some people with OA eventually need to have an arthritic joint replaced by an artificial one made of metal and plastic. The hip is the joint most often operated on, but the knee, shoulder, elbow and smaller joints can also be replaced. The usual reason for the operation is to relieve pain that cannot be helped by medicines or other forms of treatment. Most older patients do well, becoming pain-free and more independent. A few develop complications such as infection, blood clots or loosening of the artificial joint.

## Rheumatoid arthritis (RA)

This tends to have more severe effects than osteoarthritis, and poses a greater threat to independence. Its cause is not fully understood. It is more common in women than in men. The basic abnormality is that the joint lining thickens and damages the bone and cartilage around it. The individual may be generally unwell, with fever and weight loss. Other organs can also be affected, with nodules forming underneath the skin, eye problems, dry mouth and nerve damage.

RA most often starts in early middle age, though it can occur in older people, sometimes very suddenly. However, most older RA patients have 'burnt-out' disease, which has left them with poor mobility and dexterity because of joint damage.

A variety of medicines are used for RA, the commonest being the non-steroidal anti-inflammatory agents (NSAIs; see p 194). If the resident has unpleasant symptoms, it may be wise for them to ask their doctor for a referral to a hospital specialist (a rheumatologist), in case special medicines are needed.

Most older RA patients find it helpful to consult an occupational therapist about aids to daily living. Cutlery with built-up shaped handles and 'space shoes', made to fit the feet in three dimensions, are especially useful.

If the occupational therapy service is limited, the resident may want to obtain equipment privately. Various mail order services produce catalogues; a visit to a Disabled Living Centre may be a good way of trying out available gadgetry without the obligation to buy.

## Osteoporosis

Bone thinning with age may be severe enough for the bones to break more easily than usual. Softened vertebrae may squash under the weight they carry, becoming wedge-shaped; this produces severe back pain and a stooped posture ('dowager's hump'). Osteoporosis happens in both sexes but proceeds more quickly in women than in men; this means that in general an older woman has thinner, weaker bones than a man of the same age, and is therefore more likely to suffer a fracture.

Hormone replacement therapy (HRT) starting at the menopause reduces bone loss. Other treatments are being developed for women who cannot take HRT. People of either sex can help to keep their bones strong by exercising, taking adequate dietary calcium and vitamin D, and refraining from smoking and drinking excess alcohol; these last two both worsen osteoporosis.

Because of the risk of a fracture, every attempt should be made to improve the health and fitness of residents who fall; a review of medicines may be especially helpful. However, it is not sensible to try to restrict the activities of an older person who is unsteady on their feet: inactivity carries its own risks to health, and may make the quality of life unacceptably poor.

## Paget's disease

In this condition, bones become abnormal. This happens patchily in the body, most commonly in the pelvis, spine, skull and bones of the legs. No one knows the cause.

Some people with Paget's have no symptoms at all, and the condition is found by chance on an X-ray taken for some other reason. Others suffer pain, and their bodies can change in shape – in particular, the head gets bigger, the legs become bowed and the spine stooped. The abnormal bone can press on nerves, and it breaks more easily than healthy bone does. In a few cases, bone cancer develops. These complications are rare, however; in most people the disease causes little trouble, pain is easily controlled and other helpful treatment is available if necessary.

## Gout

Crystals of sodium urate form in the cavity of a gouty joint, inflaming it and causing bouts of very severe pain and tenderness. The commonest joint to be affected is the one at the base of the big toe, but gout can occur elsewhere in the body. Sodium urate crystals sometimes form lumps called 'tophi' on ear flaps, fingers and toes.

The doctor's diagnosis of suspected gout can be confirmed by laboratory tests done on the patient's blood and on fluid from the affected joint. Treatment is by tablets. Sometimes the person with gout will be advised to alter unwise eating or drinking habits, but this is not always necessary; gout can and does occur in people with a healthy lifestyle.

## Polymyalgia rheumatica (PMR)

This seems to go together with giant cell arteritis (GCA) (see p 92). Both conditions may be due to faults in the immune system. PMR causes aching pain and stiffness in the muscles around the shoulders and hips, worse in the mornings and after rest. Affected people feel generally unwell, with a low fever and weight loss.

A blood test will help establish the diagnosis, and GCA may be looked for at the same time. Treatment is with steroids, which quickly make the patient feel better. PMR tends to go away within about two years of the diagnosis being made, and when this happens, steroid therapy can be stopped.

### KEY POINTS

- Arthritis can be of several different types; the commonest and least disabling is osteoarthritis.
- People with arthritis should work with the doctor and other health carers to get the best possible pain relief and function.
- Osteoporosis means that older bones break more easily.

# THE GLANDS

Within the body are a number of glands that produce hormones. These have widespread effects on various organs and tissues, and help to control many body processes, such as the metabolism of food, growth and reproduction. If the glands secrete too much or too little of their hormones, or if the balance between them is disturbed, illness results and affects several body systems.

## Common problems

### Diabetes

This is very common in older people. Those from the Indian subcontinent are five times as likely to suffer from it as native Britons, and Afro-Caribbeans also seem to be at increased risk.

When diabetes begins in later life, it is not usually due to lack of the hormone insulin as it is in younger people with 'type 1' diabetes. Instead, 'type 2' diabetes occurs because the ageing body tissues become less sensitive to insulin. When insulin is lacking or does not work and glucose cannot enter the cells, the extra glucose remains in the blood, and some then passes out of the body, dissolved by water to make extra urine. This can cause dehydration and also incontinence: an older person who becomes incontinent should always have a blood test for diabetes.

Older people with undiagnosed diabetes are often overweight and in generally poor health. They gradually develop complications of the disease: these include eye problems (see p 91), itchy fungal infections round the genital area, signs of poor circulation, and loss of pain and touch sensation in the feet and legs. Bladder and bowel function may be affected, and men may become impotent. Because of the combination of poor sensation, poor healing and increased liability to infection, people with diabetes may develop septic foot wounds which go unnoticed and may even become gangrenous. It is therefore very important for older diabetics to have regular professional chiropody. Residents with diabetes may need help with daily foot care; gentle, thorough washing should be followed by a careful inspection for small ulcers or cuts which require prompt treatment.

Some newly diagnosed diabetics are ill enough to need to go into hospital for their disease to be stabilised, whilst others can be managed as out-patients. All people with diabetes need a special diet which they must follow. Some must also take tablets to control the sugar level, and a few may need insulin injections.

The complications of diabetes seem to be less common in people whose diabetes is well controlled, so it is worth while to follow treatment instructions carefully. More information is available from the British Diabetic Association.

## Thyroid disease

The thyroid is a U-shaped gland at the base of the neck, and its secretions control energy output in most body processes. Under-activity leads to sluggishness, weight gain, poor mental function and confusion that may be wrongly diagnosed as dementia. It may also lead to hypothermia. Treatment is by replacement of the missing hormone, called thyroxine.

Over-activity of the thyroid gland in older people causes heart failure, weight loss and poor general health. It can be treated in one or more of three ways, depending on the person's needs. Radioactive iodine may be given to switch off the thyroid cells; this has to be done in hospital. Drug treatment can also be used, and surgery is occasionally required when the enlarged gland is causing symptoms by pressing on another part of the body. Treatment for over-activity may lead to under-activity in later life, especially in someone who has stopped taking their prescribed thyroid replacement. This should always be thought of in a confused older person with a thyroid operation scar, shaped so a traditional pearl necklace would hide it.

A swelling of the thyroid gland is called a goitre, and these are often nodular in older people. Nodules may be 'hot' (functioning: secreting hormone) or 'cold' (non-functioning), and cold nodules are occasionally cancerous. The treatment of thyroid nodules depends on whether or not they are malignant, whether they are causing pressure symptoms and whether the gland as a whole is over- or under-active.

- An older person with diabetes becomes generally unwell and may be confused and incontinent. Treatment makes them feel much better.

- Complications of diabetes (eg failing sight and septic foot wounds) are less likely if:

    the diabetes is well controlled;

    the person has regular eye checks and professional chiropody.

- Older people with under-active thyroid glands may be wrongly thought to have a dementing illness.

- An over-active thyroid causes weight loss, heart problems and poor general health.

- Thyroid diseases respond well to treatment.

# CANCER

## What it is

Normally, body cells work together for the health of the whole person, but when a cell becomes cancerous or, in medical jargon, malignant, it starts to grow and divide without regard to the needs of the rest of the body. In the worst sorts of cases, bits may break off from the 'primary' growth and spread directly or by the blood stream and lymph channels. These spreading cells form 'secondary deposits', sometimes called metastases, in other organs such as the lungs, bones or the brain. Growth of the primary or of the secondaries may produce symptoms by pressing on or otherwise impairing the function of vital organs. Gradually, normal body processes may fail; the sick person will become vulnerable to infection and other complications, and will eventually die.

Cancer is less common in people from the Indian subcontinent than in native Britons. Afro-Caribbeans are especially likely to develop prostatic cancer, but otherwise get less cancer than native Britons do.

There are many different sorts of cancer, some of which are curable, some containable and a few for which little curative treatment is yet possible. Older people in particular are likely to regard a diagnosis of cancer as a death sentence, and one that will be carried out in a short time with great suffering.

The truth is rather different, for many cancers in older people do not shorten life and may cause little disability. Even when no more can be done in the way of a cure, good care can ensure that life continues tolerably and even enjoyably before death follows peacefully and without distress.

## Tests for cancer

When cancer is suspected, the patient will usually have various investigations, including blood tests, X-rays and scans. Whenever possible a bit of the abnormal tissue will be sampled so that it can be examined under the microscope; this is called a biopsy. These investigations aim to answer three questions: Does the person have cancer? If so, what sort? How far has it spread? Treatment is then planned according to the answers.

## Treatment for cancer

The three basic sorts of treatment used for cancer are surgery, radiotherapy and cytotoxic (cell-poisoning) drugs (chemotherapy). The idea of surgery is to remove the primary growth before it can cause severe local damage, and theoretically before it has a chance to spread.

Radiotherapy and cytotoxic drugs both act in the same way: they kill cells, and the more rapidly a cell is dividing into new cells, the more likely it is to be killed. The usefulness of this sort of treatment depends on the fact that cancer cells divide more quickly than normal cells, and are thus killed first.

In addition, some cancers respond to hormone treatment. The principle of this is to interfere with the action of any hormone causing tumour growth, or to oppose its effects.

## Coming to terms with a diagnosis of cancer

Sick people differ in how much they want to know about their illness, and doctors vary in how much information they volunteer and how good they are at imparting it. Often, people have to take in bad news a little at a time; if offered information too early or too much at a time, they may be unable to absorb it. Sometimes the message is confused with the messenger; if the news is bad, even the most sensitive breaking of it may be perceived as brutal. Someone's account of what they have been told about the illness may be coloured by their feelings about it, and it is wise to bear this in mind.

If a resident with cancer seems to want to know more about their illness, you should suggest that they ask someone who is properly informed. Suitable people include the doctor, Macmillan nurses and members of a hospice outreach team, depending on who is available. Other good sources of information and support are organisations such as BACUP and Cancerlink, and where appropriate specialist groups such as the Breast Care and Mastectomy Association.

General health and spiritual well-being are especially important in serious illness, and neither should be neglected. Of course people have a right to opt for whatever forms of help and treatment they prefer, but it is wise to be wary of any unorthodox treatment that seems to offer a cure. None of these has been shown to work, some are actively harmful and they may delay or interfere with more effective measures. In any case, it is best if people following 'alternative' therapies tell their doctors about them, as it is impossible to look after a patient properly without all the relevant information.

## Some common types of cancer

### Bladder

The usual symptom is blood in the urine. Investigation is by cystoscopy – that is, the passing of a thin telescope up through the urethra. This is done under anaesthesia so that the bladder lining can be inspected and samples taken for laboratory analysis. Smaller cancers can be removed either through the cystoscope or during an open operation. Occasionally the bladder is removed entirely and the ureters are transplanted into a loop of bowel which drains externally into a bag; this is called a urostomy.

People who have been treated for bladder tumours are usually recalled for regular cystoscopies so that any recurrence can be detected and treated early. Many bladder tumours are comparatively harmless, and people who have them commonly lead a normal, healthy life, eventually dying of an unrelated condition.

## Bowel

The person usually consults the doctor, complaining that bowel habits have changed or that blood has appeared in stools. The presence of a cancer may be confirmed by X-ray studies, usually involving the injection of barium up the back passage (a barium enema). Alternatively, a modified telescope may be used to inspect the diseased area and to take a sample for laboratory analysis. This is called sigmoidoscopy or colonoscopy, depending on the area examined.

If surgery is used to remove the cancer, it may be possible to join up the two ends of the bowel so that the stools may still be passed in the normal way. Sometimes this cannot be done, and the person will have a colostomy (see p 76). Some of these are temporary and are closed later at a second operation, whilst others are permanent.

## Breast

This is one of the commonest cancers in women, and usually comes to light when someone finds a lump or other abnormality in her breast. Treatment may be by any combination of surgery, radiotherapy or chemotherapy. Surgery now is much less drastic than it was. Women who have had a breast removed (mastectomy) may benefit from contact with the Breast Care and Mastectomy Association.

## Leukaemia

This is a blood disease in which very many abnormal white blood cells are made at the expense of red cell and platelet production. Some people have no symptoms, whilst others become anaemic and very vulnerable to infections. They also tend to bleed excessively because their blood clots poorly.

The diagnosis is made by examining specimens of the affected person's blood or bone marrow under the microscope. Other tests may be needed if the liver, spleen or lymph nodes are thought to be affected.

Treatment depends on the type of leukaemia and how it is affecting the patient; cytotoxic drugs are often used (see p 195). The outlook is very variable, and depends on individual circumstances; some types of leukaemia in older people progress very slowly.

## Lung

Lung cancer is usually diagnosed after a person with respiratory symptoms such as coughing up blood, shortness of breath or chest pain goes to the GP and has a chest X-ray. Surgery to remove the tumour is occasionally possible, but is uncommon in older people. Radiotherapy may be used to shrink primary or secondary tumours that cause pressure symptoms, pain or bleeding. Cytotoxic drugs are rarely used.

## Prostate

Cancer of the prostate produces the same symptoms as benign enlargement of the gland (see p 126). The clinical diagnosis is based on the patient's account of his symptoms, and the results of physical examination can be confirmed by blood tests, a needle biopsy, X-rays and scans. Afro-Caribbean men are especially prone to this form of cancer.

Treatment depends on the circumstances of the case. Many prostate cancers grow and spread very slowly, so it is sometimes best simply to keep the sufferer under careful observation and relieve his symptoms as appropriate. If and when further treatment becomes necessary, this may involve surgery, radiotherapy or medicines. As prostate cancer depends on the male hormone testosterone to help it grow, hormone treatment opposing its action is often effective (see p 195).

## Skin

Skin cancers appear as lumps, warty masses or ulcers that grow slowly. Any ulcer or lump not clearing up after three weeks should be examined by a doctor. The commonest skin cancer is the 'rodent ulcer', almost always on the face. The 'malignant melanoma' is much less common and is more serious. It looks like a mole, and may bleed or enlarge noticeably. Skin cancers are treated by surgical removal and sometimes also by radiotherapy. Treatment usually produces a complete cure. Most skin growths are benign, but where there is any doubt, medical advice should be sought. If the growth is harmless, the person can be reassured; if not, the earlier a growth is removed, the less noticeable the remaining scar will be.

108

## Womb (including cervix)

Cancer can occur either in the body of the womb or in its neck or cervix, where it can be detected by a cervical smear. Abnormal bleeding is the main symptom of this condition, either between periods in younger women or recurring after the menopause in women whose periods have stopped. Any woman who has abnormal bleeding should report it to the doctor at once so that it can be investigated further. When cancer is present, treatment is usually surgical, sometimes using a laser. This may be followed by radiotherapy using radium, which is implanted in the body for a short period during a hospital stay and then removed.

Older women may try to hide gynaecological or breast cancers out of modesty. While respecting their wishes, you should try to get them to see the doctor, as treatment often results in a better as well as a longer life.

**KEY POINTS**

- There are many different sorts of cancer.
- Good treatment and care sometimes cure cancer, and always improve the person's quality of life.
- Seriously ill people should always be told as much of the truth about their illness as they want to hear. 'Telling all' can be brutal, lying is patronising; both are harmful.

# HIV AND AIDS

The human immunodeficiency virus (HIV) causes the Acquired Immunodeficiency Syndrome, commonly known as AIDS. The virus is present in the body fluids of an infected person, and can be passed on to someone else by blood, semen or vaginal fluid and from mother to child before or during birth or, afterwards, in breast milk.

# How HIV is spread

People can be infected:

- By sexual intercourse, whether heterosexual or homosexual. 'Safe sex' techniques, such as using a condom, reduce the risk.

- By contaminated blood or blood products, such as Factor VIII used to treat haemophilia. In the UK, testing and processing of blood for transfusion and treatment mean that transmission in this way is very unlikely to occur.

- By contaminated injection needles, scalpel blades or similar apparatus. This can happen when health workers suffer 'needle-stick' injuries, when intravenous drug users share needles and syringes or when reusable equipment is not properly cleaned and sterilised.

- By organ or tissue donation; people who are HIV positive should not donate blood, tissue or organs, or carry donor cards.

- By the passage of virus from mother to child before or during birth, or afterwards via breast milk.

HIV cannot be spread by coughs and sneezes, by using the same lavatory as an infected person, by sharing crockery or cutlery or by normal social contacts.

# HIV testing

Blood testing (the HIV test) will show that the person has been infected by HIV about two months after the virus has entered the body, though 'seroconversion', as it is called when the test becomes positive, can take longer. Probably about 50 per cent of people infected with HIV will develop AIDS within 12 years. We do not know for certain whether or not everyone who is infected with HIV will eventually develop AIDS but it seems likely that most will.

# What AIDS illness is like

AIDS can take several different forms. Some happen because people with AIDS are less able to fight infection. They may develop unusual illnesses such as *Pneumocystis carinii* pneumonia (PCP). Alternatively, they may become much more severely ill than would be expected if they develop shingles, tuberculosis or candida (the fungus that causes thrush). People with AIDS also develop unusual forms of cancer, such as the skin tumours of Kaposi's sarcoma and various types of lymphoma. AIDS can also appear as persistent fever, diarrhoea and weight loss; this is especially common in parts of Africa, where it is called 'slim disease'. Nervous system disorders such as dementia can also be part of the AIDS complex of illness.

## Treatment for AIDS

Various forms of treatment are used. The drug zidovudine seems to be helpful in some cases, but its unwanted effects can be severe: they include nausea, vomiting and interference with blood cell production by the bone marrow. Appropriate antibiotics are given to fight infections, and radiotherapy can shrink the nodules of Kaposi's sarcoma.

## HIV-positive residents

An HIV-positive resident poses no risk to other residents of a Home in normal social circumstances. His or her sexual partners could catch the virus, and blood or equipment contaminated with it could infect others. If a resident who is HIV positive or with AIDS also has diabetes requiring insulin injections, disposal of injection needles will require special care, as will checks on blood sugar level by doctors and nurses. However, research shows that, even after a needle-stick injury where the patient is known to be infected with HIV, the risk to the health worker is very small. Care staff are at even less risk.

## Dealing with body fluids

If you need to mop up spilt blood or other body fluids, you should wear disposable gloves which can be discarded and use household bleach for cleaning, diluted in the proportion of one part of bleach to nine parts of water. You should get into the habit of doing this for every such incident, not just when you know the resident to be HIV positive. Blood-stained clothes and bedding should also be handled with gloves and machine washed at a high temperature.

In case you encounter such a task in the course of your working day, you should cover any cuts or grazes you suffer with a water-proof dressing until they seal themselves with a scab. If you do get blood or body fluids on your skin you should wash them off with soap and water, not bleach.

Sharp objects such as injection needles should always be handled carefully, and should be disposed of safely in a specially designed 'sharps box'. Saliva, sweat, tears and urine produced by an HIV-positive person have not been shown to be infectious. No special treatment is necessary for cutlery or crockery used by an HIV-positive resident: they can be washed in hot water and detergent in the usual way.

Hepatitis B is caught in the same way as HIV, and these precautions protect carers against both conditions.

## Combating ignorance and keeping confidences

Many people are not well informed about HIV and AIDS, and this ignorance has often reinforced prejudice; residents may be ostracised or treated unkindly because they or a relative have AIDS, or because of their lifestyle. AIDS is not a 'gay plague': in large parts of the world heterosexual intercourse is the commonest route of transmission of the HIV virus. Sensational publicity about HIV and AIDS often seems to have led to victimisation of gay men, whether infected or not; it hardly needs saying that there is no justification for this.

People with AIDS or who are HIV positive are often understandably reticent about their health. If a resident confides in you that he or she is HIV positive or has AIDS, or if you find out in some other way, you must of course be especially careful to keep the information confidential. If the news becomes known in the Home, you will need to know the facts about HIV and AIDS so as to be able to reassure the other residents that they are quite safe and at no risk of acquiring the infection. They will be watching you and noting your attitude and behaviour, so it will be important that your actions are as sensible and kindly as your words. If you or the residents need further information, you might like to get in touch with the Terrence Higgins Trust and read some of their excellent publications.

112

- The HIV virus that causes AIDS is usually spread by sexual contact or by blood.

- Normal social contact cannot spread the virus; carers of HIV-positive people run almost no risk if they take sensible precautions.

- Myths about AIDS abound; try to make sure that you and your staff are correctly informed.

Although this chapter has concentrated on illness, remember that health is the normal state for older people. Age alone produces no illness or disability – you are ill because you are ill, not because you are old.

# 5 Caring for Frailer Residents

Even in extreme old age, frailty always has a cause. Not all can be corrected, but the search for reversible factors should always be made. Steps such as treating an infection or changing medicines – especially stopping sleeping pills – can often make an older person more independent and much happier.

## Monitoring independence

Gradual deterioration can be very difficult to notice in people we see every day. It is wise, therefore, to record a new resident's mobility, continence, mental state and daily living skills, on admission and every six months to a year thereafter – more often in the more frail. A change in abilities thus revealed means that the resident's health should be investigated thoroughly.

# MAKING RESIDENTS COMFORTABLE DURING ILLNESS

This involves the sort of nursing care we would give to a sick or frail relative. Doing these things well can make a good deal of difference to the resident's comfort. If some techniques are unfamiliar to you, ask the district nurse to demonstrate them. In particular, make sure that you and your staff have been taught correct techniques for lifting and handling immobile residents.

## Preventing pressure sores

These are especially likely to develop where skin overlies bone – at the base of the spine, over the vertebrae and the heels of someone lying on their back, and over the bony points of the bottom (ischial tuberosities) of someone sitting down. Pressure at these points interferes with the circulation, and can produce a shallow ulcer, or a large cavity if more tissue is damaged. Pulling people up a bed without lifting them clear of the sheets also damages skin.

People who have difficulty getting about are especially vulnerable to pressure sores, perhaps because they are sedated, semi-conscious, confused or in too much pain to move. Some illnesses and disabilities are risk factors: these include incontinence, anaemia, low blood pressure, tissue swelling and the inability to feel pain.

If a pressure sore has formed, the GP and district nurse should be asked for advice. Sometimes a transfer to hospital will be necessary for intensive nursing and sometimes surgery. Many sores can be prevented by:

- Identifying residents at high risk, and improving their health whenever possible.
- Regular relief of pressure by moving the resident; this may be needed as often as half-hourly.
- Using equipment such as bed-cradles, foam-pads, sheep-skins, foam or gel mattresses or cushions and ripple beds as advised by the district nurse; sheets must be unwrinkled.
- Watching for skin reddening and telling the nurse at once if it happens.

## Care of mouth, nose and eyes

Encourage sick residents to drink adequate fluids; pay attention to personal preferences and make drinking easy, perhaps with a flexible straw or a cup with a spout. Offer fitter residents mouth-washes and whatever they need to clean and floss natural teeth or clean dentures; frailer residents will need help.

People who cannot do this may need staff to clean their mouths with gauze swabs soaked in sodium bicarbonate; saline-soaked swabs are used for crusted noses.

Sticky eyes should be cleaned with damp cotton wool, starting from the inner corner, working outwards in a single gentle stroke and then discarding the swab. Residents should clean their own eyes whenever possible, as it is difficult to do this painlessly on someone else. Only minimal discharge should be accepted as normal: more may be a sign of an infection, when the doctor should be called.

If necessary, ask the district nurse to teach you and your staff the above techniques.

## During convalescence

Tempt a poor appetite with small, frequent, nourishing meals including favourite foods; presentation is very important.

Good personal hygiene is vital, but morale matters too: men should shave or be shaved and women helped to keep hair clean and tidy and to use make-up if usually worn.

Make sure the resident can reach drinks and fruit, spectacles, hearing aid, radio and tissues; they will also need a means of summoning help.

# PROMOTING MOBILITY

An older person who can get up and down from bed and chair without help and can walk independently can choose where they go and when they go there. Mobility also improves health by stimulating breathing, circulation and appetite. It preserves balance, prevents limb stiffness, lifts mood and promotes restful sleep.

You should note on admission whether the new resident can walk, rise from a chair, get out of bed or go outside the Home:

- Alone (always the aim), perhaps with a walking aid.
- With supervision and verbal help; these residents need clear and consistent instructions, so staff should make sure they all work in the same way and use the same words.
- With physical help, to be avoided if at all possible; even a supporting arm makes the resident dependent.

# Keeping residents on their feet

## Walking sticks

Using a walking stick widens a slightly unsteady person's 'base', and can usually render them independent. A stick can also relieve a painful arthritic joint by taking some weight, provided the joints and muscles of the arm and hand are strong enough for weight bearing; using two sticks may spread the load. Unfortunately, sticks are often regarded as a badge of frailty, so residents may be reluctant to use them.

Wooden sticks are attractive, cheap and light. The hooked end can be used as a reaching tool or to flick switches, and can hang the stick on chair arm or coat hook. The handle can be padded with foam or felt to make it fatter and more comfortable to grip. Wood may, however, rot or splinter eventually. Aluminium sticks are stronger but also more expensive, and they look more clinical; their handles can be moulded to the user's hand. Both sorts need a rubber tip (ferrule) to prevent them from slipping; this becomes dangerous when worn, so should be replaced regularly.

To find the correct length, ask the potential user to stand in their usual shoes with arms at their sides and palms facing front. The distance from the wrist crease to the floor is then the correct length for the stick.

When used for pain relief the stick should, whenever possible, be held in the hand opposite to the 'worse' side, so as to take the weight from the bad leg in normal walking.

Multi-point sticks (three points – a tripod; four points – tetrapod or quadrupod) give a wider supporting base to someone with very poor balance, for instance after a stroke. However, they are often too wide for stair treads, are out of reach if knocked over and, as with frames, other residents may trip over them.

## Walking frames

Someone who needs two people for support or leans heavily on one helper is likely to need a walking frame to walk alone. Frames (often known as 'Zimmers') widen the user's base, improving balance, and transfer weight from weak or painful legs to stronger arms. Their disadvantages are their embarrassing obtrusiveness and their awkward bulk;

they may be impossible to use on stairs or in small lavatories. Frames must be used correctly: a frame should be lifted forward and walked into with a step from each leg: 'frame, one, two'. They should not be carried, and should never be used to aid sitting or standing from a chair, bed, etc. This is a common cause of falls, as they are unstable if used in such a way.

Wheeled frames are useful for people with Parkinson's disease who find it difficult to start and stop.

Net bags can be attached to frames for carrying some personal possessions. A high trolley on wheels may be useful for transporting cups of tea.

Sticks and frames are loaned through health authorities or social services departments; they should be returned when no longer needed. Walking aids can also be bought in some large pharmacists, or by mail order; this may be useful for residents who need a simple support when waiting times for specialist assessment are long. In more complicated cases it may be worth waiting for skilled advice on choice of aid and how to use it; staff should be shown this, too, so they can help residents consistently and with confidence.

## Wheelchairs

### For general use by residents

Your Home should have a small selection of appropriate wheelchairs for the occasional use of residents who are unable to walk far, particularly when going outside. A standard push-chair design should be adequate but different sizes will be needed for different users.

Wheelchairs should not be used to transport residents to 'save time'; it is always kinder to try to help a resident become mobile and independent.

### Residents needing a permanent chair

Residents who have a substantial and permanent loss of mobility may obtain a wheelchair for their personal use from the NHS. A skilled assessment service is provided in each health district; residents may need to go to a centre for this, or the physiotherapist or occupational therapist may visit the Home. Do not use one resident's wheelchair for others, as this can be dangerous. Return 'personal' wheelchairs to the supply centre when they are no longer needed.

## Types of wheelchairs

Wheelchairs may be:

- for indoor or outdoor use, or both;
- self-propelling (with a 'driving' rim or hoop attached to the rear wheel), or to be pushed by a helper;
- manual or electric.

The NHS will supply the type of manual wheelchair most suited to the needs of the user. Features may include one-arm drive models for those who have had a stroke; adjustable leg-rests for residents with arthritis who are unable to bend their knees; or chairs with the rear wheels set further back for the safe use of those with amputations. Motorised chairs are generally given only to people with little use of their arms, as immobile residents will usually be pushed outdoors by a capable helper. If a resident wishes to purchase their own chair, the wheelchair service may be willing to advise on suitable models (including lighter weight electric chairs) and local suppliers. Remember that space will be needed for storing motorised chairs and recharging batteries.

When the NHS supplies a wheelchair, the therapist will teach the resident how to use it safely and how to transfer from bed to chair or toilet independently. A physiotherapist or occupational therapist will be able to show staff how to assist residents who cannot propel the chair or get in or out of it alone.

Detachable trays can make some activities easier but these should never be used to restrain the occupant. Residents who have had a stroke may need an arm-rest to keep the affected fingers straight, and an extension to the brake lever so that they can operate both sides with their 'good' arm.

## Care and maintenance of wheelchairs

Wheelchairs must be kept clean, in good working order and repaired as soon as they go wrong. One member of staff should be responsible for the care of wheelchairs.

Defects in wheelchairs provided by the NHS should be reported to the local service whose staff will authorise and instruct the repair contractors to undertake the necessary repairs. The repair contractors will also be willing to advise you on the care of chairs that belong to the Home or to residents. Your staff should check that:

- tyres are properly inflated (using a car tyre pump);
- foot-plates fit the chair, stay up when folded and hold the resident's feet well clear of the floor when in use;
- the canvas is intact and sufficiently taut to give good support.

A manual should be provided with all new wheelchairs; if it has been lost, you could approach the supplier for a new copy.

## Poor mobility and illness

Illnesses interfering with balance and co-ordination (eg stroke), affecting muscle movement (eg Parkinson's disease) or causing pain (eg arthritis) all make it difficult to move about. A good medical assessment from the GP or the appropriate hospital specialist may be helpful, for instance in revising drug treatment. Ask the GP about this in the first instance, and do not be afraid to speak up if you or the key worker have information to give about the resident's needs.

## Shoes and feet

While respecting residents' choices, try to encourage them to wear bedroom slippers only between bathroom and bed; they are unstable, giving no support to the feet, and make the wearer shuffle and likely to trip up. Only permanently incontinent residents need washable shoes, to avoid a smell of urine.

Suitable shoes are made of leather, wide enough to fit and with a broad, stacked heel. They should fasten high on the instep with a lace, buckle or Velcro. You could encourage residents to buy good shoes by:

- collecting suitable mail order catalogues: a Disabled Living Centre can advise you here;
- arranging an outing to a shoe shop;
- helping a resident to claim benefits to provide the money.

Tactfully encourage someone with foot problems to see the chiropodist; remember that a new resident who has found foot care difficult may be ashamed of their appearance.

Swollen feet do not necessarily need a diuretic: ask the doctor about this. It is often better for the resident to wear support hose, to walk about as much as possible and, when sitting, to move their feet frequently. Chairs with leg-rests sometimes help but foot-stools cause pressure on heels and should not be used. Residents with poor finger function may need help to put on elastic stockings.

Try to arrange for the chiropodist to show you and your staff how to cut toenails properly. An emollient cream (eg E45) rubbed into the feet daily helps to keep hard skin from forming. (See also *The Foot Care Book*, an ACE publication.)

## Reducing the fear of falling

A resident who has had a fall may become inactive for fear of falling again; prompt action can forestall this. First, make sure that the causes of the fall have been investigated and eliminated if possible (see pp 122–124). Then try to get the resident on their feet for progressively longer walks with progressively less help. Start this programme as soon as possible after the incident; the longer it is left, the more difficult it will be to break the habit of over-caution.

## Boosting motivation

Most of us need a goal to tempt us into activity. To keep residents mobile, it can help to:

- Provide tea and coffee in the dining room, only taking them to the chair side of genuinely immobile residents. However, do not let residents become dehydrated: watch for signs such as dry mouth, furred tongue and concentrated urine.

- Set up group activities in different parts of the Home, not always in the sitting room.

- Encourage gardening with raised beds outdoors and indoor plants needing care around the Home.

- Organise outings, and encourage residents and their families to do this for themselves.

Frailer residents may be more likely to move around the scheme if strategically positioned chairs give opportunities for rests en route.

**NOTE** that the regular use of sleeping pills or tranquillisers can sap the spirit. A vicious circle can easily be set up:

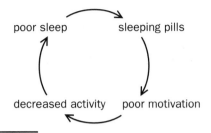

poor sleep    sleeping pills

decreased activity    poor motivation

Help your resident to avoid the use of sleeping pills whenever possible (see pp 40–43) and encourage doctors to review residents' prescriptions at least every three months.

## KEY POINTS

- Monitor your residents' independence by recording their abilities at six-monthly intervals.

- Make sure your staff are competent at basic nursing care. When residents are ill, seek advice, help and teaching from the district nurse as needed.

- Encourage residents to get about with sticks and walking frames rather than by relying on staff help.

- Appoint a staff member to be responsible for the care and maintenance of wheelchairs.

- Discourage staff from using wheelchairs to transport residents who can move alone, if slowly. Make sure they understand that this practice undermines independence and, in the long run, does not save time.

- Encourage residents to have healthy feet by making it easy for them to obtain suitable shoes and to see the chiropodist.

# RESIDENTS WITH A TENDENCY TO FALL

Older people often fall, and this gets more common with increasing age. Those who have done so in the past dread doing it again, and rightly so. Serious injuries such as fractures of the hip and wrist and head injuries can threaten independence and even life. What is more, some people are not injured but are unable to get up; lying helpless while waiting to be found is not only distressing but can also be dangerous, as pneumonia, dehydration or hypothermia can result. An incident such as this is a common reason for admission to a residential Home.

## Causes of falls

Falls can be classified as 'trips' or 'turns'; trips are due to factors outside the older person, and turns to abnormalities inside the body.

### 'Trips'

These are due to hazards such as torn and rucked-up carpets, dainty rugs that slip on polished floors and trailing electrical flex. People with poor sight are especially liable to trip, and poor lighting may make things worse. It is worth taking trouble to make the Home look comfortable and inviting rather than clinical and bare, while still avoiding trip hazards as far as possible.

### 'Turns'

Several factors often act together to produce unsteadiness and falls. The balance mechanism and the ability to right oneself after a stumble both tend to deteriorate with increasing age, and these tendencies unfortunately cannot be put right. However, good medical investigation and appropriate treatment may get rid of the falls entirely or at any rate make them much less frequent. Try to encourage residents who are unsteady on their feet to get this done, either by the GP or by a hospital geriatrician.

Anything that reduces the amount of oxygen-rich blood reaching the older person's brain will make them unsteady on their feet; simply getting up from bed or chair too quickly is one common cause. Medicines may make this worse: sleeping tablets and tranquillisers are common culprits, as are diuretics, and the unsteadiness may improve or even disappear if the tablets are stopped. Things are more difficult when residents' falls seem to be linked to the tablets they are taking to lower their high blood pressure: a separate decision has to be made in each case as to whether the falls or the high blood pressure are more dangerous.

Untreated heart disease may contribute to falls when the heart is pumping inefficiently or beating irregularly; these problems can often be put right with either drug treatment or a pacemaker. Anaemia is another treatable cause of falls. Arthritis of the neck may compress blood vessels and reduce the brain's blood supply, but it may also block the information pathways informing the brain about neck bending and head position which help in maintaining an upright posture. People with arthritic neck vertebrae should avoid sudden, sharp neck movements, and when unsteadiness is a severe problem a well-fitting support collar may be useful.

## Over-protection is dangerous, too

Though falls are risky, over-protection also poses dangers, as mobility is rapidly lost if not regularly maintained. It is very rare to find an older person who wants to do something really dangerous; more commonly, residents are over-cautious, and need encouragement to take even the most minimal risks.

If you believe a resident to be in danger, it is sensible to protect yourself from the risk of criticism by discussing the situation with the resident's family. On the whole, it is worth remembering that we tend to over-emphasise the risks of older people staying active; in fact, the tedium and depression resulting from too little change, excitement and risk are far more dangerous to the quality of life.

**KEY POINTS**

- Try to find out why a resident falls.
- Encourage unsteady residents to see the doctor.
- Check the Home for trip hazards and get rid of them.

- Do not let the fear of falls spoil residents' lives; remember that over-protection is dangerous, too.

# THE RISK OF HYPOTHERMIA

## Ageing affects temperature control

As the years pass, the body's 'thermostat' may become faulty. Older people become less able both to increase their body heat production in cold conditions and to notice that they are becoming cold. Once the body temperature starts to fall, the brain becomes sluggish, and its owner less able to make sensible decisions.

Even in residential homes or hospitals, immobile, frail and ill people can become cold. Use a room thermometer to check that room temperature does not fall below 20°C (68°F).

**KEY POINT**

- Remember the risk of hypothermia: use room thermometers.

# INCONTINENCE OF URINE

## Spoils lives but can be curable

Too often, incontinence is accepted as being due to ageing, but this is never the whole explanation. It is true that as we get older we need to go to the lavatory more often (frequency) and cannot put off the visit for as long as we used to (urgency). Less has to go wrong to make a person 80 years old incontinent than one of 40. However, at any age the fault contributing to incontinence may be correctable, and getting the person dry will enormously improve their quality of life.

## Common patterns of incontinence

You may be able to recognise these among your residents and then encourage them to seek appropriate help, with staff assistance if necessary.

### *Stress incontinence*

This generally affects women as a result of damage to muscles or nerves of the pelvic floor during childbirth; the muscles weaken still further after the menopause because of hormonal changes. Leaking urine occurs with the 'stress' of lifting or straining to get up from a low chair, or with coughing, sneezing or laughing; being overweight worsens the problem.

Pelvic floor exercises can be helpful, as can hormone treatment either in tablet or patch form or in locally applied creams. Some women benefit from a ring pessary being inserted into the vagina; these help to support the bladder and urethra in their correct position. In some cases, drugs or an operation will be the answer, and the woman should ask the GP to refer her to a suitable out-patient clinic.

### *Urinary infection*

Someone suffering from this condition has a strong desire to pass urine when the bladder contains only a small amount, though this may be less noticeable in older people. The urine often smells fishy and unpleasant, and may be frothy or even blood-stained. In younger people the passage of infected urine is painful and burning, but in an older person this is often less marked.

Someone who may have a urinary infection should consult the doctor, so that a specimen of urine can be collected and sent to the laboratory for examination. An antibiotic will usually then be prescribed. A urinary infection may be solely responsible for incontinence, and it will worsen incontinence due to another cause, so every incontinent person needs to have a urine test.

### *Unstable bladder*

This is very common in people who have had a stroke, who develop a dementing illness, who have Parkinson's disease or who suffer from multiple sclerosis. The muscle of the bladder wall becomes over-active, leading to an urgent and frequent need to pass urine. If the visit to the lavatory is delayed, incontinence is likely, and the situation will be aggravated by immobility or a urinary infection.

Treatment can often be managed by habit training. The techniques used are quite simple. Very often, just reminding someone to pass water or assisting them to the lavatory every two hours or as necessary is enough to correct the problem. A simple chart can be used to record whether the person was wet or dry at the two-hourly checks; ideally, the resident should take charge of this and fill it in themselves. When wetness persists, the times of checks and visits to the lavatory can be suitably adjusted.

The person's morale lifts as soon as the incontinence starts to improve, and a great sense of achievement is felt on marking the chart as dry. After this, the bladder can be retrained to go a little longer between visits, and reminders can eventually correspond to events of the day, such as meals and outings, rather than being prompted by the clock. Occasionally, drugs are also used to help control this kind of incontinence, but unwanted effects from these can be troublesome. Sometimes the 'insurance' provided by wearing an incontinence pad will also be necessary to make the person feel secure.

## Mechanical obstruction

In men this often happens because of an enlarged prostate gland which interferes with the free passage of urine. An affected resident will have a poor urinary stream, with difficulty in starting to pass urine and dribbling as he finishes. This leakage stains clothing and bedding and causes smell. Because of the partial blockage, the bladder becomes unable to empty itself completely; a stagnant pool of urine accumulates, becomes infected, and thus makes incontinence worse. Eventually the man becomes unable to pass urine at all and needs admission to hospital for this retention to be relieved.

In prostatic enlargement the combination of back-pressure and increased liability to infection can damage the kidneys, so someone with this condition is at risk of developing dangerous kidney failure. Because of this, someone with an enlarged prostate should be encouraged to see the doctor with a view to receiving surgical treatment. The operation is now a much simpler undertaking than it used to be, and can be safely performed on quite frail people.

In women, gynaecological conditions such as fibroids can obstruct the bladder outlet and cause incontinence; this can be treated surgically.

In both men and women, severe constipation can cause mechanical obstruction and incontinence. Someone suffering from this will require nursing or medical help to remove the mass of faeces. After removal, the person should avoid becoming constipated again by taking more fibre and fluids.

# Contributing factors

Once a person has developed a tendency to incontinence, many things can aggravate the situation.

## Immobility

A condition such as osteoarthritis or Parkinson's disease that slows up movement will make older people more likely to wet themselves while trying to get to the lavatory. Treatment of the condition and improving mobility will improve their continence. Another solution is to shorten the distance to be travelled by providing a commode or a urinal near at hand. Anxiety probably strengthens contractions of the bladder wall muscles, so anyone who is 'caught short' will have a better chance of reaching the lavatory in time by pausing to take a few deep breaths, rather than by rushing.

## Clothing

When the need to urinate is urgent, having to undo complicated clothing can result in incontinence. Wrap-over or gathered skirts are easier to manage in a hurry than tight ones. In men, difficult fly buttons can be replaced by Velcro. Advice about clothing for people with various types of disabilities can be obtained from a Disabled Living Centre.

## Lavatories

If your residents are to retain control of their bladders and bowels, lavatories must be attractive and easy to reach and use. Try to ensure that:

- There are enough lavatories, and they are correctly positioned; no one in the lounge, dining room or bedroom should be so far from a vacant lavatory that an accident becomes likely. If your residents agree, it may help to make all lavatories 'unisex'.

- The lavatories are easy to use. Where an older person has difficulty in standing up and sitting down safely in the lavatory, extra support rails and a raised lavatory seat may be helpful. The occupational therapist at the social services department will be able to arrange for this, but in some areas there are long waiting lists for this service. Rails that hinge down from the wall give safety and confidence to unstable residents, without restricting access for people in wheelchairs. Residents in wheelchairs will have to learn to transfer from chair to lavatory or commode, so the seats will need to be at the same height. A physiotherapist will be able to teach transferring skills and advise about seating.

- Stroke patients with restricted use of one hand or arm can clean themselves. Moving the toilet paper holder or supplying a pad of interleaved sheets rather than a roll may make this operation easier. A bidet may occasionally be useful; a portable form is available which fits over the lavatory bowl and can be emptied into it.

- Lavatories are easy to recognise; it may help to colour-code doors. Corridors should be well lit at night.

- Lavatories are warm enough to encourage an unhurried visit. They should also be pleasant for a modest and respectable older person to use with dignity and comfort. Scrupulous cleanliness and hygiene are vital: a partially sighted person who unwittingly sits down on a soiled seat is likely to put off further visits until near the danger point for an accident. Loss of privacy is not only intrusive: it also makes it physically difficult to empty the bladder. Doors must not be left open, or staff stay with residents, except in the most exceptional circumstances or if the resident asks for this; the risk of an accident pales into insignificance beside the certainty of loss of dignity and self-respect.

## Passing more urine – diuretic drugs and diabetes

A tendency to incontinence can also be affected by diuretic drugs ('water tablets'), which increase the amount of urine passed. The prescribing doctor may be unaware of the urinary problem if the person is too shy to mention it, even though it is often possible for a diuretic to be stopped without the person's health suffering. You should ask the resident if they would like you to inform the doctor, if you think this may be happening.

People with untreated diabetes also pass large amounts of urine. Incontinence resulting from this is quite commonly what brings the older undiagnosed diabetic to the GP for an examination. Once the diabetes is brought under control, the incontinence will improve.

# Promoting continence in Homes

## Staff attitudes and daily life

Try to foster willingness to cope with individual habits, rather than forcing residents willy-nilly into a rigid toileting regimen. Staff are sometimes reluctant to spend time and trouble helping residents to regain continence. Remember that this short-term view is false; continence promotion saves staff time in the long run, and the benefits to residents' self-respect and happiness are enormous.

Encourage residents to be physically and mentally active; wetting of chairs is much less likely when their occupants are doing something interesting. An active day is also more likely to be followed by a good night's sleep, without the need for sleeping pills, which themselves make wetting the bed more likely.

People who think they have lost control of their lives are likely to feel the same about their bladders. Anyone can feel like this on moving into a Home, and a depressed pattern of thought may become set, often in a vicious circle:

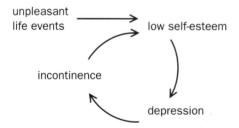

Kindly encouragement to regain maximum independence, autonomy and self-esteem along with bladder control can prevent this destructive pattern from becoming established.

## Managing fluid intake

There is a tendency among incontinent older people to restrict the amount of fluids they drink. However, this is a mistake, because dehydration is dangerous for older people, and, in fact, may worsen the incontinence. The timing of drinks may be adjusted to promote continence provided the total daily amount remains adequate: for instance, if the person commonly wets the bed, the daily fluid requirements can be taken before 6pm. Occasionally this strategy does not work, and the more concentrated night-time urine so produced irritates the bladder and causes a wet bed. In these circumstances, a late-night drink may prevent incontinence. The sensible course is to experiment with timing of drinks that together total the volume of fluid needed over the 24-hour period (see p 34), for no two bladders – or their owners – are alike.

# Getting professional help

Most incontinent people will benefit from skilled medical and nursing advice. Quite apart from the various medical conditions that directly affect bladder function, general health problems can also cause incontinence. Most physical illnesses can make an old person confused (see p 147), and so can the medicines used to treat them. Urinary 'accidents' can sometimes be the first sign of a toxic confusional state.

Incontinence is never an easy subject to broach, and it may take several attempts before sufferers are prepared to admit that they have a problem. It is often helpful to explain how common incontinence is, especially in women: 50 per cent of women who have had one child and over 80 per cent of those who have had two children will have suffered from it at some time in their lives. It also helps to assure the person that their problem is not their fault; this is especially important if, as sometimes happens, other residents have unkindly labelled the incontinent person as 'lazy'. You should also try to convince the incontinent resident that help is worth seeking, as they may wrongly believe themselves to be incurable. Incontinent people can truthfully be told that improvement is likely and cure a possibility. Even when things cannot be put right completely, modern ranges of pads and pants can make the problem less obtrusive and life more tolerable than used to be the case.

Older people may find it embarrassing to discuss the private parts of their bodies with a young doctor of the opposite sex. You could ask an incontinent resident who felt like this whether they would like you to speak to the doctor on their behalf. You could also encourage them to ask to see a doctor or nurse whom they would find it easier to approach; it should be possible to arrange this. Any necessary tests can then be arranged so that treatment can be organised.

In some areas of the country there are out-patient continence clinics where doctors, nurses, physiotherapists and other health care workers co-operate in caring for incontinent people who have been referred by their GP. Continence advisers from such clinics also work in the community in some areas, and visit people in their own homes. They are nurses who have extra training and a special interest in this sort of condition. Your district nurse or the local Community Health Council will tell you whether there is a local continence adviser in your area. You can also get in touch with the Continence Foundation for advice and books and leaflets aimed at promoting continence. Publications are also available from Age Concern England.

Where the special services outlined above do not exist, an incontinent person may be referred to a urological surgeon, a gynaecologist or another specialist. The GP and the district nurse will help to look after the person in the Home.

# Making permanent incontinence more bearable

When someone's incontinence cannot be cured, it is still possible to make things more pleasant both for sufferers and for those around them.

## Washing clothes and bedding

The smell of incontinence is probably the most distasteful thing about it. Special deodorants (eg Nilodor) can be used in appliances or on padding or can be added to the water used for shampooing stained carpets. However, the most important factors in the prevention of smell are the speed and efficiency with which wet clothing and bedding are changed and laundered. All clothes should of course be washable, and, if they become wet or soiled, should be sluiced off at once in cold water. Dirty laundry or used incontinence pads should be stored in sealed plastic bags.

An incontinence laundry service may be available locally; the social services department or Age Concern will know whether this is so. Note that the provision of a laundry service varies in different areas of the country. If you think there is an unmet need for this service in your area you should discuss the situation with the staff of your local Community Health Council.

### Protecting furniture and bedding

Plastic sheeting over the mattress is not usually sufficient, and will in any case have a bad effect on the sufferer's skin. The standard incontinence pad is often useful but is inclined to leak around the edges. The Kylie Sheet is a useful newer product, but a washing machine and tumble dryer need to be available. Your continence adviser should be able to tell the resident or their helpers which equipment will best meet individual needs.

## Using equipment

### Catheters

A person with irreversible incontinence may wear an in-dwelling catheter. This is a plastic tube passed up the urethra and into the bladder, containing an inflatable balloon that expands and keeps the catheter from falling out. The urine drains through a hole at the end of the catheter down the outer section of tubing and into a plastic bag. The bag must be fixed below bladder level to help drainage and reduce the risk of infection from backward flow. If the tube is sat on or kinked, drainage will be blocked and urine will leak where the tube joins the bag.

Occasionally a catheter will become blocked, and its wearer will be in pain because they cannot pass water. A temporary block can be relieved by milking the tube. If this does not work, the doctor or nurse should be called. If it is not possible to unblock or replace the catheter rapidly, the best course of action is to remove it by first cutting off the end to deflate the balloon and then gently pulling it out. The person will then be out of pain, but incontinent until a new catheter can be inserted.

Catheters are either changed by the district nurse in the Home or in the catheter clinic at the local hospital. The resident (and you) should know whom to call in case of emergency, and should hold a record card so that a strange doctor or nurse can read the circumstances of the particular case. Ideally, someone with a catheter should also keep a spare catheter and the sterile pack needed for its insertion in case of need.

If the person wishes to have a bath, this is possible with the bag in place or if the bag is removed and the end of the catheter is corked with a conical spigot. If the bag is left on, it must not be raised higher than the patient's bottom, as there is a risk of infection if urine from the bag flows back into the bladder.

Sexual intercourse is possible for people who are catheterised. Some prefer to have the catheter removed before sex and replaced afterwards, but others find the arrangements for this an intrusion on their privacy, and prefer to manage with it in place. Advice from the organisation SPOD can be helpful.

## *Self-catheterisation*

Some people learn to insert their own catheter whenever the need to pass urine arises. People who use these techniques are likely to cope well in normal circumstances, but you may want to check that you know whom to get in touch with in an emergency.

# External appliances

These are sometimes worn by men. The newer ones are quite satisfactory, and maintain a good fit without being uncomfortably tight round the penis. Both the appliance and the underlying skin need to be kept scrupulously clean to prevent soreness and smell. Padding or similar precautions may need to be used instead of, or as well as, the appliance during sleep.

# Urinals

Many older men find a bottle urinal useful, especially at night. These are easier to use if the man sits up and dangles his legs over the edge of the bed. Some are available with a non-return valve at the neck, and this prevents accidental spillage.

The female anatomy is more difficult to accommodate with a urinal, but there is the commonly used 'St Peter's boat', or a disposable urinal with its own plastic bag designed to fit into a handbag.

Further information about incontinence can be obtained from the local continence adviser or the Continence Foundation.

**KEY POINTS**

- Aim for continence as the norm for your Home.
- Incontinence of urine spoils lives but is often treatable; encourage residents to seek help.
- When incontinence persists, aim to preserve the individual's respect while keeping them comfortable and sweet smelling.

# BOWEL PROBLEMS

## Constipation

Many of the generation who are now elderly learned in childhood that all sorts of medical and even moral dangers lay in wait for anyone who did not have 'a good clear out' every day. This is not so: the natural frequency of passing stools varies considerably from person to person. Provided that there has been no recent change in habit, there is no bleeding from the back passage and the stools are not hard or difficult to pass, a daily bowel movement is not necessary for health. However, the onset of sudden constipation or an increased frequency of passing a motion, especially when blood is also passed, may be a sign of serious underlying disease and should always be reported to the doctor. On the other hand, as well as being uncomfortable, constipation may aggravate a tendency to urinary incontinence and may make confusion worse in someone who is mentally frail.

The intestinal muscle seems to become less efficient with increasing age, so it takes longer for food residue to travel the full length of the digestive tract. The bowels of anyone on a low-fibre diet or who does not drink enough will become sluggish. Some drugs also cause constipation, including some cough mixtures and cold medicines bought over the counter. Going to the lavatory may be very painful, with piles or a fissure: faeces become hard, so the next attempt to move them will be even more painful, and a vicious circle will be set up.

Whilst severe cases require medical advice, common-sense home remedies are useful in milder ones. Someone who tends to be constipated will be helped by increasing the fibre intake in their diet, as well as the daily amount of fluids. You might also consider asking a dietician's advice on the Home's menu. It is worth remembering, too, that bowel action seems less sluggish in people who take more exercise – yet another reason for encouraging your residents to be as active as possible.

Laxatives impair the normal bowel-emptying pattern, so try to discourage their use. When they are necessary, the doctor or nurse will advise on a suitable preparation.

## Faecal incontinence (soiling)

Though it often happens in confused people, faecal incontinence is rarely the result of mental frailty alone, and a medical search for a cause is always indicated. Sometimes the person may be suffering from diarrhoea and has simply been unable to reach the lavatory in time. The situation will be resolved when the cause of the diarrhoea is identified and treated – for instance, the over-use of laxatives or food poisoning.

The commonest cause of faecal incontinence is 'spurious diarrhoea', when the person is really severely constipated and liquid faeces leak past the obstructing mass. In these circumstances the sufferer requires a simple medical examination, which will usually reveal the cause and indicate appropriate treatment. Some very frail older people have bowels loaded with soft faeces which they are too weak to push out. Again, these people can be helped if they are examined and treated.

In occasional persistent cases of faecal incontinence, the district nurse gives the individual an enema about twice a week to empty the bowel. Between times, the patient takes constipating medicine to restrict bowel action. Protective clothing can be worn in case of accidents. Provided these measures are followed, the situation should become tolerable for people with faecal incontinence and for their carers.

- Constipated residents who are unwell or who are also bleeding from the back passage should see the doctor.

- As well as being uncomfortable, constipation can worsen urinary incontinence and confusion.

- Soiling (faecal incontinence) usually happens because of severe constipation (faecal impaction). Less common causes are diarrhoea or damaged sphincter muscle at the anus.

- Soiling can usually be put right; seek help from the continence adviser, district nurse or doctor.

# VISUAL HANDICAP

You can help your visually handicapped residents to make the most of their remaining sight.

## Registration

A visually handicapped person should register as partially sighted or blind. This is done by an ophthalmologist (a hospital specialist) on referral from the GP, and entitles the person to special benefits. The Benefits Rights Office at the RNIB (Royal National Institute for the Blind) produces leaflets describing these. People with mobility problems can ask for hospital transport, or to have the examination in the Home.

### Services for visually handicapped people

These vary in different parts of the country. You may be able to find out about them from the social services department, where there may be a special social worker for visually handicapped people. In some areas the local voluntary society for the blind may have a 'service agreement' with the local authority to do this job on their behalf. Other good sources of information are the RNIB and the Low Vision Adviser at the Partially Sighted Society. In addition there is the weekly BBC Radio 4 programme *In Touch* and its linked publications, produced by Broadcasting Support Services. These are available in print, Braille, on tape and on disk, and the

*In Touch Handbook* or some of the *Care Guides* would be good additions to your reference library; you could write for a publications list. Also, many public libraries have a directory of agencies for visually impaired people.

Ideally you and your staff, plus other helpers such as the specialist social worker, should work with visually impaired residents to find out what tasks they find difficult. You should note skills such as personal care (washing, dressing, using the toilet, shaving if male), finding the way when moving about, dealing with money and signing documents. You can then make a joint plan of ways to regain necessary skills or to compensate for their loss.

# Low vision aids and partially sighted people

The ophthalmologist who has registered someone as partially sighted may also refer them to a specialist in low vision aids. The Partially Sighted Society produces a list of Low Vision Clinics and also of optometrists and opticians who perform low vision assessments and stock low vision aids. These aids include magnifying devices such as a small telescope, neat enough to be hidden in the palm of the hand, which can be used for identifying friends in the street or reading bus numbers and street names. For close work, magnifying glasses of various designs are available. Hand-held ones are useful to carry about for occasional use; there are also spectacles with very thick lenses, and tiny binoculars to be held very close to the eyes when reading. Some low vision aids incorporate a built-in light.

## Light, colour and position

Good lighting can be very helpful to visually handicapped people. Someone with failing sight should be sure to sit sideways on to a window when using a low vision aid. At night a single central ceiling light is unlikely to be sufficient. Encourage the resident to experiment with illuminated magnifiers and with a differently positioned lamp on an adjustable arm. The sight of people with cataract is worsened by glare; on fine sunny days they will see better when wearing tinted glasses, eye-shades or hats with peaks or brims.

Colour can help orientation, safety and independence if it is used to define the join between the walls and floor, the woodwork of windows or door frames and the handles of doors. Remember, however, that people with macular degeneration may lose much of their colour vision.

Try to exploit the contrast between light and dark whenever possible, for instance by putting pale food on a dark plate, or dark objects on a table with a light cloth. Someone with poor sight may still be able to read short messages if they are written in large, bold letters with a thick black felt pen. Find out if the resident has a visual field defect – ie cannot see well to one side. If this is so, staff must take care to put objects such as cups of tea on the side where they are noticeable. Make sure that a poorly mobile person with this problem is not placed with their 'good' side to the wall, but has interesting things to see.

# Daily living and getting about

The social services department may have technical or mobility officers who will visit visually impaired people to help them get about and look after themselves. Encourage residents with poor sight to go out if at all possible, either alone or with a sighted guide. (See below for advice on doing this.)

Visually impaired residents may need reassurance about their appearance, with tactful help in drying the skin after washing, untucking a trapped skirt from knickers or doing up flies.

## Acting as a guide

A partially sighted or blind resident will need to be given a careful tour of the Home, with specific directions being given along the route from the person's room to the lounge, the dining room, the bathroom, etc. Acting as guide is sometimes difficult and can be frustrating for both parties, so it is helpful to know a few principles. For instance, blind people usually prefer to hold the arm of their guide, rather than to be frog-marched by someone holding on to them.

When walking on a flat surface, hold your arm (the grip arm) straight with fingers pointing towards the ground so that the blind person can grasp your upper arm, with their grip hand, on the inside. They can then walk slightly behind you, and can detect changes of direction by noticing your body movements. When it is necessary for the two of you to walk in single file, put your grip arm in the middle of your back, so that the blind person can change their grip hand if this is more comfortable.

When the blind person needs to walk on your other side, they should slide their grip hand across your back to catch hold of your other arm which will then become the grip arm. The techniques for helping them to sit down vary with the type of seating involved.

A novice guide may like to practise guiding techniques with a blindfolded volunteer, and it is useful to take a turn under the blindfold yourself to discover what it feels like to be guided. The RNIB produce an excellent illustrated free booklet called *How to Guide a Blind Person*.

## Listening and reading

A registered blind person who needs a radio can get one through the British Wireless for the Blind Fund, and the local social services department can advise about the procedure. The BBC Radio 4 programme *In Touch* is likely to be of special interest. Reduced rate television licences are also available; and the RNIB sells a television device that receives only sound and no picture, for which no licence is needed.

Learning to read the Braille or Moon system is an important part of a newly blind person's rehabilitation, and some determined people in their 80s have done this. There are special editions of newspapers and some periodicals in Braille and Moon, and some official leaflets can be obtained in these scripts. Registered blind people are eligible to become members of the National Library for the Blind and the RNIB's Talking Book Library, and so are those who have poor reading vision, as certified by their GP, an ophthalmologist or an optician. The subscription for the Talking Book Library includes the cost of hiring a playback machine as well as cassette tapes. The Talking Newspaper Association produces editions in most areas of the country to be 'read' by the playback machines.

Sometimes there is no substitute for reading vision. Make it easy for a visually impaired resident to ask you or your staff for help in reading letters, notices or the prices of articles in shops.

# Social contact

Call a blind person by their name as you approach them; do not get too close without warning, as this may startle them. In particular, be sure to tell a blind person when you enter and leave a room, as they cannot see you and should be spared the embarrassment of talking when no one is there. Unless your voice is familiar to the person, say who you are, and in any case explain what you are doing – whether you are bringing a letter or are showing in a visitor, for instance. If their hearing is poor, alert them to your presence by a touch on the arm. Otherwise, speak clearly without shouting. If you are giving important information such as the time of an appointment, check that you have been understood.

When introducing a blind person to a group of residents, explain the disability in a matter of fact way. Otherwise the person may be thought to be unfriendly and stand-offish when he or she is simply unable to see and respond to smiling faces. Tell the blind person who is present, and make efforts to bring him or her into the general conversation, as people who cannot see visual signals may be ignored. Remember that many of the early stages in establishing a relationship involve eye contact, which a visually handicapped person cannot achieve. The RNIB produce a leaflet 'Meeting Blind People' which is reassuring to people who are unfamiliar with anyone with this disability; the fear of doing or saying 'the wrong thing' sometimes leads people to avoid a blind person, who consequently becomes isolated.

## Activities and pastimes to enjoy

Many of the activities enjoyed by sighted people are still possible for those with visual impairment. The RNIB's catalogue of Aids and Games gives details of modified forms of noughts and crosses, backgammon, ludo, and many other games. Tactile dice are available, as are playing cards in large print and in Braille; there is even an audible ball, perhaps for games with visiting children? Many other ideas can be found in 'The Age of Adventure', another RNIB publication.

People with very poor sight can still listen to tapes or to the radio, and can make their own recordings; cassette machines with controls like piano keys are probably the easiest to operate. Blind people often enjoy the company of children or pets, caring for plants and handling flowers or fruit. Opportunities to go to meetings, church services and concerts outside the Home may be particularly welcome; staff will probably need to make the practical arrangements for such outings.

It is useful to know about services for visually handicapped residents, as they may find it difficult to gather this information for themselves. Imaginative use of available equipment and aids can increase independence and help visually handicapped people to continue to enjoy life.

**KEY POINTS**

Help your visually impaired residents to make the most of their remaining sight by:

- Encouraging them to register as blind or partially sighted.
- Providing them with information about local services, low vision aids and ways of continuing to enjoy favourite activities.
- Using light, colour, contrast and texture helpfully in the Home.
- Making sure your staff know how to guide a blind person and to prevent their becoming isolated.

# IMPAIRED HEARING

## Diagnosis first

Your residents may be inclined to accept hearing loss as 'just old age'. Try to counter this wrong idea, suggesting it may be possible to get help.

Someone with difficulty in hearing should first go to the GP. If no simple cause, such as a build-up of wax, is found to be the problem, the person will then be referred onwards to an ear, nose and throat (ENT) specialist at the local hospital, where tests will be organised. These tests usually include an audiogram, which is a map of the pattern of hearing loss. A treatment plan can then be designed.

## Getting a hearing aid

After treatable causes of deafness have been attended to, a hearing aid may be prescribed, available on the NHS at the ear, nose and throat department of hospitals or at commercial hearing aid centres. The usual NHS aid is worn either behind the ear or on the body. Behind-the-ear models have all the necessary equipment in a small and inconspicuous case, but they are less powerful than the body-worn types. The latter also have large controls which may be easier for someone with arthritic fingers to manipulate. Both types have an ear-mould, and an impression of the ear is taken by the technician so that the aid will fit properly.

Privately supplied aids may also be worn on the body or behind the ear. There are also models enclosed in the ear-pieces of spectacle frames and some worn within the ear itself. These aids can be expensive, and the purchase price does not cover the cost of repairs. They are sometimes bought on hire purchase, but residents should be very careful about signing any HP documents; they may want to get advice first from a relative or friend, or the Citizens Advice Bureau. Some commercial devices are advertised as hearing 'correctors' or 'adjusters', but these are still only amplifying hearing aids. In general, an older person is best advised to obtain an NHS aid; but in some areas they will have to wait.

Very elderly, infirm people who have difficulty in adapting to a hearing aid may sometimes benefit from an old-fashioned ear trumpet or conversation tube. Various types are obtainable on the NHS; whilst they are less efficient and more conspicuous than conventional aids, they need no upkeep, no batteries and no adjustment, and are comparatively easy to get used to. The Royal National Institute for Deaf People (RNID) or hearing clinic should be able to advise.

## Adjusting to an aid

Among publications from the Royal National Institute for Deaf People (RNID) are two booklets, *Hearing aids – Questions and Answers* and *Understanding Hearing Aids*. Both would be useful to a resident with a new hearing aid, and you might like copies for reference. NHS hearing aids always come with their own explanatory booklet. You can help by encouraging residents to read this, and may want to refer to it yourself.

Older people are much more likely to use an aid if they are given personal help in doing so. In some areas of the country there are specially trained hearing therapists attached to the hearing aid clinic to help people to adjust to hearing loss and to get the most out of an aid. In other places volunteer counsellors will visit hearing-impaired people at home. You might like to investigate the services available in your area, including the possibility of a staff member training as a volunteer counsellor.

Many people do not realise until they wear one that a hearing aid amplifies all-round, background noise as well as conversation. If the person has heard little for the past few years, the sudden din can be upsetting and difficult to accept. You could reassure residents in this predicament that they will get used to the loudness of sounds and to the aid in general, but that they will need to take their time. It is best to avoid noisy gatherings where everyone talks at once while the aid is still new, and to wait about six weeks before using it outside.

If after three months the aid still seems unhelpful, the resident should return to the clinic. Getting an aid adjusted properly and learning to use it to best effect may require several visits. Some older people may find this so tiring and disheartening that they give up trying to use the hearing aid. You may be able to help by encouraging perseverance and, whenever possible, by reducing the practical problems of clinic or hospital attendance. For instance, the time spent waiting around for transport can be reduced if taxis or volunteer drivers are used instead, and a staff member as an escort will also help.

When trying to help people adjust to an aid, you should suggest the following technique. First, they should start using it in a quiet room with someone else sitting opposite, about five or six feet away, with sufficient light for lip movements to be clearly visible. When they have become accustomed to this controlled situation, they can then progress to group conversation, remembering to turn the hearing aid down when surroundings are especially noisy. Many hearing aids have a switch marked 'T' which receives magnetic signals rather than sound and can be used with the telephone (if adapted), with some TV sets and in buildings that have an induction loop system fitted. Theatres, cinemas and churches that operate loop systems usually display an ear symbol or 'T' sign to indicate that they have this facility. Loop systems can be fitted in residents' rooms at social services department expense. They are useful in public rooms too, but the money for this has to be found privately. You can find out more about loop systems from the RNID or from the British Association for the Hard of Hearing.

It is sensible for a staff member to organise a regular weekly check that hearing aids are working. Make sure that the aid contains a battery and that it is 'live': if it is, turning up the volume should produce a feedback squeal. Simple problems can be dealt with there and then: for instance, the ear-mould may require cleaning, or the tubing or flex need to be replaced. You can find out how to do these simple forms of maintenance in 'Understanding Hearing Aids' (from the RNID). Do not attempt do-it-yourself repairs of more serious faults; for these, the aids should be returned to the supplier.

## Sources of help

The social services department may have a social worker for deaf people, who can advise about hearing aids and equipment. Clubs for deaf people and those who are hard of hearing are a good means of maintaining social contact for those who enjoy them. Information about aids, learning lip-reading, the induction loop system, specially designed articles such as visual doorbells, and rehabilitation and residential services can be obtained from the RNID. The Association of Teachers of Lipreading to Adults has details about learning this technique.

## Talking with a deaf person

It is sensible to assess a new hearing-impaired resident carefully to find out what tasks they find difficult and thus how they may best be helped to communicate. The traditional Home's lounge, with chairs round the walls and permanent TV noise, could hardly be worse for this purpose. You might like to consider running small group discussions or bingo sessions in smaller, quieter rooms especially for those hearing-impaired residents who want to join in. You should also make sure that staff understand and use the communication techniques described below.

When talking to someone with hearing difficulties, make sure they can see your face clearly so that they can lip-read. Face the person, remove sunglasses, and do not talk with a pipe or cigarette in your mouth. Good lighting is of course essential. A pad and pencil will be useful not only to indicate conversation subjects at the outset, but also to convey any information that must be accurate such as 'Hospital appointment, August 6th,

2.30pm'. Remember that the resident will need spectacles and a good light to read what you have written.

Before starting to speak, try to attract the person's attention so that they do not miss the beginning of what you say. Speak a little slower than normal and concentrate on being clear rather than loud; be aware that the natural rhythm of speech is destroyed if you speak too slowly.

If the hearing-impaired person does not understand you at first, it may help to rephrase what you say. For instance, the sounds making up the word 'August' are invisible to the lip reader, whilst the word 'summer' is easily read. Place yourself five or six feet away from the person, unless their sight is poor, in which case it may be appropriate to move closer. Of course, when a person is distressed and needs comforting, the communication received from touch and physical contact may be more important than what is heard.

**KEY POINTS**

- Encourage residents with poor hearing to get help.
- Make sure you and your staff know how best to communicate with a hearing-impaired person, and to help them adjust to a hearing aid.

# IMPAIRED SPEECH

Speech difficulties are much less common in older people than are problems with sight or hearing. Poorly fitted dentures are one simple cause, which can be put right if the dentist adjusts the fit. People getting used to a new set of dentures may gain confidence and improve their speech by reciting in front of a mirror until they are confident that the new teeth will not slip.

If a number of your residents with dental problems have difficulty leaving the Home, it may be worth enquiring from the district health authority whether they run a community dental service. Age Concern produces a Factsheet called 'Dental Care in Retirement', and you or your residents might like to send for it.

Hoarseness or loss of voice may occur with a cold or similar illness, but it should get better within two or three weeks. If it persists for longer than this, the GP should be consulted, as very occasionally something serious is amiss.

Stroke, Parkinson's disease and conditions such as motor neurone disease can also affect a person's speech. It helps if the affected person can see a speech therapist, both to receive treatment and so that relatives and carers can be advised how best to help the speech-impaired person. The self-help organisations for these diseases are a good source of information about the speech difficulties involved.

### KEY POINTS

- Remember that dental problems can affect speech.
- When hoarseness persists, it should be investigated.
- Try to arrange speech therapy for people with communication difficulties resulting from stroke, Parkinson's disease or motor neurone disease.

# 6 Confusion, Dementia and Mental Frailty

## Physical illness causing confusion

When older people get ill, they may become mentally confused. This can occur at any age but, because of ageing changes in the brain, it happens more easily in sick older people. Confusion of this sort is called a delirium or a toxic confusional state. It can result from a number of treatable medical causes such as chest or urinary infections, poorly controlled diabetes, or dehydration and the chemical upset due to diarrhoea or vomiting. It can also occur as the unwanted effect of medicines.

A physical cause is likely if the older person's muddled state has come on quickly – often over as little as 24 hours. Sometimes the illness at the root of the trouble is obvious, but sometimes a careful examination and investigations will be needed before it can be identified.

A doctor who does not know the sick resident well may not be aware that they are not usually confused. It is then very helpful if you can tell the doctor that something seems to have gone suddenly wrong. If the cause can be found, it will usually be possible to put things right, though recovery is often slow and jerky.

## Poor sight and hearing, not confusion

It is also worth remembering that someone who cannot see or hear well may appear to be confused when they are not. You may need to help your residents get treatment for sight or hearing disabilities (see pp 89–95).

## Depression mistaken for dementia

People who are slowed down by a severe depressive illness may seem to have dementia. When there is doubt as to the cause of an older person's abnormal mental state, the GP may arrange for a psycho-geriatrician (sometimes called an old age psychiatrist) to visit to give an expert opinion. Community psychiatric nurses may also be very helpful.

## Dementia – permanent confusion

Some people who become confused do not have a physical illness of this type, and do not get better. This is not due to old age, but to one of a group of illnesses called dementias. There are two common types in the UK – Alzheimer's disease and multi-infarct dementia.

## Which word to use?

'Dementia' and 'demented' are words best used in medical circles only, for two reasons. One is that, to many people, someone who is 'demented' is seriously disturbed, raving and probably dangerous. Very few older people with dementia fit this description, and many relatives would be understandably distressed if the word were applied to their elder. The other reason is that, because the dementias are incurable illnesses, it is important that, before one of them is diagnosed, all likely curable causes of confusion have been carefully considered and discarded.

In general, it is probably best to describe people who are permanently confused because of a dementing illness as 'mentally frail' or 'mentally infirm'. It is often wise, however, to make sure that the person you are talking or writing to means the same thing as you do by the words you use, as awkward misunderstandings can otherwise occur.

# COMMON TYPES OF DEMENTIA

## Alzheimer's disease (AD)

This can happen at any time in adult life. In a few early-onset cases (before the age of 60) there is a clear family pattern, the disease being passed genetically from parent to child. However, most Alzheimer's disease occurs in later life, usually past 75 and often around the age of 80. Having this condition in the family may increase the chances of a person getting it as they get older, though more than half of all patients have no family history of the condition. Environmental factors may also be important.

Late-onset Alzheimer's disease is sometimes called 'senile dementia of Alzheimer type' or 'SDAT'; however, 'senile dementia' is a term best avoided as it implies that the person's mental confusion is the result of ageing, which is not the case. Whenever in life it happens, Alzheimer's disease attacks the brain substance, replacing useful nervous tissue with 'plaques' and 'tangles' of a useless substance called amyloid. The pattern of this destruction can be recognised if a piece of brain from an Alzheimer's sufferer who has died is examined under the microscope.

People with AD do not get better and usually get worse, though the rate at which this happens varies from one person to another. The beginning of the disease can be difficult to notice, and it may come to attention because of changed social circumstances – for instance, the affected person's carer may be taken suddenly ill. AD sufferers often seem unaware of their deteriorating mental function, though they may often seem to know uneasily that something is wrong. Their disease may affect judgement skills and may change their personalities. It also shortens their lives compared to people of the same age who do not have AD. However, it is not possible to predict how long any one person with AD is likely to survive.

## Multi-infarct dementia

Here the cause is very clear. It happens because diseased brain arteries block and fail to supply blood to the brain tissue. Starved of oxygen-rich blood, these sections of brain die, and the functions they control are lost. Death of tissue because of lack of blood is medically known as 'infarction', and so the condition is called 'multi-infarct dementia' (MID). As the brain arteries block at irregular intervals, the MID sufferer tends to deteriorate in a jerky fashion, rather like going down an uneven flight of steps. This contrasts with the smooth downhill course of the person with AD.

People with MID commonly have other sorts of blood vessel disease, such as angina, heart attacks or arterial disease in the legs. They are also prone to major strokes. MID is in fact due to the effects of many tiny stroke episodes, and MID sufferers often show stroke signs when a blockage happens. These include sudden worsening of confusion, slurred speech, weakness down one side of the face and body, and epileptic fits. People with MID may be aware of what is happening to them and because of this they may become depressed. Personality and judgement skills are usually affected less in MID than in AD.

Because of the generally poor state of their arteries, people with MID do not live long. They usually die of a heart attack, major stroke or similar illness within two to five years of the diagnosis of MID being made.

## Diagnosis and treatment

There are as yet no simple and certain ways of telling whether someone has AD or MID before they die and the brain can be examined. The most sophisticated sorts of brain scanning equipment can give a right answer in about 80 per cent of cases. At the moment these scans are mainly done when there is doubt as to whether the patient has a dementia or another, possibly curable, condition causing confusion. However, once a treatment for AD is available, it will be very important to make a certain diagnosis.

The drug tacrine seems to help a few patients a little, but many patients do not benefit, and the drug is toxic to the liver. At the time of writing there is no generally effective treatment for AD, but research suggests that there is real hope of one being found before long.

Little can be done for MID once it is established. Sometimes its progress can be slowed a little if the sufferer will stop smoking and if conditions such as diabetes, anaemia and heart disease are managed carefully. A small dose of aspirin sometimes helps, but some people cannot take this because of the risk of bleeding. Young or middle-aged people can reduce their chances of getting MID in later life by not smoking, by taking exercise, keeping their blood pressure within normal limits and eating a healthy diet.

# WHAT DEMENTIA IS LIKE

With a few exceptions, people with AD and MID have similar mental difficulties.

## Loss of abstract thinking

People with dementia lose the ability to think in the abstract and make 'if ... then' connections. 'If I do not put out this cigarette, I may start a fire.' 'If I walk into the road without looking, I may get run over.' These are examples of the sort of abstract thinking that mentally healthy older people do all day and that people with dementia cannot manage.

## Loss of judgement skills

Mentally frail people also lose the judgement skills needed to put thought into practice. 'This road is very busy – I could be hurt in the traffic. Therefore I will walk down to the traffic lights and use the crossing there.' It is easy to see how the loss of abstract thought and judgement skills make mentally frail older people vulnerable to exploitation by unscrupulous people. Because of their loss of grasp on current reality, a mentally frail person may return to a garbled version of behaviour that served them well in the distant past; one example of this might be the older person who tries to boil an electric kettle on the gas ring.

## Loss of memory

Forgetfulness becomes severe enough to interfere with daily life. The sufferers may forget they have moved into a residential home and, once outside the building, try to return to an old home they dimly remember. People with dementia hide things and forget where they have put them. They may then accuse staff of having stolen from them. Others tire out their carers by asking them the same question, over and over again; they have already forgotten the answer, and to them it is a new question every time. The memory for recent events is usually much worse than that for the remote past: the affected person can tell you what happened the day war broke out but not what they had for breakfast this morning.

## Loss of contact with reality – disorientation

Mentally frail people may become disorientated, losing contact with reality and becoming very distressed. The sense of place is often lost first: they do not recognise their surroundings and find it very difficult to adapt to a new environment. This is why it is usually a mistake for a mentally frail person to move from familiar surroundings if this can possibly be avoided.

Loss of sense of time can cause great difficulties where people live close together. A mentally frail resident may wake at 2.30am and cause a general disturbance by insisting that breakfast is late.

Mentally frail people who no longer identify other people reliably may fail to recognise close relatives or carers. A remark such as, 'Go away, you're not my daughter!' can be very hurtful to a visiting relative. On the other hand, mentally frail people may think that they recognise total strangers, and trustingly invite them in.

## Personality change

The personality of the dementia sufferer may change. This is more noticeable in people with AD, and is very distressing for relatives and friends to watch. While some mentally frail people become over-active, others become slow and apathetic. They lose all their previous interests and enthusiasms, and do little but sit around. It can be difficult to tell the difference between someone like this and someone badly slowed down by severe depression. The sufferer may need to see an old age psychiatrist to establish what is wrong.

## Sudden tears and laughter

Some mentally frail people are very easily moved to laughter or tears, but the cause of the emotional outburst is soon forgotten. Incidents like these often seem to be more upsetting to carers than to the mentally frail people themselves.

## Loss of inhibitions

As dementia progresses, 'inhibitions' tend to be lost. 'Disinhibited' mentally frail people are no longer able to control their feelings. They start to behave in ways that those around them find difficult to accept. Private things such as nose-picking or masturbation may be done publicly. Someone who feels angry may become aggressive, and if sexually aroused they may harass other people. It is important to remember that the person's feelings are normal: it is the way in which they are expressing them that is not.

What the person was like before the start of the dementing illness affects the way they behave when they become mentally frail. Someone who has always had trouble controlling a quick temper is more likely to become aggressive than someone who is by nature sweet-tempered and placid.

## Confusion level varies

A person with dementia is more confused at some times than at others. Carers often find this difficult to understand and to cope with. People with MID are most confused at the time a brain artery blocks, get a little better as swelling goes down and then worsen again when another blockage occurs. How well they function mentally will depend on how long it is since the last blockage happened, as well as how badly the whole brain has been damaged.

People with AD have good and bad days, so what they can understand and how much they can do for themselves genuinely varies from day to day. When tired, upset or unwell they may perform very poorly. On the other hand, they can with an effort appear almost normal if they want to impress. An inexperienced person can sometimes be deceived by this, and it may be a great help to a visiting doctor or social worker if you are available to explain the true state of affairs.

## Do they know what's happening to them?

It is difficult to tell how much insight people with dementia have into their condition. Between episodes of MID, sufferers may be aware of what is happening to them, and become understandably depressed. People with AD lack some of this awareness, but seem to know that something, somewhere, is badly wrong; this may explain some of the agitation and need for reassurance they often show. Staff who can meet this need by competence and kindness are a great help to mentally frail residents.

## 'Dementia? I don't believe it'

People almost always deny bad news when they first hear it, and often have to be told the same thing several times before they take it in. Relatives will sometimes appear to shrug off the very bad news that their elder – your resident – is showing signs of dementia. If this happens, it does not help for you to press them harder. Relatives will be more likely to acknowledge the nature and severity of their elder's illness if they are not forced or hurried into doing so.

Mentally frail residents themselves may also refuse to admit there is anything wrong. They may insist that they are perfectly able to look after themselves when it is obvious that this is not so. They will sometimes tell elaborate and superficially convincing false stories about their daily pattern of life – what psychologists call 'confabulation'. If pressed to do tasks or perform mental tests to the point at which they fail, they become very distressed or extremely angry – a 'catastrophe reaction'.

It is important to realise that someone behaving in this way is not deliberately trying to deceive. To people with dementia the world is a mysterious and terrifying place. They have no grasp of current reality and cannot remember recent events for long enough to help them cope with the problems of the present. They fall back on their memories of the past – of themselves as caring and coping people, who were able to do so much, so well, years ago.

# CARING FOR MENTALLY FRAIL RESIDENTS

Though the underlying illness cannot be cured, good care for people with dementia makes a great difference to their lives. This section gives suggestions on coping with some of the more common difficulties you may encounter when caring for your mentally frail residents.

# Balancing rights and risks

On the one hand, older people have as much right to keep control of their own lives as anyone else has. On the other hand, people who for any reason cannot look after themselves properly have a right to be protected from danger. Trying to balance these rights is an uncomfortable task for anyone close to a mentally frail person. Clear thinking on the lines suggested below will not make the problems disappear, but may help carers to retain their peace of mind while allowing mentally frail older people maximum freedom with minimum risk.

## Too much safety can be dangerous

No life can be altogether risk-free: everyday activities such as using electrical equipment, crossing roads and travelling by public transport all have their small dangers. Oddly, though, young and middle-aged people worry more about the dangers their elders run while being active rather than while being passive. There is great concern about the risk of falls when old people move about freely. Much less is said and written about the grave health risks of not being mobile, especially when such false 'safety' is brought about by sedation or restraint in a chair with a locking tray. Older people have not had safe lives; they should be encouraged to live as they wish even if this means taking risks.

## Protecting others

In general, we all expect to be allowed to choose the risks we run ourselves, but not to be permitted to endanger other people. Older people in poor health may choose to live alone because they consider the danger a small price to pay for independence; this action is justified because no one except the older people themselves is put at risk. On the other hand, someone whose driving ability is impaired is banned from driving because of the risks of accidents to other people; this applies whether the cause of the disability is poor sight at 50 or dementia at 80.

## Covering ourselves

Those who care for mentally frail older people often worry that they will be blamed or disciplined if someone they look after comes to harm. Staff do have a right to protect their reputations, and it is usually possible for us to 'cover ourselves' without necessarily restricting the old person's activities. In fact, if we do not recognise our worries in these situations, our unconscious anxieties will make us more likely to restrict mentally frail people without realising that we are doing this for our benefit rather than for theirs.

## Thinking it through

When considering possibly dangerous behaviour, it helps to list carefully the three sorts of risks that concern us. These are:

- risks to the mentally frail people themselves, or to their property;
- risks to other people;
- risks to ourselves.

The next step is to consider whether these risks can be reduced, or whether the dangerous behaviour can be modified in any way. For instance, providing adaptations and equipment in bathrooms may make it perfectly safe for a frail and unsteady person to bath and toilet themselves in privacy.

Once this has been done, the three sorts of risks can be re-evaluated, and the conclusions used as the basis for a future plan. This plan should be put together in consultation with the mentally frail resident and all those who have an interest in their welfare. A meeting to do this should give everyone a chance to exchange information and also to express their feelings; it is entirely understandable that staff should want to protect an older person they are fond of, but they must not be allowed to do so unless it is what that individual would have wanted. (An advocacy service may be useful here.) It is sometimes helpful to remember that it is very different to decide that risk taking is justified to improve quality of life, rather than just to let things slide and hope for the best.

## 'Wandering'

Mentally frail residents who 'wander' – that is, leave the Home and cannot find their own way back unaided – are often a source of anxiety to staff, and the approach to risk taking described above can usefully be applied here.

The risks are almost certainly over-estimated: the evidence shows that the chances of a 'wanderer' coming to harm are very small indeed, and no risk is posed to anyone else.

## Identifying patterns

It is often possible to work out ways of improving older people's safety without making their lives miserable with undue restraint. To do this it is necessary to find an underlying pattern to the wandering behaviour, and knowing the resident's background and past history will help in this. Some people have a 'target' that they always make for – an old home or place of work, for instance. The jaunt can be made less risky if the people at the target destination recognise the confused person and are able to let those who look after them know where they are. Other mentally frail older people revert to an old pattern of behaviour. They may, for instance, get restless around tea time because of a long-past need to take the dog for a walk in the early evening. If a short, accompanied walk can be arranged at the appropriate time, the older person will often settle happily, and have been perfectly safe throughout.

Other patterns include the sensible errand that goes wrong: the confused person reaches the post office or shops, but, being disorientated, cannot find the way home. A companion on the outing can ensure a safe return, and relatives or other residents may be prepared to accompany the older person. Some 'wanderers' are seeking stimulation, avoiding noise or trying to 'walk off' pain or discomfort; if the cause can be identified and eliminated, the problem may disappear.

## Sensible precautions

It is usually sensible for mentally frail people who may wander to have their names and a contact telephone number about their persons. Identity bracelets and Medic Alert lockets are now sufficiently widespread to be an acceptable and non-stigmatising way of doing this. Do not include the older person's living address in case the information falls into the hands of criminals. A recent photograph may help passers-by to give you accurate information if you are out looking for a lost resident. It may also help to give the person's details to the local police station to help officers bring them safely home. The need to do this should of course be explained to the resident concerned and their consent obtained whenever possible.

To protect yourself, you should arrange to meet the resident's concerned relatives or friends so that you can explain the facts carefully to them. Make sure they understand that, though you will do your best to help reduce the risks their elder is running, you are unable to control the daily comings and goings of your residents. You can use this opportunity to listen to the family's worries about the older person's welfare and to reassure them when they over-estimate danger. You should also write to your managers with details of the situation, including a brief description of your dealings with the relatives.

You will find suggestions for further reading about risk taking and coping with challenging behaviour in the Further Reading on pages 274–275.

# Wrong ideas, muddled behaviour and confused talk

Sometimes a mentally frail resident seems to be talking nonsense, or wants to act in a foolish way on the basis of a wrong idea. This is especially common during the dark hours when there are fewer outside clues to events in the real world, and when carers are often too tired to feel at their best. Here is a simple and easily remembered plan for coping with incidents like these.

## Is it true?

First, beware of the unlikely truth. A personal collection of examples includes a man of 88 who was thought to be confused when he asked ward staff to tell his mother he had been admitted to hospital. She proved to be alive and in good health at the age of 112. It is usually wise to check on the facts of the case and to visit the scene; as well as alerting you to improbable facts, this will also help you to recognise misunderstandings and misinterpretations (see below).

## Neither support nor confront confused thinking or behaviour

Never support a wrong idea or statement by agreeing with it or behaving as if it were true. Do not, for instance, chase out imaginary intruders or wild animals. Mental state tends to fluctuate, and when the fog of confusion lifts a little, the mentally frail person is likely to remember what you said and did and to feel puzzled and distressed by it.

On the other hand, there is no need to upset or annoy the confused person by confronting them with their mistake and a bald recital of the true facts. It is rarely necessary to comment on the objective truth of what is said. Remember that to the confused person it is a true account of what they think is going on, and listen carefully to what they say, bearing in mind what you know of their past lives and present circumstances.

## Misunderstandings, misinterpretations and feelings

Good observation and attentive listening will help you to work out the background to a confused resident's seemingly irrational behaviour. Some problems arise from misunderstandings: one old man was reported to have 'attacked the bath nurse' when from his point of view he had awakened suddenly from his afternoon sleep to find a strange woman trying to tear his clothes off. It is important to keep in mind that mentally frail people have a short memory span and a poor grasp on reality. This means that they need more, rather than less, explanation of who visitors are and what they have come for.

Many people with apparent 'hallucinations' are in fact misinterpreting things they really see and hear. Real events are distorted by confused understanding, poor sight and hearing. Also, the extra noises of tinnitus may be thought to be coming from outside the person. They may then be wrongly interpreted as, for example, noise from the neighbours or from squatters in empty rooms. Removing the stimulus can sometimes make the problem disappear. In one case a resident's complaint of 'a man in my room' was traced to a misperception of her own image in a mirror; moving the mirror to the inside of the wardrobe door got rid of the intruder and of her distress. Again, if a resident can be persuaded to accept treatment for tinnitus, the wrong ideas based on it may disappear.

Mentally frail people often express their feelings in a confused way. Half-remembered wartime horrors or a half-forgotten nightmare may be at the root of the trouble when shadows or dimly seen objects are perceived as wild animals or lurking intruders. Some people may be helped by talking about the events underlying these feelings, but this needs some care and skill; you may want to discuss this with a community psychiatric nurse. When you do not know the underlying cause, it is best simply to deal with the feeling – to calm the fears and soothe the agitation. Confused people can be comforted more easily if they are separated from the apparent cause of the trouble, so moving to a different but still familiar room may help.

## Restore contact with reality or distract

Whenever possible the confused person should be brought back to reality, with as much understanding and respect as possible. An example might be, 'That hat and coat over the chair did look like a burglar, Mrs Jones – it had me fooled too for a minute. Still, there was no one there really.' This will work only if the mentally frail person knows the speaker well and trusts them. A familiar member of staff will find this easier than a new or temporary one, though it may still be impossible when the older person is either very confused or very upset. In these circumstances, it is best to try distraction – perhaps some conversation on a topic known to interest the resident, conducted over a cup of tea. Later, when trying to settle the resident, a useful phrase is 'everything is all right now'. This provides reassurance without risking an argument about what did or did not happen earlier, often now disappearing into hazy memory. In a similar way, someone on a mistaken errand can often be stopped for long enough to forget about it if told 'There's time for a cup of tea'. By the time the tea is drunk there is no longer a need for a confrontation about whether, for instance, the long-adult children really need fetching from school, and the confused person can easily be persuaded to stay indoors.

Here is an example of the system in action. A hospital patient, an old man with moderate dementia, left the ward during a thunderstorm. He was eventually found in the coal cellar, which he refused to leave. The doctor called to him found that he thought the bangs and flashing lights were the effects of an air raid, and he would not 'come out of the shelter' while it was going on. The doctor stayed with him, reassuring him that he was safe until the storm passed. The patient was then happy to accept the assurance that 'everything is all right now', and was accompanied back to the ward.

Here is a summary of what to do:

1 Find out if there is a basis of *truth* in the apparent confusion.
2 *Do not support* the confused behaviour.
3 *Do not confront* the older person with their mistake.
4 Ask why this is happening. Look for *misunderstandings, misperceptions* and *feelings*.
5 Bring the person back to *reality* if possible.
6 If this is not possible, use *distraction*.

# Stimulating a failing memory

Dementia interferes with the memory for recent events. This means that a mentally frail older person will find it difficult to retain new information: having been told the doctor will call, the confused resident soon forgets about the planned visit and goes out for a walk. People with dementia find it difficult to learn new skills: however easy the remote control of a TV seems to us, the mentally frail person is unlikely to be able to master it.

## Using memory cues

Mentally frail people can often be helped by the same sort of memory joggers we all use, especially in the early stages of the disease. A mentally frail older man may, for instance, be able to act on the information on the card in his pocket which reads, 'If lost, ring this number'. An up-to-date noticeboard in the Home is useful for mentally frail residents to consult. The board should include the name of the Home, a perpetual calendar reading, for example, Sunday 5th June, a note of the next meal and a list of the day's events. A panel of staff photos with names underneath may help residents to keep track of identities; some Homes do the same with pictures of residents.

## Helpful design and furnishing

Ideally, residential homes should be designed with the needs of mentally frail residents in mind. Clever use of fittings and decoration can also be helpful. Colour-coding the carpeting on different floors and attaching personally chosen pictures to otherwise identical doors can help confused people to find their way to their own room. The two ends of a corridor can be made obviously different by displaying plants, pictures or ornaments to act as landmarks.

New residents should be encouraged to bring small possessions and items of furniture with them on entering the Home. Fitting out rooms with these not only helps to preserve individual identities but also supports a fragile memory: an old and familiar commode is more likely to be identified and used correctly than a new one.

There is considerable scope for mental prompting inside individual rooms. A carefully sited clock with a clearly visible face and hands helps the resident to keep track of time. Door labels, colour coding and direction arrows assist someone with poor bladder control as well as a faulty memory to find the lavatory in time to prevent an accident. Labels on photographs saying, for example, 'Granddaughter Jane with great-granddaughter Sarah' may help the resident to keep track of generations of relatives. If brought out beforehand, such photographs can help the resident recognise infrequent visitors or identify the writers of letters or callers on the telephone. Muddled residents who spend a large part of the day in a chair will find it easier to keep in touch with the world around them if they can see out of the window. You may want to experiment with these ideas or with others of your own to find out what will help your residents.

## Useful ways of talking

Callers who talk in an information-giving way reinforce links with reality. 'Good morning, Mrs Smith, have you had your breakfast? It's a cold morning, but that's only to be expected with Christmas three weeks away.' This sort of talk can help a confused person to understand what is going on around them and to cope better with life. You will need to adjust the speed and level at which you give information to match the resident's varying mental state: sometimes you will need to go slowly, whilst on good days little prompting may be needed. It always helps to point out things that the resident can confirm by their own observations, such as the weather, the colour of the sky or the state of the plants in the garden. Seasonal music, food smells or objects are helpful: conkers mean autumn, mince pies Christmas, and daffodils spring, for instance. When the resident comes from a different ethnic or religious group from your own, you may want to ask advice from their relatives, friends or community leaders as to what would be appropriate here.

# Accusations of theft

### These may be true

Mentally frail people quite often accuse other people of stealing from them. Occasionally these accusations are justified: unscrupulous people do sometimes take advantage of older people who are too confused to notice and complain, or who are unlikely to be believed if they do. More often the lost property has not been stolen, but misplaced or hidden and its whereabouts forgotten.

## Why false accusations are made

Confused older people who make false accusations of this sort are not deliberately trying to make trouble for those who have access to their belongings. 'I've been robbed' is the conclusion the muddled brain comes to when it attempts to make sense of what seems to have happened: the lost article is not where it ought to be, so someone must have taken it away. Everyone loses things, but only mentally frail people allege that burglars have stolen their false teeth. In other words, it is not the act of misplacing the object that is abnormal but the bizarre explanation given for the loss.

## Finding lost property and protecting yourself

If you or your staff are wrongly accused of having stolen a resident's property, it is best not to argue but to sidestep confrontation by saying 'I'll help you look for it'. It is often useful to know where the resident has previously put things they regard as precious, as people often use the same or similar hiding places over and over again.

If you do not own the Home, it is wise to notify your managers about these incidents, in case a complaint is made against you. In most cases you should speak to the relatives as well, and make a note of the conversation. This is not only for your own protection, but also to enable relatives to take steps to care for their elder's property. If you think it possible that money or property really has been stolen, you should let your managers know at once, as the police should be called in.

# Repetitive questioning

Some mentally frail people ask the same question repeatedly, over and over again. This is particularly exasperating for anyone who spends a great deal of time with the confused person. There are no magic solutions, but the suggestions below may help.

It sometimes lowers the emotional temperature to remember that this behaviour is another symptom of the dementing illness. Mentally frail questioners are not trying to be irritating: because of their short memory span, it is a new question every time to them. Sensing the carer's irritation often makes things worse, because they feel even more unsure of themselves; they may then be asking as much for reassurance as for information. It is always sensible to give the requested information clearly and fully once. It will sometimes help to write down the answer and give the paper to the confused person for reference; for instance, someone who repeatedly asks, 'What's for tea?' can be given a 'menu'.

If this does not help, the person's attention can sometimes be distracted to an easy task that they are able to perform, such as putting plates on the table. Reference to an old and pleasant memory can also break the cycle of repetition. An example might be 'Do you remember when we had the opening and you had tea with the Mayor?'

When older people stop repeating themselves and talk of other things, this should be 'rewarded' with extra attention. General reassurance is always worth persevering with, such as 'Everything's all right, Mary, and the kettle's just boiling.' As a last resort, the carer should withdraw.

# Poor personal hygiene

Many of those who are now confused residents of Homes have in the past worked hard under difficult circumstances to keep themselves and their families clean and decent. This makes it all the more poignant when such people neglect themselves, becoming dirty and smelly. Confused people are often unaware of their unhygienic state, but staff may be besieged by other residents and their relatives, all demanding that 'something must be done'.

## Why does it happen?

There are several reasons why someone with a dementing illness can get into this state. Loss of recent memory means that they forget the recurrent need to change clothes and to wash. Having forgotten where clean underwear is kept, they keep to those whose whereabouts are known – the ones they have on. Loss of reasoning and judgement skills make it difficult to run a bath successfully, or to assemble the towel, soap and face flannel needed for a wash. They cannot do these tasks alone and, being modest, dislike staff help with such intimate matters. In addition, loss of contact with reality means that the days slur into one another. Taken together with memory loss, this disorientation makes it difficult for confused people to keep track of when or whether a bath has been taken or their clothing changed.

## When to intervene

Keeping clean is a very personal matter, and staff often wonder when, if ever, it is proper for them to interfere in this aspect of their residents' lives. They know they are not supposed to function as a sort of hygiene police force, enforcing high standards of personal care and cleanliness whether residents want to co-operate or not. Loss of insight and inhibitions can mean that mentally frail older people are blissfully unaware that they are unpleasant to be with; pointing out that they are dirty forces them to confront their own inadequacies, and this can make them very angry and upset. Even so, it is sometimes right to intervene: perhaps when a neglected person is increasingly lonely because others do not want to get too close, or has become the puzzled butt of unkind jokes. In the close quarters of a Home, one resident's poor hygiene may well affect the comfort and well-being of others, whose rights and quality of life must also be considered.

## Offering acceptable help

It may fall to you to broach the subject of personal hygiene with the resident. Your tact and knowledge of their personality will be important if your message is to be heard and accepted. Every effort must be made to preserve the resident's self-respect, as undermining this will make things worse. Bathing help or personal care often seems to be acceptable as a 'package deal', offered together with hairdressing and an outing to buy new clothes, if this can be arranged. If the resident is incontinent or if you think a physical illness or problem with medicines might be worsening their confusion, you might like to suggest a consultation with the doctor.

One common source of failure is the tendency of would-be helpers to try to impose their own hygiene methods on unwilling residents. Many of those who are now elderly and confused grew up in homes without bathrooms, and even in middle life will have been accustomed to getting into a bathtub only once a week. Though showers are becoming much more familiar and acceptable, many older people still regard them as new-fangled, chilly and likely to gush steam or ice water in an unpredictable way. In the past, many ordinary people seem to have relied on a leisurely and thorough daily strip wash as their basic way of keeping clean. In later life, a return to their old habits may be the easiest way of improving their personal hygiene. A reminiscence session may be an easy and acceptable way of finding out what is likely to work, and relatives may also be able to give useful information.

## Making things easier

It helps to make the process of washing, showering or bathing as easy as possible, both physically and mentally. The occupational therapist will be able to advise about and arrange for equipment such as tap turners and rails round baths, if these have not already been fitted. Unfortunately, in some areas there may be a long wait both for assessment and for the aids to arrive and be fitted. Useful articles such as bath seats can be borrowed from the Red Cross, and most can be bought privately if funds permit. A Disabled Living Centre such as London's Disabled Living Foundation will be able to advise you about useful equipment. Using such aids may give the resident more privacy by enabling them to wash themselves with minimal help.

## Tactful prompting

Verbal reminders may be more necessary for some confused residents than actual physical help. Unobtrusive replacement of dirty clothing with clean, or the request for more washing for the machine 'to make up a load' are tactful ways of getting clothes changed without a confrontation. When the resident seems to tolerate one helper better than another with intimate hygiene tasks, it is only sensible to go along with this. Preserving the resident's dignity and self-respect throughout is vital.

# Medicines and confused older people

## Medicines causing confusion

Almost any medicine can cause confusion, but the commonest culprits are sleeping pills (hypnotics) and tranquillisers, which tend to accumulate in the body. Occasional causes include anti-depressants, some medicines given for Parkinson's disease, some ulcer-healing medicines and high doses of steroids.

An older person can also become confused if the sleeping pills or tranquillisers they have been taking for some time are stopped suddenly. It is often a good idea for such medicines to be stopped, but this should be done gradually, under medical supervision. Stopping the medicines used to treat conditions such as thyroid disease or diabetes can also cause confusion if the underlying disease gets out of control.

Someone who has had a long-established problem with their medicines may appear to have a dementing illness, but may recover completely if things are put right. It is always important to consider medicines as a possible cause of confusion.

## Medicines used to treat confusion

Confusion can sometimes be cured by getting rid of its physical cause: for instance, if someone becomes acutely confused because of pneumonia, the antibiotics that clear the chest will also clear the head. Less often, chronic confusion has a treatable physical cause: an example is the replacement of missing thyroid hormone in thyroid deficiency.

As yet there is no drug to halt the degenerative changes in the brain of someone with Alzheimer's disease. However, medicines such as tacrine correct some of the faults in the brain chemistry that come about in Alzheimer's, and some patients' abilities improve, while others deteriorate more slowly on treatment. Not everyone benefits, and a large minority have to stop taking the medicine because of unpleasant unwanted effects such as digestive upsets and liver damage. Tacrine is far from being a 'miracle drug' for Alzheimer's; much more research is needed on this and other medical ways of helping sufferers. Various medicines are offered for multi-infarct dementia, but there is no evidence that they help.

Some people with dementing illnesses seem upset, or behave in ways that make them difficult to care for. Agitation, restlessness, insomnia, hallucinations and delusions are examples of symptoms that can be helped with the right sort of medicines, such as thioridazine and promazine. However, the dosage and timing need to be carefully adjusted to the particular patient's needs if unwanted effects are to be avoided: these include drowsiness, incontinence, poor co-ordination, falls and disturbances of movement.

# Alcohol and confusion

Acute confusion can follow a drinking bout. Because tolerance of alcohol decreases with age even in life-long drinkers, the amount consumed may not seem large.

If a regular drinker stops suddenly, the abrupt alcohol withdrawal can also cause confusion. In really severe cases the terrifying and dangerous condition of delirium tremens (DTs) can occur. Withdrawal of alcohol from habitual drinkers is best done under medical supervision.

Long-term alcohol abuse can lead to brain damage. This happens partly as a direct toxic effect of the alcohol on the brain and partly because of nutritional deficiency, especially of vitamin $B_1$ (thiamine). Another factor is the high risk of head injury in people who fall over when drunk.

Some people who have drunk moderately all their lives lose control of their drinking when they develop a dementing illness. This happens because of both loss of self-control and loss of memory – they may truly think that the drink in their hand is the first today because they can remember no other. Because alcohol causes further loss of inhibitions, dementia sufferers who also drink are particularly likely to show inappropriate sexual behaviour or to become aggressive. Such people are very difficult to help, and often the best that can be done is to limit damage as far as possible.

# Speaking up for your residents – advocacy

You may be in a good position to act as advocate for your residents. You may, for instance, be able to give information about useful services or explain how to use them to the best advantage. Residents may need encouragement to push themselves forward, or your support in making themselves heard. However, sometimes you may find yourself in a difficult situation. Perhaps the confused resident enjoys loud music late at night when wakeful, or has low standards of personal hygiene. Other frail residents – perhaps supported by their relatives – are troubled by their behaviour and would like them to move; not surprisingly, you feel unable to put forth a good case for each opposite point of view. In these circumstances an outside person can usefully act as the confused person's advocate. You may be able to find out about advocacy services in your area from local or national branches of organisations such as Age Concern and MIND, or by asking at the Citizens Advice Bureau.

## Working with the relatives of mentally frail residents

Sometimes an elderly couple will come into the Home when one partner is physically frail and one mentally so. When this happens, you should encourage the mentally intact partner to do as much with and for the mentally frail person as they seem able and willing to do. In some cases, however, the relationship may have broken down, and in others you may have to protect the alert but frail partner against the exhaustion of repetitive questioning or injury from bursts of aggression. Sometimes breaks such as holidays apart give a welcome respite.

Some older people come into residential care because an ageing spouse, though able to care for themselves in the community, can no longer cope with the difficulties arising from their partner's increasing mental frailty. The 'ex-carer' is likely to have a great many feelings, some of which conflict with each other – relief at lifting of the care load, guilt at giving up, love for the sufferer mingled with exasperation, plus a great deal of poorly focused anger. Sometimes this last will be directed at care staff in a constant drip of criticism. This should not be taken personally, but seen as an expression of pain and real need to believe the carer's own work was worth while. While real shortcomings in your Home's care should of course be corrected, unfounded complaints should simply be listened to without over-reaction. Some 'ex-carers' may benefit from the chance to express their feelings in a carers' group; you could find out about these in your area from the social services department, health centres or voluntary agencies such as the Alzheimer's Disease Society, the Relatives Association or the Carers National Association.

How much relatives and friends want to care for their elders in the Home, and how much and in what ways the resident wants them to help, will vary from one situation to another. You should be guided by the wishes of those concerned as to what you suggest or encourage. Contrary to popular opinion, there is no evidence that relatives are less attentive to their elders' needs than they used to be. In any case, we can never know the rights and wrongs of family relationships, as we only come on the scene late in the last act of a long play. Though it is never right to interfere, you may occasionally be able to help relatives' efforts to visit and care for their elder. Providing information about dementing illnesses may help them to understand and better tolerate upsetting behaviour such as aggression or inappropriate sexual activity: the Alzheimer's Disease

Society produces excellent literature and Age Concern England have published *Dementia Care: A handbook for residential and day care*. You could encourage relatives to continue to visit a seemingly ungracious resident who in fact finds it difficult to express her very real affection for her family. Reminding the resident of the approaching visit and drawing her attention to family photographs will make it more likely that she will recognise and welcome her visitors when they arrive. You may be able to suggest appropriate presents for a mentally frail resident to generous but puzzled relatives who know less about their elder's abilities and the scope for interest and enjoyment within them than you do; the Winslow catalogue may provide some ideas. Dispelling the outdated but still prevalent notion that 'they aren't allowed out', you can encourage residents' visitors to take them out for a while, underpinning your suggestions with practical advice on coping with difficulties such as poor mobility or an unreliable bladder.

People with caring skills – you and I, for instance – have special difficulty when we have to act the role of relative rather than professional. You may find relatives who belong to the caring professions especially difficult to deal with because of this. Such people need to be helped to express their concern in an appropriate way, by providing their elder with loving support and companionship rather than using their working skills.

You should inform concerned relatives and friends when a resident is genuinely at risk in some way – perhaps through unsafe smoking habits. The family need to know what is going on, what the dangers are and in what ways if any you can intervene. Loving relatives naturally feel protective, and because of this may want to curtail perfectly reasonable behaviour. You may need to emphasise that all human life is risky, and that on the whole older people suffer more from unwise restraint and limitation than from recklessness. It is rare for an older person to be injured through being unwisely active, while many are hurt or made miserable by being over-protected.

## Together or apart?

There are no easy answers to the dilemma of whether mentally intact and mentally frail people should be cared for together or apart. Mentally frail people who are cheerful and show no challenging behaviour may be accepted by alert residents and benefit from their company. When care is good in such settings, mentally intact residents feel reassured that they will not lose their dignity if they too should deteriorate. On the other hand, it can cause real distress to alert but physically frail people to be threatened by someone who is confused and aggressive, to encounter someone who masturbates publicly, or to have a near neighbour with unpleasant eating habits, poor personal hygiene or a tendency to rummage through others' personal possessions. In this situation, mentally frail residents suffer too: no longer benefiting from the stimulation of integrated care, they are more likely to be disliked, avoided and isolated.

The main danger of segregating mentally frail residents in special units is that staff become overwhelmed and care standards fall. When resources allow continued good care, however, this can be tailored to the confused residents' needs without the anxiety of 'failure to achieve' in comparison with mentally intact residents.

Compromise solutions often seem to work best. Whenever possible, try to have alert residents well in the majority, though this is becoming ever more difficult to achieve. Do all you can to reduce or eliminate upsetting behaviour patterns like screaming and aggression, and to establish continence as the norm for your Home. Try to provide all residents with privacy when they want it, and with a lockable drawer or cupboard to keep possessions safe. In a grouped living setting it may be possible to place residents with others of similar abilities and habits without some becoming stigmatised. A choice of sitting spaces can allow informal segregation as and when residents wish it. You will find it useful to explain the nature of dementia and the reasons underlying bizarre and distressing behaviour to your mentally intact residents, as understanding a little of what is going on often reduces fear and increases tolerance. Lastly, try to ensure that mentally alert residents do not feel neglected; they should be given their fair share of staff time and attention, in an atmosphere where residents of all levels of mental functioning are treated with kindness and respect.

# LOOKING AFTER YOUR STAFF

Caring for mentally frail people is always difficult, and staff need help and support to do it properly. Training is the first essential: the basis of care for confused people should be included in the induction course which all staff must have. Further 'refresher' training will also be needed, perhaps by day release or distance learning; see the ACE publication *Good Care Management* for a full discussion of training opportunities. You could also arrange for in-house training from a visiting expert, tailored to the special needs of your staff; a community psychiatric nurse or clinical psychologist can be useful here.

Informal, on the job training should go on all the time; new recruits, especially, will be watching you and other senior members of staff, listening to what you say and noting what you do. Some Homes find it useful to use established members of staff as mentors for new ones, and to arrange for staff visits to local resource centres or other places where care for mentally frail people is known to be good. You could also set up a library of publications for reference (see Further Reading).

Emotional support is very important; staff will need to express anger, sadness and frustration, and group meetings are a useful forum to let these out. Strong feelings are especially likely to be aroused by residents with challenging behaviour such as aggression or inappropriate expressions of sexuality. Such meetings also serve a practical purpose, as they allow staff to agree a consistent pattern of care for coping with such residents.

In between times, try to be as approachable as possible when a staff member is in practical or emotional difficulties. Be alert to signs of strain and encourage those affected to take necessary breaks. Remember, also, that you too need a listening ear, relaxation and refresher courses.

## KEY POINTS

- An older person who becomes confused because of a physical illness may be wrongly thought to have dementia.
- Depressive illness and the effects of sight and hearing loss can be mistaken for dementia.

- The commonest types of dementing illness in the UK are Alzheimer's disease and multi-infarct dementia. At present there is no cure for these illnesses.

- Confused people are more muddled at some times than at others; how much they realise about their mental state also varies.

- Confused people and their relatives may 'cover up' and try to deny that anything is wrong. They do not mean to deceive but are protecting themselves from the unpleasant truth.

- Take sensible precautions without being over-protective; too much safety endangers quality of life.

- Caring for mentally frail people is always difficult, and your staff will need help and support to do it properly.

---

Giving good care to mentally frail people requires both technical competence and human warmth. Having trained your staff to intelligent efficiency, foster compassion by your own attitude; kindness in a voice or a touch of a hand often gets through to someone who is too confused to understand much else. .

# 7 Residents and their Medicines

The information in this chapter should make it easier for you to help your residents to get the most out of their medicines, whether they take care of their own drug treatment or need help with it from you and your staff. Chapter 8 gives a list of commonly used medicines, with the reasons they are used and their more common unwanted effects.

# GENERAL KNOWLEDGE ABOUT MEDICINES

## Different names for medicines

Every medicine has a 'generic' name, which is usually an abbreviated form of its chemical name. When a doctor writes a generic name on the prescription form, the dispensing pharmacist will usually supply the cheapest form of that preparation in stock. In some circumstances, however, doctors might prefer to use a particular drug company's preparation because, for instance, it is swallowed more easily, quicker acting or better absorbed. They would then specify the drug by its 'trade' name. A drug that is marketed by several different companies will have several different trade names. Because 'proprietary' drugs (prescribed by trade names) usually cost more than the generic preparation, doctors are encouraged by the Government to prescribe generic drugs.

Sometimes a resident may become upset because the doctor seems to have changed the usual tablets or the pharmacist to have dispensed the wrong ones. Confusion may result because a generic preparation has been dispensed instead of the accustomed proprietary one, or vice versa – for instance, a person may be disturbed to be given digoxin (generic name), having become used to seeing Lanoxin (trade name) on the bottle. The person can be reassured that the two are, in fact, the same substance. If in doubt, ask the pharmacist.

## POMs and OTCs – the difference

Prescription-only medicines ('POMs') cannot be bought over the counter in a chemist's shop (pharmacy); they are supplied only on a doctor's prescription. The pharmacist will then dispense them in a container labelled with the person's name. The medicines then become that person's property, and should not be used to treat anyone else.

Over-the-counter ('OTC') medicines can be bought without a doctor's prescription. Such items as indigestion mixtures, travel sickness remedies, mild pain killers and laxatives come into this category. Some OTCs can only be sold in a pharmacy when the pharmacist is in the shop; they have a letter P on the packaging. Others are more freely available, on the general sale list (GSL).

Some residents may buy their own OTC remedies, and of course they have every right to do so. However, OTC medicines are not necessarily harmless alone, and they may also interact with any prescribed medicines the resident is taking. Pharmacists can advise about this; some keep a record system which notes the patient's use of both prescribed and OTC medicines, making possible interactions easy to spot.

In general, it is sensible to discourage the use of OTCs, as it is unwise for an older person to attempt self-diagnosis, and money spent on these remedies might be better used elsewhere. Most minor ailments get better spontaneously within a few days; if a resident has symptoms that persist for longer than this, you should suggest that they see the doctor.

Do encourage your residents to be honest with the doctor about the medicines they are taking. For example, they should say if they have stopped taking a prescribed medicine they found unhelpful, or if they have started using an over-the-counter drug or complementary therapy. Failure to do this could lead to unwanted effects from treatments that do not mix.

Some Homes keep a small stock of OTC remedies from a list agreed between the doctor, the pharmacist and the Home's staff; for example, indigestion remedies, mild pain killers and laxatives. The medicines may be supplied on a bulk prescription or bought; their use should always be recorded carefully. Because it is difficult to tell whether a 'minor ailment' is truly that or the symptom of something more serious, OTC remedies should never be used to treat a resident for more than two days without the doctor being consulted. Also, if the resident already takes prescribed medicines, the pharmacist should be asked whether they and the proposed OTC medicine are safe to mix.

## Controlled drugs

Controlled drugs are medicines whose use is regulated by law. The likeliest ones for you to come across are the strong pain killers, such as morphine. For information about these, consult your pharmacist.

## Unwanted effects of medicines

People tend to become confused about the 'side effects' of drugs. These are better described as 'unwanted effects' because most drugs have more than one effect, and which of them are wanted and which are unwanted can vary from one occasion to another. There is no such thing as a good or bad drug, only one that is used well or badly by the doctor and/or the patient.

Using a medicine is no different from using a knife; either can cause damage if used carelessly or by someone with poor sight, or if used for suicide or murder – misuse is not the fault of the knife or the medicine but of the person using it.

Older people are especially prone to the unwanted effects of medicines, for a number of reasons. Because of ageing changes in the body, medicines may be removed more slowly from the body than in younger people. This means that normal adult doses may accumulate and produce toxic effects, and therefore older people often require smaller doses of medicine than younger adults with similar illnesses.

In addition, some doctors seem insufficiently well informed about the needs of older people, and may prescribe with insufficient thought and care. People sometimes reinforce this by being reluctant to leave the surgery without a prescription as a 'talisman', even when the doctor has suggested that this is unnecessary.

Each time a medicine is used, its likely benefits must be balanced against the possible risks. For a serious illness, it may still be sensible to use a medicine with quite serious unwanted effects, if the illness is more dangerous than the medicine. It would not, however, be sensible to use the medicine for a minor illness, because the balance of risk would be against it.

## Older people from ethnic minorities and their medicines

Some sorts of British medicines and ways of taking them are unacceptable to older people from certain ethnic groups. Here are some points to remember:

- Muslims who fast during Ramadan may need their usual medicines altered so that they can be taken twice a day or less often.

- Devout Muslims, Hindus, Sikhs or Buddhists may be reluctant to use preparations containing alcohol, whether they are to be swallowed or applied to the skin. The pharmacist will be able to find out the ingredients of a particular preparation, and can if necessary help the doctor choose a suitable alternative.

- Gelatin capsules are made from animal bones and hides, including those of cows and pigs. Medicines in such capsules will not be acceptable to religious Hindus, Sikhs and Muslims, to many Jews or to vegetarians or vegans of any faith or none. Again, it will usually be possible to find an alternative.

- Older people from ethnic minorities find some British medicines unacceptable; seek advice from community leaders, if necessary.

If you are unsure about the cultural requirements of older people from ethnic minorities, you should seek advice from appropriate community leaders.

# Complementary or alternative medicine

Residents of course have every right to decide what sort of medicines they want to take, and when or whether to use complementary, alternative or traditional treatments as well as or instead of orthodox scientific Western medicine. Beliefs about health and illness vary a great deal, especially in people from different cultural backgrounds. Older people from ethnic minority groups commonly use several types of medical care; one common pattern would be to use traditional remedies for chronic, vague disorders and orthodox Western medicine for acute illness or injuries.

As a general rule, complementary therapies that can be shown to have useful effects may also be harmful in some circumstances. Other types of treatment which seem to do little good probably also do little harm; they may, however, delay the use of effective treatment.

## Herbal remedies

Many of the drugs now available in a conventional form were originally derived from plants. For example, digitalis (digoxin) came from foxgloves, aspirin from willow bark and colchicine from the autumn crocus.

Western herbal medicines may be obtained from a herbalist or over the counter in health food shops. Herbal remedies are especially popular with the Chinese community, where they are believed to act by restoring the 'energy balance' in the body. They may help in some cases of eczema, but some preparations have been found to contain steroids as well as herbs: this makes the effectiveness of the herbs difficult to assess.

Unwanted effects from herbal treatments may be serious or even fatal. They include kidney and liver damage, with reports of liver cancer, blood disorders and skin rashes. Herbal preparations may also interact with orthodox Western medicines in someone who uses both.

## Homoeopathic preparations

The practice of homoeopathy is based on several principles. One is that 'like cures like': giving a medicine that reproduces or supports the symptoms will encourage the body to throw off the disease. Another theory is that the minimum dose has the greatest effect: homoeopathic preparations contain only very diluted solutions of their active ingredients. They are therefore unlikely either to relieve symptoms or cause unwanted effects. Their use might, however, delay effective treatment, and they are best prescribed by a qualified doctor specialising in homoeopathy.

## Osteopathy and chiropractic

These varieties of 'manipulative medicine' seem to have good effects in some cases of back pain and of joint diseases. They are among the most popular of the complementary therapies, and many orthodox doctors find them both acceptable and useful.

Osteopathic and chiropractic manipulations can cause damage to bones, joints and nearby structures such as nervous tissue in the spinal cord or peripheral nerves. It is important that the medical diagnosis is known before manipulation is attempted, and good practitioners usually make sure that this is done.

## Acupuncture and Shiatsu

This Chinese therapy involves the insertion of fine needles at points on the body corresponding to the condition or organ under treatment. In Shiatsu, finger pressure is applied to acupuncture points. Both are said to work by releasing the body's natural pain killers, called endorphins. Studies suggest that the techniques may be helpful in a small proportion of cases, but the effects are not consistent.

An important unwanted effect is the spread of hepatitis B or the HIV virus if contaminated needles are not properly sterilised before reuse.

## Traditional Asian medicines

Muslims may consult a hakim or traditional healer and take the medicines he provides. These may contain metal compounds: toxic amounts of arsenic and mercury from these sources have caused serious disability from nerve damage, and even some deaths.

## Faith healing

Reputable faith healers offer spiritual support in addition to orthodox medicine, rather than attempting to replace it. The healer will suggest that the sick person consults a doctor for diagnosis, and he or she will not countermand the doctor's advice.

Someone who stops orthodox treatment, such as tablets for epilepsy, after a healing in the wrong belief that they are no longer necessary, can suffer serious harm. In addition, some people who are not cured develop a crippling sense of guilt: they come to believe that, lacking sufficient faith for a healing, their illness is all their own fault.

# IS THE TREATMENT WORKING?

It can often be very difficult to tell how effective a treatment is, whether it is orthodox or complementary. Many people have long-standing, recurring conditions (eg arthritis, eczema, migraine) whose symptoms wax and wane mysteriously. They may be affected by the person's psychological state, their diet and workload, chemicals they are in contact with, changes in the weather and other even less well understood factors.

When someone gets better, it is easy to attribute the improvement to whatever orthodox or complementary treatment was in use at the time, and to disregard other possible influences. There is also the 'placebo effect': in about a third of cases, something the person believes to be effective will produce an improvement in symptoms, whether or not the 'treatment' contains active ingredients. Placebos have their drawbacks, however: the improvement does not always happen, and is usually short-lived when it does. Also, once a symptom has responded to the placebo 'medicine', the patient finds it difficult to accept that a psychological element is the cause of the trouble; this can then interfere with effective psychological treatment. In any case, many doctors prefer to work in partnership with their patients, and think it is paternalistic and insulting to deceive a patient with a placebo.

As orthodox medicines are powerful for both good and harm, good scientific testing is needed to ensure that they are used well. Many people think complementary therapies should be tested in the same way: then they could be used if effective, or, if useless, discarded.

# SOURCES OF HELP WITH RESIDENTS' MEDICINES

You should get to know the other people who are concerned with your residents' drug treatment, so that you communicate freely and work well together.

## The role of the GP

Prescribing doctors may not need to see residents every time they write prescriptions for them. However, it is unwise for 'repeat prescriptions' to be allowed to run for more than three months. Try to make sure that the resident sees the doctor if this time has elapsed or if their condition has changed since their last prescription was written.

Do not expect the doctor to prescribe large amounts of medicines: 28 days' supply is enough for residents on continuous treatment, and in many cases much shorter courses will be needed.

If the doctor writes the amount and frequency of the doses of medicine on each prescription (eg 'Two tablets twice a day'), this will appear on the label of the medicine package. If this information is omitted from the prescription, the pharmacist can only write 'As directed', which is much less helpful to you and your staff. You may be able to suggest to the doctor that dosage details are included on the prescription.

The prescribing doctor should give the following information to the resident, and to the staff if they help with medicines:

- why the medicine is being given;
- when it should be taken;
- what it is expected to do;
- what unwanted effects should be looked for and reported.

## Help from pharmacists

Residents who are fit enough to leave the Home can of course choose where to have their prescriptions dispensed, and others may ask their relatives to go to the pharmacist on their behalf. Remaining prescriptions will go to whichever local community pharmacist (the pharmacist in the pharmacist's shop) has contracted with the Family Health Services Authority (FHSA) to serve the Home. He or she will visit the Home with the pharmacist from the local health authority, to agree on the service your residents need. In addition, the local pharmacist may visit the Home regularly to:

- deliver dispensed medicines and tell staff how to help with them and store them safely;

- educate staff about the wanted and unwanted effects of the medicines;

- see that records are kept correctly, stored safely and that the information in them tallies with the existing stores of medicines;

- remove unwanted medicines for disposal;

- liaise with doctors about medicine doses, interactions and unwanted effects as necessary;

- relabel medicines if the dose is changed or if the original label becomes illegible;

- work out with the doctor and head of the Home ways in which urgently needed medicines can be obtained in an emergency;

- ensure that residents who spend part of their time away from the Home (eg at a day centre or with relatives) have medicines and information about them available so that their treatment is not interrupted.

The pharmacist will keep careful records of all work done within the Home.

## Monitored dosage systems (MDSs)

Some pharmacists will operate these systems, which are increasingly used in Homes. They all work in a similar way: a week's tablets are split into the doses to be taken at specific times on each day. The tablets for each occasion (Tuesday morning, Tuesday lunchtime, Tuesday evening, Tuesday bed time and so on) are then sealed into compartments of a cassette or the bubbles of a blister pack. The sorting, filling and sealing are all done by the dispensing pharmacist. At the point of taking the tablets, the resident or their helper simply has to identify the correct compartment or blister; there is no need to decide which tablets should be taken or to count out the dose. The cassette or blister pack also works as a sophisticated 'memory box', so the resident or their carer can check whether the tablets have been taken. If the resident needs to go into hospital, they can take the pack or cassette with them in the ambulance; hospital staff can then find out quickly what treatment has been prescribed and which tablets have been taken.

MDSs are often free to residents and to Homes. Pharmacists purchase them and they bear the costs of operation because they benefit from dispensing revenues.

For further information about help available from pharmacists, ask your local Family Health Services Authority (address and telephone number in the telephone book).

## Help from nurses

The practice or district nurse may be able to teach a resident how to manage their medicines correctly; this may be especially useful with eye-drops or inhaled medicines. Nurses in an increasing number of hospital wards now make a point of training patients to cope with their medication themselves before discharge. If this is not the case in your area, you may be able to suggest that this policy should be adopted.

## Medicines and independence

Residents should take charge of their own medicines if they possibly can. Drugs prescribed for them are their own property, and controlling them helps residents to feel in charge of other aspects of their lives. It is especially important for residents to remain independent of help when they plan to return to the community, for instance after a period of respite care.

A trial period of responsibility for medicines is a useful test of a new resident's abilities, if these are in doubt. After the trial period you, your staff and the resident, with advice from the doctor or district nurse and pharmacist if necessary, should decide whether help is needed, and, if so, of what sort. For instance, you could ask the pharmacist to dispense medicines in bottles or packs that are easier to open if the resident has difficulty with child-resistant tops or blister packs. If all residents who look after their own medicines are asked to consent to checks on their correct use from time to time, problems can be dealt with early. Each such resident should have a lockable drawer or cupboard to keep the medicines in.

When a resident cannot manage their own medicines, you should explain that you and the staff will look after them carefully and give them out according to the doctor's instructions. You will need to be especially tactful when someone who was previously capable becomes forgetful and can no longer be relied on to take their medicines.

When help is needed, the minimum possible should be given. In some cases, supervision and prompting will be enough, but in others staff may need to take complete responsibility for the safe keeping and administration of medicines. Try to find ways of leaving the resident some independence; for instance:

- By providing a monitored dosage system or filled memory box for forgetful residents. If reminded that the medicine is due, they may be able to do the rest themselves.

- By improving labelling for partially sighted residents. Large print and Braille labels, plus advice, are available from the Royal National Institute for the Blind (RNIB), and the social worker for the blind (see p 136) may be able to make further suggestions.

- By asking an occupational therapist's advice when poor dexterity is the problem. It may sometimes help to use a monitored dosage system, or to ask the pharmacist to dispense into containers with screw tops, preferably with prominent flanges; child-resistant tops and blister packs should be avoided.

- By teaching residents about their medicines. People find it difficult to tell apart the drugs they take every day to prevent illness and those that they take from time to time to relieve a troublesome symptom. The visiting pharmacist can label medicines as, for instance, 'Heart pill – one each morning', or 'Pain killers – two when necessary, up to eight per day'. This can be followed up with a careful verbal explanation.

Be very careful what you say if a resident asks you for advice about their medicines, as it is very risky for residents to be given conflicting advice by different people. All but the simplest queries are best referred to the pharmacist or doctor, to avoid worsening the confusion in the resident's mind.

# CARE OF MEDICINES IN THE HOME

## Storage

Nothing else should be stored in medicine cupboards and trolleys; this means there is no need to open them except to give out medicines. Cupboards should be kept locked, and trolleys locked and immobilised; the keys must be kept securely. Medicine cupboards and storage trolleys should be kept in staff areas, where residents do not normally need to go. Where possible, you should have a lockable refrigerator in which only medicines are kept.

Individual residents' medicines should not be pooled in bulk containers. They should remain in the individual labelled bottle or MDS compartment until the dose is due; then the resident should be given the medicine straight from the labelled container. Medicines prescribed for one resident should not be used to treat another.

Choose a method of drug storage that is easy to manage in your Home. For instance, if there are many stairs, drug containers that build into stackable trays are useful but drug trolleys are not.

Do not improvise your own memory aids from egg cups or ice trays, as it is easy to make mistakes in using them.

## Designated officer (DO)

A member of staff known as the 'designated officer' should be in over-all charge of those medicines for which the staff take responsibility. He or she should make sure that proper, full records are kept (see below). The DO should also check that the systems of storing and giving out medicines are safe and efficient, and that staff have proper training. He or she should work closely with the pharmacist.

The DO should have a named deputy to cover absence from the Home.

# Records

Records are kept to make sure that medicines entering the Home can be accounted for at all times and that they are given correctly. Records must be clear and accurate enough for members of staff who do not know the residents well to use them without making mistakes. Some MDS cassettes include a list of the medicines inside and a small photograph of the resident for whom they were prescribed.

Three sets of records should be kept: a Medicines book, medication profiles and an administration record.

## Medicines book

This helps to track all the medicines that enter or leave the Home and for which staff take responsibility (ie prescribed medicines and homely remedies if these are kept). Medicines that residents have dispensed or buy for themselves over the counter and then look after themselves are not included.

When a medicine comes into the Home, its description and the quantity should be recorded; if it has been prescribed for a particular resident (ie not a household remedy stock bottle), the resident's name should also be noted. When a medicine leaves the Home, its amount and description should again be written down. Its destination should also be recorded: for example, accompanying the resident to hospital, going to the pharmacist for disposal.

A well kept Medicines book should show when a medicine cannot be accounted for by normal use, and must therefore have been given to the wrong resident, given to the right resident but in too large a dosage, or has been stolen or mislaid.

## Medication profile

Each resident should have one of these. If residents are looking after their own medicines, lists of what they are taking may be kept with their consent. If residents prefer to keep their treatment private, this should be noted on their profiles.

When staff are helping a resident with medicines, the medication profile should include the following:

**Information about the resident:** full name and date of birth; photograph if available; details of any known drug sensitivity (eg to penicillin or aspirin).

**Information about the medicine:** its name, form (eg tablets or syrup), the amount dispensed, the strength of the preparation, the dose (how much is to be given at a time), and by what route (eg by mouth, rectally etc), the times of doses and whether it should be taken before or after food.

**Time factors:** the date the medicine was dispensed, when it was received and when treatment with it was started.

## Administration record

If the resident is looking after their own medicines, this fact should be noted on the administration record.

For residents helped by staff, the record should show: the name of the medicine, the timing of the dose, the amount given and the amount the resident actually took if this is different. Each entry should be initialled at the time the medicine is given, and household remedies should be included as well as prescribed medicines.

If a resident refuses to take some or all of their medicines, staff should not pressure them to do so. They should note the resident's refusal on the administration record and report it at once to the designated officer on duty. The DO can then inform the pharmacist and doctor, and ask advice on further action.

---

**NOTE** It is most important that the doctor is told when a resident is not taking their medicines; if this is not done, the doctor may unwittingly take action that could be harmful.

---

If the medication profile and the administration record are not on the same sheet, they should be kept together.

Medicines records must be available when medicines are being given, and also whenever a doctor or pharmacist visits the Home. The doctor should check the details on the medication profile, and initial and date any alteration to treatment; for example, a change in dose, or a medicine being stopped altogether. The head of the Home is responsible for making sure that records are kept correctly, and that they are stored for at least three years after the resident has died or left the Home.

Occasionally, a doctor may give verbal instructions for a change in a resident's medicines, perhaps over the telephone. These instructions should be noted in a standard way – for instance, the DO or their deputy should sign the entry, adding the date and time at which the instructions were given, and the note should be countersigned by the doctor as soon as possible.

## When and how to dispose of medicines

Medicines should be disposed of:

- When their expiry date is reached; this happens very soon for some eye preparations, skin ointments and syrups.
- When a course of treatment is finished, or the doctor stops the medicine.
- When the resident for whom the medicines were prescribed dies. However, they should be kept for seven days after death in case the coroner's officer wants them.

Medicines for disposal should be returned to the community pharmacist, who will dispose of them safely. Their leaving the Home for disposal should be recorded, and the designated officer and the pharmacist should both sign the Medicines book.

Visiting doctors and nurses who give injections should deal with their own used equipment. Disposable syringes should be broken and dismantled, and needles put safely in a 'sharps' box.

*Never:*

- keep half finished medicines in case they come in useful for other residents;
- put unwanted tablets or bottles of liquid medicines in the dustbin or refuse sack.

## Treatment prescribed outside the Home

Residents who visit hospital clinics may be prescribed new treatment. Usually only a small supply of this will be dispensed, and residents will be expected to obtain further supplies through their GP. Poor communication about altered drug therapy can lead to dangerous mistakes. If residents are in charge of their own medicines, you should enquire tactfully whether they understand any changes that were made; if they do not, they may value your help and support in making any necessary telephone enquiries. If staff normally help the residents with their medicines, you should make sure that hospital staff tell you, as well as the GP, when changes are made in drug treatment. It will be especially useful if the hospital pharmacists and the community pharmacists supplying the Home keep in touch. There may be a local protocol under which hospital pharmacists pass on information to the community pharmacist who has contracted with the Home.

## Transfer or discharge of residents

A resident's treatment should not be interrupted if they leave the Home, so you should ask the doctor to prescribe enough medicines to bridge the gap before they can obtain further supplies. If they are going to another Home, they should take their medicines profile and administration record with them, as well as their medicines.

## Timing of medicines

The timing of medicines may be very important, for instance in the treatment of diabetes and Parkinson's disease; the doctor or pharmacist can advise. Independent residents can arrange timing for themselves, but residents who need help should also be given their medicines at the best time. This may not necessarily fit in with 'medicine rounds', but the benefit to the resident may more than justify the inconvenience to the staff.

## Medicines and challenging behaviour

Medicines are of course intended for treatment; they should never be used to 'control' or 'punish' a resident. Challenging behaviour should be discussed with the doctor in the first instance; when appropriate, referral can be made to a community psychiatric nurse, old age psychiatrist (psycho-geriatrician) or clinical psychologist. Sometimes a change in drug treatment may be recommended, but other forms of treatment may be more appropriate, and expert advice will help with this.

## Giving medicines safely

Staff concerned should follow these steps:

1 Check the resident's identity.

2 Find the corresponding medicines record and check the name. (Special care is needed when temporary or agency staff are giving out medicines, or when two or more residents have the same or similar names.)

3 Find the entry on the medicines record for the medicine you are about to give. Make sure that:

   the dose has not been changed recently;

   the medicine has not already been given by somebody else.

4 Find the right medicine container and check it against the record.

5 Measure or count the dose from a labelled bottle or pack.

6 Give the medicine to the resident.

7 Record that the medicine:

   has been given to the resident and taken by them *or*

   has been given to the resident but not taken (in this case, dispose of it safely); *or*

   has not been given, in which case state why.

## Staff training

Training courses about medicines matter, as they teach new staff how to work with them and help to keep established staff up to date. It is especially important that designated officers are able to give out medicines safely and keep clear, accurate records. Before they do so, the doctor, district nurse or pharmacist should test their competence. The pharmaceutical officer and community pharmacist can help with more theoretical aspects of training and some practical ones. In addition, district nurses can show staff how to apply 'topical' medicines such as eye-drops and skin creams properly.

A recent edition of the *British National Formulary* should be available in the Home for reference; the pharmacist will help you get one. Other useful reference books are mentioned in the Further Reading section.

# DRUG PREPARATIONS

Active medicines come in many different forms. Sometimes the substance has to be given in a particular way, but if a resident has difficulty in using one preparation, it is worth asking the doctor or pharmacist if it or a good substitute comes in a more convenient form.

## Medicines taken by mouth

Tablets or capsules are usually designed to be swallowed whole with a good draught of water; in some cases, milk or similar drinks will interfere with the medicine's action. Tablets difficult to swallow whole can sometimes be chewed up in a mouthful of food, but check with the pharmacist first. Alternatively, the same medicine may be available in liquid form.

Sublingual preparations are put in the mouth and allowed to dissolve under the tongue rather than being swallowed. Glyceryl trinitrate for angina taken in this way relieves the pain quickly and reliably.

## Inhaled medicines

Used in chest disease, these are designed to get the medicine to its site of action with the minimum of waste and unwanted effects in the rest of the body. The medicine may fail to work if the inhaler is not used properly, so the resident should ask to be shown this.

## Locally applied ('topical') medicines

These can be as powerful for good or ill as medicines that go inside the body, and need just as much care in use. The district nurse can be asked to demonstrate the use of eye- and ear-drops and to check that they are being put in correctly. The nurse may be able to suggest equipment to help the residents to do this for themselves. When using topical medicines, residents or their helpers may need to find out where on the body patches should be applied, when they should be attached or removed and whether ointments or creams on the skin should be covered with dressings.

# Injections

Injections are usually given by doctors or nurses rather than by patients themselves, with the exception of insulin. Diabetics who need insulin may find self-administration more difficult if their sight worsens or their fingers become clumsy. Staff who help with this should be taught to do so by the district nurse, who will confirm that they are able to do so safely.

# Rectal or vaginal medicines

Suppositories (for the rectum) and pessaries (for the vagina) are solid preparations that are usually bulkier than tablets designed to be swallowed. They dissolve slowly after insertion, and are mostly used to treat local conditions such as constipation or infections. However, the rectal route is sometimes used to release a medicine slowly into the whole body. The person responsible for inserting the suppository or pessary should make sure they know exactly how to go about it.

**KEY POINTS**

- Medicines can be prescribed by 'generic' names (shortened chemical descriptions) or by one of the 'trade' names manufacturing companies give to their own brands.
- A medicine that seems to be different may just be a different brand or name. Check with the doctor or pharmacist.
- While respecting their right to choose treatment, try to discourage residents from self-medication with over-the-counter drugs which they can buy without a doctor's prescription.
- Encourage residents to be honest with the doctor about whatever medicines they are taking.
- Medicines that have useful effects also have unwanted ones. Older people are especially vulnerable to the unwanted effects of medicines.
- You can get advice about residents' medicines from the doctor, nurse or pharmacist.
- Whenever possible, residents should take charge of their own medicines. When help is needed, give the minimum possible that will make things safe.

# 8 Some Commonly Prescribed Medicines

This chapter describes some of the medicines that older people take most often – for:

| | |
|---|---|
| **abnormal blood clotting** | **indigestion** |
| **anaemia** | **infections** |
| **arthritis** | **mental illness** |
| **cancer** | **Paget's disease** |
| **chest diseases** | **pain** |
| **constipation** | **Parkinson's disease** |
| **cough** | **peptic ulcer** |
| **diabetes** | **shingles** |
| **diarrhoea** | **sleep problems** |
| **epileptic fits** | **thyroid problems** |
| **gout** | **vitamin deficiency** |
| **heart disease** | and **steroid therapy** |
| **hiatus hernia** | |

Unwanted effects of medicines should always be reported to the doctor. Whenever possible, residents should do this themselves; you may need to speak on behalf of confused or very frail residents.

# For abnormal clotting

## Anti-coagulants

These are used to prevent a blood clot from forming, or, if it is already there, to prevent it from spreading further. Treatment needs to be taken strictly as prescribed, and dosage is adjusted according to results of frequent blood tests. The resident should always carry a card with details of tests and treatment to show to a new doctor. This is necessary both because of possible complications of anti-coagulant therapy and because new medicines can interfere with previously stable anti-coagulant therapy.

Unwanted effects include bleeding, especially into urine or the gut. Fainting and collapse may occur due to hidden, internal blood loss; this needs urgent medical treatment.

# For anaemia

## Iron tablets

These are used to treat anaemia due to iron deficiency. They should be taken as prescribed, usually with food.

Unwanted effects include nausea, diarrhoea or constipation. These should be reported to the doctor, as a change of preparation may enable iron treatment to continue without complications.

## Vitamin B$_{12}$

This is used for the treatment of pernicious anaemia and is given by injection into muscle. Once pernicious anaemia has been diagnosed, B$_{12}$ injections will be needed for life, at approximately three-monthly intervals. B$_{12}$ has no known unwanted effects.

# For arthritis

Pain killers such as paracetamol taken regularly may be sufficient to give relief in mild cases.

Non-steroidal anti-inflammatory agents (NSAIs) are used in more severe cases to relieve pain and inflammation. Examples are benorylate, ibuprofen and diclofenac.

The main unwanted effect of NSAIs is digestive upset, ranging from mild indigestion through pain, nausea, vomiting and diarrhoea to severe bleeding. These medicines are not usually given to people with active peptic ulcers. Some people with a healed peptic ulcer who really need an NSAI take it with an acid-reducing drug such as ranitidine. This makes the ulcer less likely to flare up again. NSAIs should always be taken with food or milk. Anyone who has digestive symptoms while taking an NSAI should stop taking the medicine at once and should consult the doctor.

It is sometimes difficult to decide whether the genuine help many arthritis sufferers receive from their NSAIs is outweighed by the risk of unwanted effects. Residents who have arthritis may want to discuss this with their doctors.

# For cancer

Two sorts of medicines can be used to halt the growth of cancerous cells in primary and secondary tumours; these are cytotoxic drugs and hormone therapy.

## Cytotoxic drugs

These poison cancer cells by interfering with their growth or metabolism. They are most effective against leukaemia and lymphoma (tumours of lymph gland tissue), and tend to be less useful for solid tumours.

Unwanted effects come about because normal body cells are partially poisoned too. Common complaints are of sickness and vomiting, lowered resistance to infection because of a lack of white blood cells, and loss of hair. Treatment with cytotoxics is usually supervised by a medical oncologist with special knowledge and experience of their use.

## Hormone treatment

This may be used to treat tumours of the reproductive organs such as the prostate or breast. Treatment involves either blocking the action of a hormone that causes growth or using one with the opposite effect.

Breast cancer may be treated by tamoxifen, which opposes the action of the female hormone oestrogen. Unwanted effects are uncommon, but people whose cancer has spread to their bones may find their pain becomes worse for a short while, after which the bone deposits shrink and the pain gets better.

Prostate cancer is helped to grow by the male hormone testosterone, so treatment aims to prevent this effect. One way of doing this is to remove both testicles surgically, but medicines can give the same effect. They include goserelin, buserelin and diethylstilboestrol (DES). The main unwanted effects are impotence, shrinkage of the genitals and enlargement of the breasts. These may get better if and when treatment is stopped.

# For chest diseases

## Bronchodilators

These relax the bronchial tubes so that air can pass in and out of the lungs more freely. They may be given as tablets or by inhalation as an aerosol spray. Some drugs given by aerosols need to be taken regularly to prevent illnesses, rather than to relieve symptoms. Steroid therapy for chest disease is sometimes given this way.

Inhalers are very effective if used properly, so technique is most important. If a resident does not seem to be benefiting from an aerosol spray, you should suggest that they consult the doctor, nurse or pharmacist, who will demonstrate how to use it properly. It is unwise to use inhalers more often than prescribed, as this may be dangerous.

Unwanted effects of bronchodilators include hand tremors, nervousness, headache and, occasionally, fast heart beat. Slow-release preparations taken by mouth to control wheezing overnight sometimes interfere with sleep.

## Oxygen therapy

Residents with chronic lung disease and those who are terminally ill and short of breath may need to breathe oxygen all the time. Continuous long-term oxygen is best provided by an oxygen concentrator, a machine that extracts the gas from room air. The person usually breathes it through nasal cannuale, tiny tubes inserted into the nostrils. These are more comfortable to wear for long periods than masks, and do not have to be removed to allow the person to eat, drink, talk or cough up spit.

Intermittent oxygen is given to increase exercise tolerance and to reduce the discomfort of being short of breath. The resident may breathe it from a static oxygen cylinder; this can also be used to refill portable equipment if the resident is well enough to move about.

The dose of oxygen can be crucial for a person's well-being; receiving too much or too little can make them seriously ill. The amount the person gets is affected by the rate of flow of the gas, as shown on the flow meter, and sometimes by the type of mask used. It is therefore important that no one alters the rate of flow or changes the mask without asking medical advice.

When someone is using oxygen, there is an increased risk of fire; you may want to ask the fire officer about this. In particular, it is very important that a resident taking oxygen agrees not to smoke. In any case, apart from being dangerous, the smoke counteracts the good effects of the oxygen and makes it useless.

# For constipation

## Laxatives

These should be avoided as far as possible, as they impair normal bowel-emptying patterns. When necessary, a doctor or nurse may advise a suitable preparation, but sometimes a resident may wish to take their own. Older people are often very attached to the laxative they have always taken, and occasional use is probably not very harmful.

For occasional use:

- Lactulose is a syrupy preparation which produces soft, easily passed stools; it is harmless, but rather expensive.
- Methylcellulose granules are harmless and cheap but unpalatable to take, and not always effective in severe cases.
- Senna is supplied as tablets or granules; the effective dose varies from person to person. Unwanted effects include abdominal pains and dangerous loss of salts and water.
- Bisacodyl is similar to senna and can be taken as a suppository.
- Glycerol suppositories lubricate the actual passage of stools and stimulate the bowel. They may cure mild cases, or be useful when taken with another drug for more severe constipation.

To be avoided:

- Senna teas or 'brews' vary in strength, and overdosage is common. Unwanted effects include abdominal pain, diarrhoea, faecal incontinence and disturbances of body chemistry.
- Liquid paraffin has as its unwanted effects leakage at the anus and faecal soiling, impaired absorption of fat-soluble vitamins A and D, and the production of tumours.
- Epsom and other 'health' salts can result in excessive loss of fluid and salt, and faecal incontinence because the stools are difficult to control.

A high-fibre diet often renders laxatives unnecessary. Large amounts of unprocessed bran should not be taken because it interferes with absorption of nutrients and, rarely, can cause bowel blockage. A spoonful added to soups or cereal is harmless and helpful, however.

# For coughs

## Suppressants

These are used to suppress a dry cough. Simple linctus is mild and harmless but comparatively ineffective. Codeine and pholcodine are strong, effective drugs and should be taken strictly as prescribed. Unwanted effects include constipation and retention of mucus. They should not be used for a wet cough, as phlegm may then accumulate and clog the lungs.

## Expectorants

These are used to help bring up thick mucus, and are usually taken in hot water on waking in the morning. They have little if any unwanted effects, but probably do little if any good.

## Steam inhalations

These are cheap, readily available and useful for liquefying thick mucus; however, there is a risk of scalds. It is not necessary to add anything to the water, but a scenting agent such as Friar's Balsam can be used if liked.

# For diabetes

## Oral hypoglycaemics

These are used together with a prescribed diet to lower the sugar level in the blood. They must be taken strictly at the times and in the dosage prescribed, as changes of dose or timing of the tablets or missing a meal may cause dangerous hypoglycaemia.

Unwanted effects include flushing of the face on drinking alcohol, loss of appetite, sickness, vomiting and symptoms of hypoglycaemia ('hypo') such as drowsiness, irritability and confusion. As this condition impairs thinking abilities, you will have to act on behalf of a hypoglycaemic resident; call for help at once and take emergency action (see p 224).

## Insulin injections

These are used for people with diabetes whose condition cannot be controlled by diet or tablets. They must be given exactly as prescribed in both dose and timing. Older diabetics with poor sight may have difficulty with this, and will need help from a visiting nurse.

Few older diabetics need insulin injections all the time, but people usually treated with diet and tablets may need insulin for a short while during an acute illness or to tide them over a surgical operation.

Unwanted effects include hypoglycaemia, infections and other skin complications at the injection site.

# For diarrhoea

In acute cases, medicines are much less important than ensuring that the person drinks enough to replace the lost fluids. Drugs are occasionally used when diarrhoea is very inconvenient or has lasted for more than 24 hours.

Absorbent chalk mixtures and kaolin preparations are popular and harmless. Methylcellulose is useful for people with colostomies. Drugs that reduce gut activity include codeine, morphine or opium compounds, diphenoxylate and loperamide.

Unwanted effects include faecal impaction, sedation and the risk of dependence. In addition, these drugs may slow the rate at which the body gets rid of toxins, and, by masking symptoms, suggest that the illness is less severe than it is. Older people should not take these drugs except on medical advice.

# For epileptic fits

## Phenytoin, carbamazepine, sodium valproate, etc

These medicines need to be taken very regularly, in dosages tailored to the person's requirements. They should *not* be stopped suddenly.

Unwanted effects include impaired absorption of folate and vitamin D from food in people on long-term phenytoin. These substances need to be replaced.

# For gout

Acute attacks are treated with NSAIs. Some people with persisting high levels of urate in their blood need continuing treatment to lower it. Allopurinol slows the formation of urate, whilst probenecid and sulphin-pyrazone help the body to dispose of it, helped by plenty of fluids to flush out the kidneys.

Unwanted effects are rare, though allopurinol may cause skin rashes. An acute attack of gout may be caused if allopurinol is started without 'cover' from an NSAI.

# For heart disease

## Digoxin

This is used to stimulate the heart and/or to regulate its rhythm. It should be taken regularly every morning to maintain a constant level in the blood.

Unwanted effects include slowing of the pulse, confusion, nausea, vomiting and yellow vision. These are usually a sign that the dose is too large, so such symptoms should be reported to the doctor as soon as possible.

## Vasodilators

These expand (dilate) blood vessels – that is, they cause vasodilation. Examples include nitrates such as glyceryl trinitrate and isosorbide dinitrate, and calcium channel blockers such as nifedipine and diltiazem.

Glyceryl trinitrate (GTN) and other nitrate preparations are used to treat angina. Tablets should be put under the tongue at the onset of pain or, better still, before embarking on the sort of activity that provokes pain (eg walking uphill, sexual intercourse). 'Sustained-release' preparations of isosorbide dinitrate give long-lasting protection and these should be taken as directed, usually regularly. Nitrates are also available in aerosols and in forms absorbed through the skin.

Unwanted effects of nitrates include throbbing headache, flushing, faintness and fast heart beat. People should take GTN tablets while sitting down and should spit out the remains of the tablet once the pain is relieved, to reduce unwanted effects.

Someone with frequent angina attacks may do better with treatment designed to prevent them from occurring. Beta-blockers are sometimes used for this (see below). Another alternative is a calcium channel blocker; these medicines reduce the heart's activity as well as dilating blood vessels. They also lower the blood pressure, so can be used to treat high blood pressure.

Unwanted effects of calcium channel blockers vary, depending on which preparation is used. If the heart's action is depressed too much, the patient may develop heart failure or heart rhythm disturbances. Faintness, flushing, headache and swollen ankles may also occur.

Vasodilators have been tried in the hope of improving the blood supply to the legs of people with arterial disease or the brains of people with multi-infarct dementia. Unfortunately, they do not seem to work.

## Beta-blockers

These include propranolol, oxprenolol, atenolol and timolol, used to prevent angina, to treat thyroid over-activity and to lower high blood pressure. They can also prevent the recurrence of a heart attack. Beta-blockers should be taken as prescribed for the special circumstances of the person and the illness.

Unwanted effects include worsening of asthma or heart failure, cold hands and feet, sleep disturbances and tiredness. They may also mask the effects of hypoglycaemia (low blood sugar) in people with diabetes.

## Diuretics

Examples include bendrofluazide, frusemide, amiloride and triamterene. Often called 'water pills', these are used to remove water from the body as urine in heart failure and oedema (watery swelling). They are also used to treat high blood pressure.

Diuretics are usually taken first thing in the morning so that the need to pass water does not lead to a disturbed night. Potassium (chemical symbol K) is lost in the urine and may need to be replaced in people taking diuretics. Some tablets with 'K' in their names contain both substances.

Unwanted effects include muscle weakness, confusion and unsteadiness due to potassium loss, and incontinence because extra urine needs to be passed. Some diuretics make gout and diabetes worse.

# For hiatus hernia

The pain or heartburn happen because stomach acid runs back into the gullet and irritates it (reflux oesophagitis). Reflux preventers such as alginic acid with an antacid (eg Gaviscon, Gastrocote) form a thick jelly layer on top of the acid in the stomach. This makes it less likely to run back into the gullet, and coats the sore area protectively if it does.

Antacids or ranitidine reduce acid damage. Preparations such as metoclopramide are used to help the muscle encircling the gullet base to stop stomach acid from running back. Unwanted effects such as muscle spasms, involuntary movements and difficulty in moving can be serious.

# For indigestion

## Antacids

These are an effective treatment for discomfort due to unwise eating or anxiety. Liquid preparations are more effective than tablets, though less portable. Two over-the-counter preparations are magnesium trisilicate, which also has a slight laxative effect, and aluminium hydroxide, which tends to constipate. One to three teaspoonsful should be taken up to three times a day between meals and at bed time.

Unwanted effects include interference with absorption of other drugs. Some types of antacids may worsen heart failure. The resident should check with the pharmacist or doctor if in doubt about this.

# For infections

Anti-bacterial drugs, commonly called 'antibiotics', kill bacteria but not viruses such as those that cause colds or 'flu. The choice of antibiotic depends on the likely cause of the illness, so the doctor will sometimes take a specimen of the patient's blood, urine, spit, etc, to find out which germ is responsible.

Anti-fungal agents are used to treat infections such as thrush. These can be very serious in people with low resistance, such as those with AIDS.

Anti-viral agents are occasionally used against herpes viruses (see 'Shingles', p 207).

Antibiotics must be taken at intervals throughout the day. The course of tablets must be finished even if the patient feels better before the bottle is empty, in order to make sure that the infection is thoroughly cured. If the resident does not improve after taking the tablets for 48 hours, they should let the doctor know.

Unwanted effects include nausea, diarrhoea, skin rashes and thrush (sore mouth with white patches, or severe itching of vagina, vulva or penis). Some people are allergic to antibiotics, especially penicillin. It is wise to tell the doctor at once if this seems to be happening, and to make sure the doctor knows and has a record if an antibiotic has caused upset in the past.

# For mental illness

## Anti-depressants

These are usually taken in a single dose in the evening, and rarely need to be split into separate doses through the day. Their anti-depressant effect may not be felt until two to three weeks after starting treatment, but sleep and appetite improve sooner. Treatment is continued for weeks or months.

Unwanted effects may be troublesome, though newer drugs may have fewer. Minor ones, which usually disappear within a few days, include dry mouth, giddiness on getting up quickly and drowsiness. More serious effects such as painful red eyes with blurred vision (a sign of glaucoma), difficulty in passing water or confusion should be reported to the doctor at once. You may need to do this on behalf of a resident who is too unwell to act unaided.

### Anti-psychotics

These neuroleptics or major tranquillisers are usually given for an established psychiatric condition such as schizophrenia, often as a regular monthly injection. They are used with great caution, if at all, in people over 70. A resident who has been on these drugs for a number of years will need careful reassessment by a psychiatrist. A community psychiatric nurse (CPN) may be very helpful in day-to-day care.

Serious unwanted effects include the production of abnormal movements and of a condition like Parkinson's disease. They may also lead to falls and to impaired temperature regulation, so residents taking them are vulnerable to hypothermia in cold weather. Because of their underlying illness, people on these medicines may be unable to take proper care of themselves. If this is happening, you should notify the doctor or CPN.

### Anxiolytics

These minor tranquillisers such as diazepam or chlordiazepoxide are rarely necessary in older people, and unwanted effects are especially troublesome. These effects include confusion, falling, incontinence and worsening of depression.

## For Paget's disease

Simple pain killers are all that some people need. Further treatment may be necessary for uncontrolled pain, or when overgrown bone is causing pressure symptoms or deformity.

Calcitonin is a hormone that relieves these symptoms. It is given by injection as a course of treatment. Unwanted effects are usually mild; they include nausea, vomiting and flushes. An alternative is disodium etidronate, which can be given by mouth on an empty stomach. Unwanted effects include nausea, diarrhoea and a metallic taste in the mouth. It can make the bones thin and fragile if taken for too long.

# For pain

## Mild analgesics (pain killers)

Mild household remedies such as paracetamol and aspirin are often bought over the counter to treat ailments such as headaches and muscular pain. Expensive compound preparations have little advantage over cheaper forms, and compound tablets containing constipating agents such as codeine are best avoided.

These mild analgesics can be taken 'as required' up to the limit stated on the packaging. If the painful condition does not get better quickly, it is wise to consult the doctor.

Paracetamol has few unwanted effects in normal dosage, but is very dangerous in overdose. Seek help at once for anyone who seems to have taken excess paracetamol, as treatment is effective only in the early stages.

Aspirin can irritate the stomach lining and cause bleeding. This is less likely if it is taken after food or in a soluble, 'buffered' or 'enteric-coated' form. On balance, paracetamol is probably more suitable than aspirin as a mild pain killer for an older person.

## Strong analgesics

Strong pain killers, mostly related to morphine, are used for short-term relief of acute pain, such as that of a heart attack, and to control pain in people who are dying. When used for terminal care, these pain killers are given according to a specially designed plan, so that pain is not allowed to develop.

Unwanted effects include nausea and constipation, which may need further medicines to put them right. Cough is suppressed and breathing becomes shallower.

The use of these drugs is strictly controlled by law; ask your pharmacist about this. Dependence is of no practical importance in terminally ill people; they should not be denied effective pain relief because of a false fear of 'addiction'.

# For Parkinson's disease

## Levodopa

This is given to relieve difficulty in starting to move. It must be taken strictly as prescribed, as the dose is tailored to each person's requirements. Changing meal times or taking extra vitamin $B_6$ (pyridoxine) can interfere with levodopa therapy.

Unwanted effects include nausea, vomiting and movement disorders; these should be reported to the doctor. Fluctuations in effect can sometimes be smoothed out by adding the newer drugs bromocriptine or selegiline.

## Anticholinergics

These are used when the main problem is tremor or dribbling of saliva. Examples are benzhexol, procyclidine and orphenadrine.

Unwanted effects include dry mouth, confusion, drowsiness, constipation, retention of urine, blurred vision and glaucoma in predisposed people. These should be reported to the doctor.

---

**NOTE** Drugs given for Parkinson's disease should never be stopped suddenly. The doctor should be informed if the person is unable to take the tablets because of illness, or if he or she 'seizes up' and finds movement difficult; someone with moderate to severe Parkinson's disease is likely to need assistance in obtaining medical help.

---

# For peptic ulcer

## Reducing acid

The commonest preparations are ranitidine and cimetidine, which are usually given in four- to six-week courses until the ulcer is healed. A small 'maintenance' dose is also sometimes prescribed.

Unwanted effects are uncommon but may include diarrhoea, dizziness, rashes, confusion and impotence.

## Protecting the stomach and duodenal lining

Bismuth preparations (eg De-Nol) coat the ulcer and help it to heal. They should not be taken within two hours before a meal and half an hour after it, as the medicine will stick to the food rather than to the ulcer. Tablets may be more acceptable than the liquid form.

Unwanted effects are only serious in people with poor kidney function. Mild effects include the darkening of stools and a tendency to constipation.

Sucralfate acts in a similar way and can also cause constipation.

Liquorice preparations such as carbenoxolone protect the lining of the stomach and duodenum, reinforcing it against acid attack.

Unwanted effects happen because the drug retains salt and water in the body. This worsens high blood pressure and heart failure, and means that the drug is not usually suitable for older people.

# For shingles

Anti-viral agents such as acyclovir and vidarabine are occasionally given to people in severe pain or with reduced resistance to infection.

Unwanted effects include skin rashes, digestive upset, liver and blood disturbances, headache and tiredness.

Idoxuridine painted on to affected skin may shorten the period of pain, but will work only if it is started as soon as the rash appears and is applied regularly thereafter. It stings the skin and may damage it.

People with shingles often need pain killers. Some doctors think that steroids help to shorten the time during which pain is felt. Shingles affecting the eye (ophthalmic herpes) needs special treatment prescribed by an eye specialist.

# For sleep problems

## Hypnotics

These sleeping tablets or sedatives should be used for short periods only. When difficulty in sleeping is a long-term problem, other strategies should be tried (see p 42). Hypnotics should be taken after retiring to bed, to reduce the chance of a fall.

Unwanted effects include confusion, decline in mental functioning, falling and incontinence. These should be reported to the doctor as they are indications that the drugs should be stopped, usually gradually. A normal sleeping pattern is then slowly regained.

# For thyroid disease

## Under-activity

This is treated by replacing the missing hormone, thyroxine. Once started, treatment continues for life, and it is important that someone taking thyroxine never runs out of supplies.

Unwanted effects include irregularities of the heart beat, angina, headache, restlessness, weight loss, flushing and diarrhoea. Thyroxine has to be used carefully in people who also have heart disease.

## Over-activity

This is treated with medicines such as carbimazole or propylthiouracil, which reduce production of thyroid hormones. These may be used alone, or together with radio-iodine or surgery.

The commonest unwanted effect is an itchy rash. A rare but more serious complication is suppression of white blood cell production. This may cause a sore throat, so people taking carbimazole or propylthiouracil are told to report such symptoms to the doctor.

# For vitamin deficiency

Vitamins should be given only when a normal balanced diet cannot be taken, when extra vitamins are required because of illness or when they cannot be absorbed properly from the diet. Vitamins should not be used as a tonic; very large doses, as in mega-vitamin therapy, can produce serious toxic effects.

- Vitamin A may be needed by people who cannot absorb dietary fat.

- B group vitamins are used to correct malnourishment, and can be taken as tablets or by injection. Unwanted effects are few in the prescribed dosage. Thiamine (vitamin $B_1$) is needed by people who abuse alcohol.

- Vitamin C is used to prevent scurvy and to promote healing, and can be given as tablets or in vitamin-rich fruit or fruit juice. Unwanted effects include diarrhoea and dyspepsia. Large doses may cause kidney stones or gout.

- Vitamin D is used to prevent osteomalacia, the painful weakness of bones caused by dietary deficiency and lack of sunlight. It can be given as tablets, often with calcium, or by periodic injections. The dose should not be exceeded, nor should vitamin D be taken by healthy people unnecessarily, when it can be dangerous. There are no unwanted effects if the recommended dosage is taken.

- Vitamin K may be needed by people who cannot absorb it from food. It is important in blood clotting.

## Steroid therapy

Steroids are used in the treatment of many conditions, including giant cell arteritis, polymyalgia rheumatica, asthma and rheumatoid arthritis. They may be taken as tablets, as inhalations or as skin creams. Therapy is tailored to the person's needs; it should be taken strictly as prescribed and *NEVER* stopped suddenly. Unwanted effects include acute confusion, raised blood pressure, heart failure and diabetes when steroids are given in high doses. Someone taking steroids for a long time may suffer from thinning of bones, back pain from spinal fractures, peptic ulcers and fungal infections. Steroid creams or ointments may cause thinning of skin, which becomes fragile, bleeds easily and is slow to heal.

**NOTE** People taking steroids should carry a card with details of their treatment and dosage. They should be careful never to run out of their medicines. The doctor should be notified if someone taking steroids becomes ill, as the dosage may need to be altered. The resident is likely to be too unwell to do this, so you may need to call for help on his or her behalf.

Modern medicines, used properly, can be of great benefit to older people, but doctors, patients and other helpers need to work together to achieve this. Encourage your residents to take responsibility for their own health; you may like to suggest that your residents increase their confidence and competence with medicines by referring to the section on Medicines in *Keeping Well* (see Further Reading).

# 9 What to do in an Emergency

## Forewarned is forearmed

This chapter summarises the action you should take when residents are taken ill or have accidents. However well prepared you may be in your own mind for something going wrong, you may be surprised by the strength of your feelings of alarm and distress when emergencies happen. A little knowledge will make you more effective and comfortable when working under this sort of stress.

First aid techniques cannot be learned from books: proper training courses are necessary. There should always be someone with first aid training on duty in the Home, and staff should take refresher courses to keep themselves up to date.

## Preparing yourself

A few simple preparations will help things run more smoothly in a crisis.

First make sure that your list of emergency telephone numbers and register of residents' personal details are readily accessible and up to date. Check that your deputy or relief is also able to use the information system quickly and efficiently when under pressure. Secondly, check on the contents of your first aid kit; ready-made ones may be incomplete, or may contain equipment that is too small to be of much practical use. Yours should include:

- Sharp scissors for trimming dressings, strong enough to cut through clothing if necessary.

- Packets of non-adherent sterile gauze wound dressings, 10cm (4in) square.
- Cleanser such as surgical spirit, cetrimide or sterile normal saline.
- Clean gauze and cotton wool, for extra absorbency around sterile dressings or for padding.
- Sterile cotton wool in small packets for cleaning wounds.
- Sticking plaster and tape for securing dressings.
- Adhesive plaster dressing strip (plaster with attached lint-strip); this may be cut to size to dress small wounds.
- Incontinence pads; the need for at least one of these may arise unexpectedly, as when a patient suffers a stroke. They are also useful in a variety of messy situations, and may be placed beneath the head of someone who is vomiting or under a bleeding wound.
- Crepe bandages about 10cm (4in) wide – at least two. These are used for support bandaging of sprains and strains, for securing dressings and steadying injured limbs until help arrives.
- Tweezers or forceps for removing splinters.
- Safety pins.

## Taking charge

When you are forced to take charge in a medical emergency, try to appear calm and reassuring, however you are feeling inside. Calmness does tend to seep inwards, until you actually feel as self-controlled as you appear. The sick or injured resident will then feel less anxious, and bystanders will be more likely to behave sensibly and helpfully and not get in the way. Stop for a moment, take stock and plan ahead.

## Getting professional help

In the case of severe illness or accident, you should call the affected person's doctor and/or the ambulance as soon as their most urgent needs have been attended to – that is, you have made sure that the breathing is not obstructed, that bleeding is controlled and that broken bones have been immobilised.

When phoning the GP, say who you are, the telephone number you are ringing from and give a full address. This is essential; though residents may know the Home as 'Churchill House, Cedar Street, New Town', the doctor may have '286 Cedar Street' on the medical records. Vital time is wasted when emergency services have to search for an inadequately described or poorly signposted building. Give the name of the resident and a brief account of what is wrong – for instance, 'We found Mrs Jones on the floor unconscious and she's breathing very noisily'.

Difficulties may arise outside normal working hours, when the doctor's calls may be referred to another doctor or to an answering service. If you have to leave a message about an emergency with a deputy, find out how long it will take to reach the doctor.

Though the best policy in an emergency is to call the person's GP first, you should call the ambulance if:

- the person is very ill and there is no time to lose;
- hospital attention will obviously be needed eventually – eg when a broken bone is suspected;
- if the doctor or a deputy suggests this should be done, perhaps because he or she cannot reach you quickly.

Do not call an ambulance without careful thought. To be jolted around, examined by strangers in an emergency department and then jolted home again, often after a considerable delay, is not a pleasant experience for an older person.

When dialling 999, there may be a delay at busy times before the headquarters answers. You will first be asked which service you require; when you are put through to ambulance control, the controller will ask at once for your telephone number so that if you are cut off by mistake, you can be reached again. As when telephoning the doctor, you must give the name of the injured or ill person, an exact address and an explanation of what has happened. If you suspect a heart attack, say so, as an ambulance with special equipment may be available. Do not put the phone down until the person taking the emergency call has all the information needed.

## Pitfalls to be avoided

It is easy to make mistakes when under the stress of an emergency, so here are some reminders:

- Check that the sick or injured person's airway is open; unconscious people are safest in the recovery position (p 237).

- Don't try to give a drink to someone who is unconscious, as it may drown them, or to someone who may need an anaesthetic shortly. A person with a broken arm who has been given a cup of tea may have to wait in pain for several hours while their stomach empties before the arm can be set.

- Don't use a tourniquet above a wound, as it may worsen the bleeding and endanger the healthy parts of the limb.

- Don't attempt cardiac massage unless you are sure the heart has stopped.

- Don't attempt to move someone who is too badly hurt or unwell to get up alone, except to maintain the airway: serious damage may be done if the person's neck, back or limb bones are broken. If he or she must be moved away from further immediate danger, get another helper to steady the head and back during the transfer, and try to immobilise injured limbs as well as possible. You will be taught techniques for this at the first aid course.

- Don't use hot water bottles to try to warm up someone who is unconscious or who is suffering from shock; this may cause burns and will also draw the blood supply away from vital organs to the skin.

- Don't put yourself at risk, for instance, by entering a smoke-filled room, touching an electrocuted person without turning off the current or by attempting heavy lifting without adequate help.

# AN ABC OF EMERGENCIES

This section summarises the action you should take in the emergencies you are most likely to come across. The conditions are arranged in alphabetical order.

# Abdominal pain

See also 'Diarrhoea and vomiting', page 224.

This is a common complaint in older people. Mild constipation or indigestion can be the cause, but sometimes the situation is more serious. Even quite mild attacks of diarrhoea and vomiting can lead to salt and water depletion and to illness and disability in frail people. Constipation that can cause abdominal pain merits advice on how it can be treated and prevented.

**Remember** also that, as with many other conditions in older people, symptoms of severe abdominal illness tend to be less acute than in younger people. This can sometimes produce a false sense of security. You should therefore make sure the doctor is called to a person complaining of abdominal pain unless:

- the pain is mild and passes off within half an hour or so;
- the person has previously been investigated and treated for abdominal pain, and is having one of the usual attacks.

In the early stages of abdominal illness, it is often difficult for the doctor to tell exactly what is wrong. A return visit may be necessary to reassess the resident and find out how the condition has developed. During the gap between visits you should notify the doctor if the resident gets worse; it may be useful to ask the doctor whether there are any special signs you should look for.

**SUMMARY**

Call the doctor to anyone with abdominal pain, except when the episode is trivial and short lived.

# Bites

Animal bites that break the skin carry germs that may cause infection. The resident will need to see a doctor for the wound to be cleaned properly and to make sure that tetanus protection is up to date. While waiting for the doctor, clean the wound with soap and water, and control bleeding by applying direct pressure and raising the part that is bleeding above the level of the heart. If the wound is extensive or the resident's condition is otherwise worrying, call an ambulance without further delay. Human bites that break the skin should be treated in the same way.

**SUMMARY**

Skilled cleaning, wound closure and tetanus protection may be needed. Call for help; clean the wound and control bleeding till help arrives.

# Bleeding

See also 'Cuts, grazes and puncture wounds' (p 222).

## Nose bleeds

The person with a nose bleed should sit in a chair and bend forward over a bowl to catch the blood dripping from the nose. Tell them to pinch the nostril on the affected side, to breathe through the mouth and to maintain the pressure for at least ten minutes. If the patient gets tired, a helper should take over 'pinching duty'. Any blood in the mouth should be spat out, as it may cause vomiting if it is swallowed. After ten minutes, the pressure can be released, but if bleeding has not stopped, pinching should be continued for a further ten minutes. If bleeding has not stopped after a third period of pinching, call the doctor or an ambulance.

**SUMMARY**

Try to control bleeding by nostril pressure. If this does not work, call for help.

## Gums

This problem can occur after a tooth extraction or following an injury to the mouth. As for a nose bleed, the person should sit forward holding a bowl to catch any blood dripping from the mouth. Get them to put a pad of clean gauze over but not in the tooth socket. This should be thick enough to squash the blood vessels in the gums when bitten on. The pad should not touch the socket, or it will pull the blood clot away when it is removed, and bleeding will restart.

Once the pad is in place, pressure should be maintained for ten minutes. Then gently remove the gauze, but if the bleeding has not stopped re-apply the pressure for another ten minutes. If bleeding persists, ring the dentist or the GP.

**SUMMARY**

Control bleeding by gum pressure. If this does not work, call for help.

## Varicose veins

An ambulance should be called, because the person will need hospital attention. In the meantime, ask the resident to lie down, raise the leg and prop it up on a pile of books or a stool. Remove any tight clothing such as garters, support hose or girdles which could act as tourniquets and make bleeding worse. Cover the bleeding point with a pad of gauze secured with adhesive tape or bandage.

**SUMMARY**

Call an ambulance.

While waiting, keep the resident lying down with the leg raised; control bleeding by pressure on the bleeding point.

# Blisters

These form on an area of skin that has been burned or been rubbed, for example by a shoe; the top layer of skin becomes separated from those underneath by fluid. If blisters are left alone, the top skin layer forms a natural, sterile dressing while healing goes on underneath. Eventually a new layer of skin forms on the raw area and the fluid is re-absorbed. Blisters should never be pricked, as this lets germs in. If padding is necessary to protect blisters from further injury, the covering should extend beyond the blistered area.

**SUMMARY**

Do not prick or burst blisters. Apply padding for comfort if necessary.

# Bruises

A bruise happens when blood vessels are damaged and leak into the surrounding tissues. Placing a cold compress on a bruise will make the blood vessels contract and reduce swelling. (See under 'Stings', p 235, for how to make a cold compress.)

Occasionally, bruising may conceal a more serious injury such as a broken bone or damage to internal organs, or the blood loss into the bruise may be sufficient to make the person feel faint and ill. If you think either of these things may have happened, or if the bruise is on the head, call the doctor.

---

**SUMMARY**

Apply a cold compress to minor bruises.

Seek skilled help:

- if the bruise may overlie a serious injury;
- if the person seems unwell;
- if the bruise is on the head.

---

# Burns and scalds

## Severe

A burn or scald is severe:

- if the burned area is more than an inch (2.5cm) square;
- if it goes deeper than the outer layer of skin;
- if the burn was caused by electricity;
- if the burned person seems unwell or is very frail.

When someone has been scalded, immerse the affected area in cold water and remove soaked clothing when it is cool enough to handle. Then send for a doctor or ambulance at once.

If a resident's clothes catch fire, douse the flames with water or lie the person down and smother the flames by wrapping tightly in a coat or blanket. Do not roll the resident over and over, as this may burn previously undamaged areas. When the flames are out, soak all layers thoroughly so that smouldering clothing does not continue to burn the skin.

While waiting for help, cover any exposed burnt skin with clean, smooth fabric such as a sheet or pillowcase, but otherwise leave the burnt areas alone. If the sufferer feels cold, add a layer of blankets. Give only small sips of water or ice to suck for thirst, as larger amounts may cause vomiting and will delay treatment under anaesthetic.

---

**SUMMARY**

Cool and remove clothing soaked in boiling liquid.

Douse flames with water or blankets.

Call the doctor or ambulance.

Leave the burnt area alone.

---

## Minor

These can be treated at home. Cool the burnt skin at once with plenty of cold water, either by holding it under a running tap or by plunging it into a basin or bath. If water is not immediately available, use another clean liquid such as beer or milk. Remove the victim's rings, watches and tight clothing from around the affected area before it starts to swell.

Small burns should be left open to the air if possible. Clear fluid will ooze from the burnt area and dry to form a germ-proof dressing which should be not be disturbed. If a protective covering must be put on to prevent clothes rubbing, use non-adherent gauze. Do not apply any proprietary lotions or creams, butter or bicarbonate of soda to a burn without first getting medical advice.

---

**SUMMARY**

Cool with plenty of cold water.

Leave open to the air if possible.

Apply nothing to burnt areas without medical advice.

---

## Chemical burns

Burns caused by chemicals such as caustic soda or bleach should be thoroughly rinsed under a running tap for about ten minutes. Remove contaminated clothing without letting it touch undamaged skin.

**SUMMARY**

Rinse well under running tap.

Care is needed if chemicals are left on clothing – do not contaminate the resident or yourself.

# Chest pain and heart attacks

Chest pain can have a minor cause such as a muscular strain, but it may be a sign of more serious heart or lung disease. Except in the most trivial episodes, call the sufferer's doctor.

## Angina

This is a tight, squeezing chest pain which may extend from behind the breast bone into the throat or down the arms. First get the person with angina pain to sit down. He or she should take one glyceryl trinitrate (GTN) tablet or use a GTN spray, if these have been prescribed; the directions for use should be followed carefully. If the pain is not relieved in ten minutes, they should take another tablet or more spray. If the resident is not better within ten minutes of the second dose, call the doctor or the ambulance.

During the 20-minute period when the medicine is supposed to be working, call the doctor or ambulance:

- if the pain becomes very severe;
- if the person becomes short of breath;
- if the person starts to lose consciousness.

If angina attacks occur frequently, the resident should see the doctor in case the drug therapy needs adjusting or more investigations need to be done.

## Heart attack

A heart attack in a young or middle-aged person produces crushing central chest pain, similar to the pain of angina but usually occurring during rest rather than during exercise. The person becomes pale, sweats and may vomit. If damage to the heart is severe, they may become rapidly unconscious and even die.

An older person who is having a heart attack may show the same symptoms, but in many cases will not. They may have no pain, but instead may become confused, develop the signs of a stroke, become short of breath, faint or have an epileptic fit. If these things happen, you should summon medical aid urgently.

Until the doctor or ambulance arrives, stay with the resident, give reassurance and make them as comfortable as possible in a sitting position, either in a chair or propped up on pillows in bed. If they become unconscious and no pulse can be felt, it is likely that the heart has stopped beating. If this happens – and only if you know how to do it properly – start mouth-to-mouth respiration and cardiac massage.

## Pleurisy

This happens when a chest infection spreads to the membrane covering the lung. The pain will be sharp, stabbing and worse when breathing in. Call the doctor.

---

**SUMMARY**

Call the doctor for all but the most trivial attacks.

While awaiting help, assist the resident to take medicines prescribed for angina.

If the resident collapses and has no pulse, consider starting resuscitation.

---

# Choking

This happens when a small piece of food or vomit enters the wind-pipe. In mild cases the sufferer will be coughing but still able to breathe. Take control of the situation. Tell the person to take a deep breath slowly and cough as hard as possible. If two coughs do not clear the obstruction, remove any false teeth, insert your index finger and attempt to dislodge the obstruction. It may also help the person to bend forward across your supporting arm with the head below waist level, while someone gives sharp slaps with a hand between the shoulder blades.

In more severe cases of choking the person may be unable to breathe and will become blue in the face. Get behind the resident and put your arms around them with one fist pressed into the stomach. Grasp your fist with your other hand and pull suddenly inward and upward. The force of the air being expelled from the lungs is usually enough to dislodge the obstruction from the windpipe, and the blockage will shoot out of the mouth. This technique, called the Heimlich manoeuvre, should be learned by attending a first aid class.

---

**SUMMARY**

**Mild cases**

Encourage coughing.

Remove the blockage by hand.

Bang between the resident's shoulder blades while they lean forward.

**Severe cases**

Use the Heimlich manoeuvre, described above.

---

# Cramp

To relieve the pain of cramp, stretch the contracted and painful muscle until the contraction passes off. Cramped toes, for instance, will need to be uncurled and held straight, with the palm of your hand beneath the sole of the foot. Alternatively, get the person to stand one pace from the wall, put their hands on the wall and stand on their toes. If the cramp recurs, repeat the manoeuvre. If residents are much troubled by cramp, they should consult the doctor, as drug therapy is sometimes helpful.

---

**SUMMARY**

Stretch the painful muscle.

For recurrent cramp, consult the doctor.

---

# Cuts, grazes and puncture wounds

A sharp knife causes a clean cut, whilst irregular objects tear the skin. A graze occurs when the superficial layers of the skin are scraped away, leaving a raw area which may be dirty. A puncture wound happens when a sharp pointed object such as a nail breaks the skin. Such injuries may have serious consequences if they are deep enough to damage internal organs or if the wound is dirty, as tetanus germs grow easily in the deeper layers of tissue.

## Severe

Call the doctor or ambulance. In the meantime do not remove any object that is stuck in the wound, as it may be acting as a plug and reducing bleeding. Try to control the blood flow by pressing on the wound through a pad of clean material, or on the area around any object protruding from it. Help the person to lie down, and raise and support the injured part.

## Minor

You will probably be able to cope with these yourself. Wash your hands and put on sterile disposable gloves whenever giving first aid to open wounds. Wash the area surrounding the wound with soap and water, then clean the wound either by rinsing under the tap or by wiping with clean, wet swabs. Remember to wipe from within the wound outwards, and use a new swab for each stroke. If a blood clot has already formed, it should not be removed, or bleeding may start again. After cleaning, the wound area should be patted dry, and a small plaster and gauze or ready-made dressing applied.

A graze or cut that bleeds little and is not in an area where it will be rubbed by clothing is better left exposed to the air. If a dressing is necessary, it should be removed after a few hours or on the following day, when the bleeding has stopped. Check whether the resident needs a tetanus injection, and encourage them to see the doctor if tetanus protection is not up to date or if there is doubt about this.

If a wound becomes more painful, swollen and red, pus oozes from it or red lines or swollen glands are found nearby, it has become infected, and the doctor should be notified.

**SUMMARY**

**Severe cases**

Call the doctor or ambulance.

Press to control the bleeding.

Do not remove protruding objects.

**Minor cases**

Clean the wound with soap and water.

Apply a dressing if necessary till the wound is dry; then leave open.

Encourage a check on tetanus protection.

# Diabetic emergencies

If someone with diabetes takes too much insulin, too many tablets or misses a meal, the blood sugar falls and they become hypoglycaemic. People with diabetes call this reaction a 'hypo'. The hypo sufferer feels faint, dizzy and confused, and sometimes irritable and aggressive. Because of these mental changes, they are often unable to take sensible action without help. They urgently need sugar, which you should give in the form of sugar lumps, sweets, glucose tablets or a heavily sweetened drink. If the hypo is not quickly corrected, the diabetic will become unconscious. If this happens, do not try any longer to give sugar by mouth, but call the doctor or ambulance without delay.

Someone with diabetes may become drowsy and confused for other reasons than having a 'hypo'. However, giving sugar to such a person will in any case do no harm. If it does not produce a rapid improvement, call an ambulance at once.

**SUMMARY**

A diabetic with 'hypo' signs needs sugar urgently: watch for faintness, confusion, irritability and aggression.

Rapid recovery is usual; if it does not occur, call an ambulance.

# Diarrhoea and vomiting

An older person with a 'tummy upset' should eat nothing and drink only clear fluids – not milk – until symptoms have subsided. It is probably advisable for the resident to stay indoors, and to rest in bed if they feel weak or sleepy. A light diet should be started cautiously with dry foods such as salty crackers, working gradually up to a normal diet.

The doctor should be called if diarrhoea and vomiting persist for more than 12 hours, or if the person develops abdominal pain or otherwise seems seriously unwell. A frail older person should see the doctor sooner as they may become seriously ill from fluid loss and need careful rehydration. Tummy upsets may take residents 'off their legs'; if this lasts for more than a few days, call the doctor.

---

**SUMMARY**

Clear fluids at first, then gradual return to normal eating habits.
Call the doctor if:

- symptoms persist for more than 12 hours;
- the resident is frail;
- abdominal pain develops;
- the resident is not soon back to normal.

---

# Epilepsy

See 'Fits' (p 228).

# Eye emergencies

## Serious diseases

The symptoms of these include:

- sudden complete loss of vision;
- disturbances of the field of vision, such as the sensation of a curtain closing across it or of seeing black patches in it;
- seeing flashes of light or coloured haloes around objects;
- pain and redness of the eye.

These require an urgent expert opinion, ideally from the emergency department of a eye hospital.

## Major accidents

When a resident's eye is injured, for instance by a sharp object or a burning spark, call the ambulance. While waiting for help, ask the resident to close the injured eye; then cover it with a pad of clean gauze, secured with a bandage or adhesive tape. Tell them to shut the good eye too because if it moves the damaged eye will follow it. The resident will now be unable to see, so they must be guided if moving about.

## Chemicals in the eye

Call the ambulance. While waiting for it, try to wash the chemical away by holding the person's face under a gently running tap, or by pouring water from a jug. Do not allow the contaminated water to run over the person's face. Once the eye has been fully rinsed, wipe it with a clean gauze pad.

## Minor accidents

Particles of grit or an eye-lash may stick to the eye-ball or lodge within the lower lid. They are easiest to remove with a damp wisp of cotton wool or tissue, moulded to a point, and by working towards the inside corner of the eye. If this procedure is not rapidly successful, the eye should be covered with an eye-pad or square of clean gauze and the person sent to the doctor or the hospital.

Skilled help will also be necessary when an object becomes embedded in the eye-ball or when it overlies its central part, the black pupil and the coloured area surrounding it; do not attempt to remove these yourself.

---

**SUMMARY**

Urgent expert help is needed if a resident:

- has lost the whole or a part of the field of vision;
- sees black patches, haloes, 'floaters' or flashes of light;
- has a painful, red eye;
- has been injured by a sharp object, a spark or a chemical in the eye.

Small objects in the eye can be removed with damp tissue if they lie over the white of the eye. If this is difficult, seek expert help.

---

# Fainting

This is a sign that, for a short time, insufficient blood has been reaching the brain. It usually happens to someone who has been standing still for a long time, especially in warm surroundings. People who faint crumple gently to the ground, but 'fall soft' and are usually little hurt. They will look very pale and will have a slow, weak pulse. They should be left lying down, as this will help to get the blood back into the brain. It is also useful to raise the legs and rest them on a stool or other suitable object. Loosen tight clothing at the neck or waist and allow them plenty of fresh air. Call the doctor if they are not soon better.

It is wise to keep a discreet eye on an older person who has fainted, for a few days afterwards. Occasionally a faint can be a sign of illness; if you are concerned, consider calling the doctor.

**SUMMARY**

Leave the affected person lying down and raise the legs to restore blood flow to the brain.

Call the doctor if recovery is not rapid.

# Falls

If you find someone on the floor unconscious, you should summon help at once, and in the meantime care for them as described on page 237. If the resident has been lying for some time in cold surroundings, care for hypothermia may also be needed (see p 231).

Someone who has fallen may not be seriously hurt but simply be unable to get up. Never attempt to lift someone by yourself as you may injure your back in the process. If there is no one else strong enough to help you in the Home, you should call the ambulance.

Provided the person who has fallen can roll to a chair, you may be able to get them up unaided in stages, with rests in between. The resident should first get the stronger elbow into the seat of the chair; then, by putting the other elbow on the chair as well, they can pull up into a kneeling position. Then, by transferring weight to the strongest foot, they can get up to the level of the seat, twist round and sit down.

**SUMMARY**

Do not lift alone.

Help fallen residents to roll to a chair and get up in stages.

If the resident is unconscious, injured or cold, refer to the relevant sections of this book for further advice.

# Fits (epilepsy)

This condition may start in childhood and persist into adult life, or begin at any age. Fits often follow a pattern. At the onset people may experience an 'aura', which is a feeling that a fit is about to occur. After this they will become unconscious and fall, sometimes crying out. They then go rigid and may stop breathing, becoming blue in the face. After this, their limbs will jerk, their breathing will become noisy and they may froth at the mouth. As this stage passes off, the muscles relax, breathing quietens and they gradually return to normal, though they are likely to be sleepy and confused for several hours.

If you are present at the beginning of an attack, try to break the person's fall and then put something soft under their head. Loosen any tight clothing and keep the airway clear by rolling the person on to their side and pulling the jaw forward. Do not try to put anything into the mouth, or to restrain involuntary movements.

If this is the person's first fit – as far as you know – call the ambulance as soon as possible. This may not be necessary for residents you know to have fits, provided they recover rapidly and completely. However, you should suggest that they let the GP know about the episode, as a change in treatment may be necessary to prevent a recurrence. Even people known to have epilepsy require urgent treatment if several fits happen one after the other, if they are injured during a fit or if they are slow to recover consciousness. People with epilepsy are well advised to wear a locket or bracelet giving details of their condition and medication. These are available from the Medic Alert Foundation.

**SUMMARY**

Try to reduce harm by:

- breaking the person's fall;
- protecting the head;
- keeping the airway clear.

Call the doctor for:

- a resident's first fit;
- fits that occur one after the other;
- a resident who is injured or slow to come round after a fit.

# Fractures (broken bones)

Old bones are fragile and brittle, and may break under an impact that would leave younger bones undamaged. Confused older people may not appear to suffer much pain from a fracture. It is therefore important to be suspicious that bones may have been broken even when injury seems comparatively trivial, and to seek medical aid accordingly.

## Signs to look for

When a bone has been broken, the person may have heard or felt it snap. The affected bone will usually be painful and tender to touch, and it is usually difficult or impossible for the person to move the injured limb. This may be distorted into an unnatural position, and may also be swollen and discoloured by bruising. Moving it may produce a grating noise as the broken bone ends grind across each other. Try to prevent this from happening, as soft tissues around the broken bone may be damaged.

Fracture of the femur (thigh bone) is a common injury in older people, especially women. The person who suffers it is almost always unable to get up from the floor. The affected leg may look shorter than the normal one, and be lying with the toe pointing outwards, away from the other leg.

## What to do

All suspected fractures need prompt medical attention, so call the doctor or ambulance. While waiting for help, remember that, in a serious accident, breathing difficulties and severe bleeding take precedence over broken bones – otherwise the end result may be a perfectly splinted corpse!

Do not move the casualty before medical help arrives unless they are in immediate danger. If you must move them, immobilise the broken bone by splinting. Ambulance staff are expert at this, so you need not be concerned with it except when you cannot get emergency help right away. Whatever object is available should then be used – for example, a board, a walking stick, a broom handle or a rolled-up newspaper. It should be firmly padded to prevent further injury. The splint needs to be applied so as to immobilise the joints above and below the broken bone, so that the bone ends cannot move about. For instance, with a break in the lower leg, the knee and ankle must be steadied.

Control bleeding from an open fracture by direct pressure on the wound, without displacing the protruding bone. If the casualty does not need to be moved, you can apply a sterile gauze dressing lightly over the wound, but do not interfere with it further. If movement is absolutely necessary, pad the bone ends with sterile gauze and support them to prevent pressure, movement and tissue damage from the sharp ends.

### SUMMARY

Remember that old bones break easily, and call for help if suspicious.

Make sure that the airway is clear.

Control any bleeding.

Do not move the casualty unless absolutely necessary.

When movement is unavoidable, splint the break and pad any visible jagged ends of bone.

# Headaches

These are very common and usually not serious. Suggest that the resident crushes two tablets of paracetamol before taking them with a good draught of water, or takes their preferred headache remedy according to the directions on the packet or bottle. If you keep a stock of 'household remedies', you could supply a suitable mild pain killer. The resident should then rest in a place with subdued lighting until the pain passes off. If the headache persists, or if the resident seems otherwise unwell (eg is confused or vomiting, finds light uncomfortable, or when the scalp is tender to touch), call the doctor.

**SUMMARY**

Suggest household remedies for mild headaches.
Call the doctor if pain persists or the resident seems generally unwell.

# Head injuries

All but the most trivial bangs to the head require expert medical attention. Someone who has been knocked unconscious, even for a short time, may need to be admitted to hospital for observation. If you think the resident may have been unconscious, the doctor must be called, even though the person seems quite well at present.

A scalp wound will bleed very freely and this may be alarming. Try to remember that, because of the good blood supply to the scalp, the wound will also heal rapidly and well. While waiting for the doctor or ambulance, bleeding can be controlled by applying pressure to the wound. If underlying bone damage is suspected and this causes pain, press either side of the wound. If the person becomes unconscious, follow the guidelines on page 237.

**SUMMARY**

Call the doctor to all but the most trivial cases; residents who have been knocked unconscious must see a doctor.
Press to control bleeding from scalp wounds.

# Hypothermia

This medical emergency can occur in a Home if the heating fails or is turned off, or if a resident becomes ill.

In hypothermia the deep body temperature falls below 95°F or 35°C, measured with a low-reading thermometer; temperature readings taken with an ordinary clinical thermometer may be misleading. Normal body temperature fluctuates around 98.4°F (37°C). In someone with hypothermia, a covered part of the body such as the armpit or abdomen may feel cold to the touch. The colder people are, the less likely they are to be fully conscious. Many people become hypothermic because of injury or illness, and this may add to the dangers of the situation.

Hypothermic people need urgent medical attention, so you should call the doctor or ambulance. While waiting for help, the room should be warmed and the resident 'insulated' to keep in body heat. Wrap them in a 'space' blanket if you have one; if not, aluminium cooking foil makes a good substitute. They should then be 'over-wrapped' with blankets or whatever else is available, not forgetting the head and hands. Keep them lying down. Avoid putting hot water bottles round them; these may cause the skin blood vessels to open up suddenly and release a rush of cold blood, which could impair the heart beat. There is also the risk of burns. Do not give a hot drink to anyone who might need an anaesthetic.

**SUMMARY**

Remember the risk of hypothermia.

Call the doctor or ambulance to an affected resident.

Warm the room and wrap up the resident to conserve their heat.

Avoid hot water bottles; be cautious with hot drinks.

# Poisoning

This is sometimes accidental but may be deliberate (see 'Overdoses and suicide attempts', p 233). Do not waste time trying to decide which; instead, call the doctor or ambulance at once. While waiting for help, care for an unconscious resident as described on page 237. Ask a conscious resident what happened, so that if possible the poisonous substance can be identified and the container sent with them to the hospital. Someone should stay with a poisoned resident all the time until help arrives, and should be ready to start resuscitation. It is unwise to try to make a person who has been poisoned vomit.

**SUMMARY**

Call the doctor or ambulance.

Stay with the resident and be prepared to resuscitate. Do not induce vomiting.

Send the poisonous substance to hospital with the person if possible.

# Psychiatric emergencies

## Overdoses and suicide attempts

If you believe an overdose to be deliberate, you must take the situation seriously. Unsuccessful suicide attempts are often later repeated and may then prove fatal. Call the doctor or ambulance and, while waiting for help, care for the resident as described under 'Poisoning' (p 232).

## Acute confusion

Someone who becomes suddenly confused needs urgent medical attention. Call the doctor, stay with the confused resident and try to reassure them until help arrives.

## Aggression

Some confused people may become violent. You should be aware of the risk of this, especially with people who have been aggressive in the past, or who abuse alcohol or drugs. Good management can often prevent outright violence and defuse the situation. Here are some suggestions as to how to cope:

- Keep your distance, and do not crowd the person.

- Do not be the first to touch: your would-be reassuring arm round the shoulders may seem like an assault to the confused person, who may hit back.

- Remember that the confused person is probably more frightened than you are. Try to appear calm and in control, acting neither in a threatening way nor as a nervous victim.

- Keep talking in a calm but firm voice. Avoid arguments and confrontation; distract attention from a touchy subject by talking about something else. Do not talk down to the confused person, but allow them to 'save face'.

- Watch for warning signs of approaching violence such as restlessness, pacing up and down, fist clenching, faster breathing, destroying objects or looking for weapons.
- Keep your escape route open behind you, and if violence is imminent, leave at once.

**SUMMARY**

Call the doctor to people who become suddenly confused.

Remember the risk of aggression; reduce risk by using the guidelines above.

# Splinters

When a small bit of wood or metal gets stuck in the skin, wash the area around it with soap and water. You can remove the splinter using forceps or tweezers that you have first sterilised in a flame or cleaned with disinfectant. Pull in the opposite direction from the way the splinter went into the skin. If the splinter does not come out easily or starts to break up, you will need medical help. An anti-tetanus injection may be necessary if the splinter was introduced from an object out of doors.

**SUMMARY**

Clean the skin; remove the splinter with clean forceps or tweezers.

Check whether an anti-tetanus injection is needed.

# Stings

## Severe

A sting can be serious if it is inside the mouth, as can happen if someone bites an apple with a wasp sitting on it. Stings are also dangerous in a person who is allergic to them, or if someone is stung by a great many insects at once – for instance, when accidentally disturbing a wasps' nest. In these situations, call an ambulance at once. In the meantime do not leave the victim alone, watch them carefully in case breathing or circulation deteriorate, and give ice to suck to reduce swelling inside the mouth.

# Minor

These are frightening rather than dangerous. Treatment will depend on the type of insect responsible. Bees leave a small sting embedded in the skin; this can be removed with a pair of tweezers held as close to the skin as possible. Avoid squeezing the sac at the top of the sting because this will force more poison into the skin. A wasp injects its irritant directly, as with a syringe and needle, withdrawing afterwards; you may be able to wipe away some of the venom from the surface of the skin.

## Treatment

With both sorts of stings it may help to swab the skin with weak bicarbonate (baking soda) in water, and to apply a cold compress or ice-pack to reduce swelling. You can make a cold compress by soaking some absorbent cloth such as old towelling in iced water and then wringing it out until it is wet but not dripping. Then wrap the absorbent cloth in another cloth such as a tea towel and apply it to the affected part. Alternatively, you can make an ice-pack by putting ice cubes in a plastic bag and sucking the air out with a drinking straw. A packet of frozen peas also makes a good ice-pack.

A certain amount of pain and swelling are to be expected on the day when a sting occurs and for about 24 hours after. If the patient is frail or becomes unwell, the doctor should be notified.

### SUMMARY

**Severe stings** (sting in mouth, allergy to stings, many stings)
Call the doctor or ambulance.
Stay with the resident until help arrives.

**Mild stings**
Remove the bee sting.
Swab away wasp venom.
Apply cold compress or ice-pack.

# Stroke

The usual signs of a stroke are the development of paralysis of the limbs and face on one side of the body, with slurring of speech and dribbling of saliva from the corner of the mouth. Stroke sufferers may also wet or soil themselves because of loss of control of the bladder and bowels.

## Severe

The most severe cases of stroke prove fatal, and you may find the resident unconscious or already dead. Note the time and send for the doctor or ambulance without delay. Until help arrives, follow the instructions about unconsciousness on page 237.

## Less severe

The resident may be found in bed one morning, unable to get up because of partial paralysis. Alternatively, sufferers may be confused and unsteady on their feet and have slurred speech. The doctor should be called; after examining the resident and verifying that a stroke has occurred, the doctor will usually admit them to hospital.

# Sunburn

You should take the affected person to a cool place and give them plenty of water to drink, while sponging the burnt area gently with cold water. In severe cases, call the doctor.

**SUMMARY**

Cool surroundings, water to drink and cold sponging help.
Call the doctor to severe cases.

# Transient ischaemic attacks (TIAs)

These produce stroke symptoms which disappear within 24 hours. The doctor must be told about these, as prompt treatment may prevent a later 'completed' stroke from occurring.

**SUMMARY**

Call the doctor or ambulance.
If the resident is unconscious, follow the plan below.

# Unconsciousness

Anyone who has lost consciousness and does not rapidly regain it is severely ill, and you should call the doctor or ambulance at once. While waiting for help to arrive, the most important thing is to make sure that the resident is breathing normally. Put them in the recovery position, lying prone on the stomach with one arm and leg bent in support, and facing towards the side of the bent limbs. This position makes the jaw and tongue fall forward, keeping the airway open, and allows vomit or secretions to drain out of the mouth.

Someone should remain with the unconscious person all the time until medical help arrives, and should be prepared to start resuscitation if necessary. Control any bleeding, and cover the person with a blanket to keep them warm and prevent hypothermia. Never give an unconscious person anything by mouth; they will be unable to swallow it and may drown. If the person recovers consciousness while waiting, reassure them and allow them to rest until help arrives.

You can help the doctor to find the cause of the condition and start the right treatment by giving information as to how the present incident happened, how long unconsciousness has lasted and what the person's previous health has been like. If they are taken directly into hospital and you do not accompany them, you should give a short written account of medical details to the ambulance staff, to be shown to the hospital doctor.

Common causes of unconsciousness include head injury, heart attack, stroke, epilepsy and diabetes.

**SUMMARY**

Call the doctor or ambulance.
Place the resident in the recovery position and keep the airway open.
Be prepared to resuscitate if necessary.

Cover the resident to keep in warmth.

Provide useful information to the doctor or hospital.

---

# Finding someone dead

When you find someone dead, notify the GP. While waiting for the doctor to come, do not move the body or interfere with its immediate surroundings. However, it may be wise to lock the doors and draw the curtains if this will prevent someone else from happening upon the scene and being upset by it. If the death has occurred in a communal room, it may be advisable to station a staff member outside the entrance to prevent accidental shocks to other residents.

Once the doctor has seen the body and confirmed that death has occurred, they will advise on the next step. A doctor who is the resident's GP and has attended them in the last illness can sign the death certificate without further delay. If the doctor says that the coroner needs to be consulted first, this does not necessarily imply that there is anything suspicious about the death. Some deaths must be referred to the coroner in this way – for instance, if the death follows an accident such as a fall, or could be connected with the person's past occupation. Usually the doctor will be able to give the certificate after talking with the coroner. Occasionally, the coroner will order a post-mortem examination to establish the cause of death, and on rare occasions an inquest will be necessary.

If you do not understand what is going on with these complicated legal arrangements, be sure to ask, as this may save needless anxiety for you and the relatives. You may also like to refer to the section on bereavement in Chapter 10 (see pp 248–252).

**SUMMARY**

Call the doctor.

Do not move the body.

Prevent others from coming on the scene unexpectedly.

# LEARNING FROM AN EMERGENCY

Many people expect too much of themselves when accidents occur, and scourge themselves with guilt afterwards, but you should resist both these temptations. After the emergency, however, comes the time to take stock. There is a lot to be said for writing down a full account of what happened while it is still fresh in your mind. You should set it down 'just as it comes', including feelings and difficulties; grammar and spelling can be tidied up later. This account may be of practical use to the police or the coroner if, sadly, a fatal incident has occurred. Writing everything down will also help you to come to terms with your feelings of distress. Talking about the incident is also useful: try to find a suitable person doing similar work; they will be the best person to listen, and you will be able to do the same for them on another occasion.

Be kind to yourself after a bad experience, and do not try to be too 'wonderful'. However, the return to normal should not be too long delayed, as following an accustomed routine can be very comforting to the spirit. After a few days have passed it will be sensible to go over the incident again yourself, looking for avoidable factors. This should not be done with the intention of finding a culprit or scapegoat, but so as to try to prevent the trouble arising again or to reduce the severity of the consequences if it does. For instance, you may find that useful equipment needs to be replaced or repaired, that your deputy needs clearer instructions or that residents' understanding of fire precautions needs to be improved.

This has been literally a chapter of accidents, and, taken in at a single gulp, makes alarming reading. In most Homes such dramatic events will be infrequent, but if you are wise you will be prepared both practically and emotionally for them to happen. Knowing what to do when things go wrong is obviously of practical importance, and the confidence this knowledge brings gives a feeling of security that benefits staff and residents alike.

# 10 Terminal Illness and Bereavement

In the nature of things, you are likely to be involved with the care of dying people and with bereavement. This chapter covers practical aspects of care and also includes basic information on common patterns of behaviour in dying people and in mourners. It aims to make you feel a little more comfortable in what is inevitably a distressing situation.

## People's reactions to the prospect of death

Some people die quickly after a brief illness, and the question of adjustment does not arise. Others, however, have to face a period when they suffer an illness and know or suspect that they will die before long. They react to this situation in various ways, often showing the feelings described below. Some people progress through them in stages, but more often they move back and forth between them. For instance, someone who one day seems to have accepted what is happening may be angry all over again on the next day, or may even be denying that they are seriously ill.

### Denial

Sometimes the seriously ill person avoids the truth, does not ask questions and does not want the facts to be spelt out. If the doctor or another carer tries to talk about the illness and its outcome the patient will be deaf to the information, and may later strenuously deny that anyone has raised the subject. You should be aware of this stage of denial whenever a seriously ill resident tells you that 'no one told me anything'. This may be a true account of his or her perceptions, but will not necessarily mean that no one has tried to explain what is going on.

Those around the dying person may collude in this behaviour. If a man who is dying and his wife both deny the truth about his illness, each of them has to cope with it alone – a sad ending to a relationship that may have involved 40 or more years of mutual help and comfort. Again, relatives sometimes try to persuade the doctor to concoct a tale of likely recovery because 'Mother would never be able to take it'. Mother almost certainly can, but the family are wondering whether they can bear the stark reality of helping Mother to die. However, you should remember that denial is a useful defence until the hearer is ready to take in the truth; it is useless and unkind to try to break it down.

## Anger

People may not expect a terminally ill person to be angry, and it can be very difficult for carers and relatives to cope with and understand. A religious person may direct the anger at God, and a minister of religion may be the best person to help. More commonly the anger finds a human target, often chosen at random. The victim may be a carer or doctor whose kindness and competence may come under attack, or a relative may be picked on.

The anger stage can be worked through if the person can express their feelings to someone who can tolerate them as a sign of pain, rather than being hurt or offended or withdrawing love and attention. For the person on the receiving end of the anger – and it may be you – this is not at all easy. Perhaps you may find it helpful to think of the person's feelings as a bit like pus bursting from a boil – until the nastiness is out, the sore cannot heal.

## Withdrawal

Denial and anger may be followed by withdrawal, when the dying person gives up hope, stops fighting and comes close to despair. If relatives and carers conspire to protect the person from this stage, they will have to face it alone, when instead they need support from someone who understands the situation but is not overwhelmed by it. All the helper can do is to be with the dying person in their misery.

Unpleasant physical symptoms are especially distressing for someone going through this stage, so try to make sure these are being treated. People sometimes gain comfort from making practical arrangements for relatives who will be left behind. You may like to suggest this, though great sensitivity is likely to be necessary if, for instance, the resident has not yet made a Will. You could also encourage them to think about the amount of meaning and purpose there has already been in their life. It will also help if they can be reassured that they will die peacefully and also will not be left alone.

## Regression

Some dying people become babyish and demanding. Their carers may find this irritating, and then feel guilty. On the other hand, they may enjoy 'babying' the dying person, who then comes to resent their attitude. Dying people should be treated as adults and expected to behave as such, within the limits of their illness.

## Acceptance

This is not necessarily a miserable or depressing stage, and you can help the dying person through it with dignity.

Feeling helpless is a recipe for depression: even the smallest effort to keep up a good appearance helps lift the spirit. Three days' growth of beard ruin a man's self-respect. Most women like to wear their own attractive day or night clothes and to have their hair set or tinted, even in the last weeks or days before death. Personal possessions reflect our personalities, so the clutter on the bedside table can be very reassuring.

Patients who accept their approaching death are often eager to be used as 'teaching material' to help doctors and nurses learn more about terminal illness. Many people say that this enables them to find some meaning in their experience.

# CARING FOR SOMEONE WHO IS DYING

## Where to die?

The rest of this chapter assumes that the resident is dying in the Home. This will not always be the case, however: for instance, some residents will be in hospital when they reach the final stage of their illness. Many hospitals, despite limited resources, still manage to do their best – and a very good best – for terminally ill patients. Some have a team of specialists who will advise general ward staff on particular problems of medical and nursing care.

However, in general, the acute medical or surgical ward is not an ideal place for someone who is about to die, as it requires different skills from those needed for the proper care of someone who is terminally ill. Acute wards are like garages, geared to a rapid in-and-out curative service. Something more like a gardener's attention to the process of nature is required in the care of someone who is dying.

Many residents, given the choice, will want to die in their own beds. While personal wishes should be respected whenever possible, sometimes when community resources are scarce and the resident needs a lot of specialised help, there is no alternative to hospital care. When this is so, neither the relatives nor you should feel guilty, but should concentrate on finding ways in which the dying person's life can be lived as richly as possible until its end, within the limits of the situation. Do not be afraid to ask for extra visiting privileges or outings because you feel that they may disrupt ward routine. You are likely to find ward staff more approachable and flexible than you think, provided the care of other patients is not jeopardised.

Hospices are especially useful for people whose dying is plagued by unpleasant symptoms such as pain or breathlessness. Also, staff can concentrate on the patient's total needs, without the distraction of operating lists or the pursuit of unlikely cures.

Two objections are sometimes made to hospice care. First, many hospices are religious foundations, and some people fear that they will find the spiritual climate oppressive. However, this rarely seems to be a problem in practice. Secondly, some people expect a hospice to be gloomy and forbidding. In fact, there usually seems to be a feeling of peaceful competence, often made livelier by staff children in playgroups.

Though hospice places are scarce in some areas, many hospices operate an outreach scheme, whose members visit patients in the community to provide specialised advice and care. You can find out about this from the Hospice Information Service.

# Relief for pain and other symptoms

If pain or other symptoms are distressing, the district nurse and the GP will be an important source of help, but they may need to supplement their knowledge and expertise by calling in the nearest hospice outreach team. The Hospice Information Service will tell you where this is. An outreach team can also be a great support to family and friends during the last illness and afterwards. If in-patient care eventually becomes necessary, families can be consoled by knowing that the decision to move the resident from the Home was made by people who know those involved and understand the situation. A short admission to hospice or hospital may help to get symptoms under control and enable the resident to remain in the Home thereafter.

# Help with nursing

District nurses from the primary health care team will come into the Home to assess the resident's needs and either provide care directly or train your staff to carry it out under their supervision. Mouth care and attention to pressure areas are especially important for terminally ill people, and you should make sure your staff know how to do these tasks properly. Pain relief is more effective if pain killers are given regularly to keep the pain away; check with the nurses about this, as the dying resident must not be forced to wait till convenient 'drug round' times.

# Talking with someone who is dying

Most – though not all – doctors try to tell their terminally ill patients as much about their illness as they are able to take in. A dying person may have been told everything, but have blocked it out during the denial stage. If you think your resident is ready to be told more, you should tell the GP. This will of course be much easier if you have built up a good relationship with the doctor, so that your judgement of the situation will be valued.

There may be times when you will want to opt for the easy way out by 'jollying along' a dying resident. For instance, if they say 'I'm not getting any better, in fact I seem worse', and you reply, 'Now cheer up – you'll be as right as rain by Easter', this makes their situation lonelier and more difficult, whilst an inarticulate but sympathetic grunt or repetition of what they said would allow them to continue to talk and be reassured about not being left alone.

Another difficulty may arise if relatives try to involve you in a conspiracy to keep the truth from the dying person. Try to help them with their own difficulties in facing up to the impending death; if necessary, arrange a meeting between the relatives, the GP and you to discuss the situation.

No one should have the impression that dealing with dying people involves learning the right thing to do, as there are no 'right' answers. What matters is the quality of your relationship with the person who is dying and how well you communicate your concern and common humanity. Listen hard to what the resident says, as sometimes their attitude may surprise you. While some 90 year olds are not at all ready to die, some younger residents may say they have had good lives but are tired and would like a long, long rest. People usually fear dying more than death; someone who wants to know exactly what will happen to them is not necessarily being morbid. They may want reassurance that they will not suffer unbearable pain or the distress of feeling suffocated, and that they will not be left to die alone. Very often, words are unimportant; listening and just being there are what really matter.

You may find it helpful to read an excellent book called *I Don't Know What to Say – how to help and support someone who is dying* (see p 275).

## What to do at the death bed

Someone who is dying should not be left alone. Relatives may be watching beside their elder, or a special friend may want to sit with them for a while. Staff should visit frequently to check whether anything is needed, and if no one else is present should stay with the dying person.

Remember that hearing is the last sense to be lost; even people who appear to be unconscious may be aware of what is said around them. Perhaps a priest or other minister of religion may be able to comfort the dying person or the family by prayer or other means. However, great sensitivity is required in this situation, as considerable distress may be caused, for instance, if Christian symbols and practices are used for someone of another faith. Get advice about this if you are unsure about the procedure for a resident from a different religious or ethnic group from your own. (Also see the Further Reading section of this book.)

The spiritual and emotional aspects of the situation need to be under-pinned with common sense. Relatives and friends watching beside a death bed need comfortable chairs; they may welcome a drink being brought into the room and perhaps a sandwich. They will also need access to a nearby lavatory.

Position the dying person however they seem most comfortable, but be prepared to turn them frequently. Give frequent drinks or ice to suck, and clean the mouth if necessary; provide food if it is asked for. Offer the commode or urinal frequently and continue with any medicines that are helping to keep the person comfortable; the doctor will be able to tell you which are unnecessary at this stage and can be stopped. You could also ask the doctor to prescribe further treatment if the resident seems dis-tressed by pain, cough or difficult breathing, or if noisy breathing is upsetting the relatives. If the dying person is conscious, ask if you can fetch anything for them, as devotional books or objects or the photograph of a loved one can be a great comfort. Encourage relatives and friends to help care for the dying person; if relatives and friends are present, try to make your own work as quiet and unobtrusive as possible.

An expected death is rarely gruesome – the person gradually stops breathing, and becomes pale and cold, quite peacefully. Those present should remove excess bedding, leaving just one pillow and a covering sheet. The body should be straightened with the arms by the sides, and heating in the room should be turned off. The eyelids should be gently shut, the mouth held closed by a pillow or book under the chin, and the doctor should be notified.

If the next of kin is not there you should let him or her know that the death has taken place. Some people advise making a brief phone call giving only the facts and a brief expression of sympathy, suggesting the relatives call back when they feel they want to talk for longer and can take in information. Family and friends may want to see the body to pay their last respects, and great distress can be caused if all is not as it should be. Details of last offices vary in different religions and cultures, so if neces-sary find out from a religious leader what you should do. (See also the Further Reading section of this book.) As a general rule, wearing dispos-able gloves, you should wash the person's face and hands, tidy their hair and put in their dentures, as this improves the facial appearance.

# Caring for other residents

Older people are not fragile blossoms but sound fruit; they do not need to be shielded from the facts of life or of death. Behaviour in the Home around the time of death should reflect this: you may need to tell the undertakers not to whisk the coffin out the back way, but to take it slowly out of the front door if this is what your residents prefer.

Residents should be informed when one of their number is terminally ill; they are likely to find evidence of good, dignified care reassuring rather than depressing. You should allow them to decide to what extent they wish to be involved each time a death occurs. They may want to sit with a dying friend, to visit the body to pay their last respects, to go to the funeral or to help organise a memorial service in the Home. However, any resident who prefers to ignore any or every death should be allowed to do so. You and your staff should be prepared for residents to show grief and also to talk about their own deaths in the week or so after a funeral in the Home; needless to say, such talk should not be discouraged as 'morbid', but regarded as a mature and sensible way of coping with reality.

# Organising the funeral

The funeral is usually arranged by a close relative of the dead person. Age Concern England produce a useful Factsheet on this subject. Residents who wish to do so should of course be encouraged to attend. Do not discourage them as a well-meaning but misguided attempt to stop them becoming upset. Religious services and family gatherings are important rites of passage that enable the survivors to adjust to the fact of death and to express their grief.

In British society a funeral service seems to help mourners most when it includes references to the dead person's life and personality. This is of course difficult for clergy to achieve if the deceased has not entered the church doors since their marriage 50 years ago. However, you may be able to pass on useful personal details and suggestions about favourite hymns or pieces of music that will help make the service more personal.

If you need to advise other residents about the rituals usually followed by a particular faith that is unfamiliar to you, get advice from someone who knows. For instance, Orthodox Jewish mourners sit 'shiva', a seven-day period of mourning in the home; visits from gentiles during this period are welcomed, though men should take along a hat to wear during prayers, while women, however liberated, should be prepared to be self-effacing.

You may find the book *Caring for Dying People of Different Faiths* useful (see p 275).

## The process of mourning

Immediately after the death, bereaved people are commonly numbed, and may even be surprised not to feel more sadness. They may behave like robots while performing the necessary duties of registering the death, arranging the funeral and so on. This stage usually lasts a few days, often until after the funeral, to be replaced by attacks of acute grief interrupting a constant feeling of sadness. These bouts are often brought on by chance reminders as, for instance, when a widow receives a letter addressed to 'Mr and Mrs'.

This stage of grieving feels very like fear or acute anxiety. Some mourners are unable to eat or sleep, and lose weight, though others grow fatter through 'comfort eating'. They may complain of palpitations, headaches and an upset stomach, and may be irritable and nervous. All these symptoms will be worse during grief attacks. Bereaved people are often unable to concentrate on anything and wander aimlessly indoors and out. They may constantly scan people's faces as though searching for the dead partner or friend.

A mourner may call aloud for the dead person, and think constantly about the time immediately before the death, saying, 'I go over that morning again and again'. Hallucinations of the dead person's presence are very common – for example, a widow may 'hear' her husband's key in the lock at his normal time of homecoming, or even his voice. Strangers in a crowd may be mistaken for the dead person and approached, with embarrassing results. Remember that behaviour like this is normal; if necessary, reassure mourners that they are not 'going mad'.

Gradually, attacks of grief occur less frequently, and bereaved people gradually start to enjoy life again. If they feel guilty about this, try to tell them that the dead person would not have wanted them to go on grieving for ever.

After some time – often a year or more in a close relationship – the survivors begin to put together a new life, and should be encouraged to do so. Eventually, reminders of the dead person are no longer painful and will evoke happy memories. Nevertheless, relapses of grief are to be expected at the anniversary of the death and at other significant times, such as Christmas and birthdays; they may also be stimulated by new losses.

## Supporting staff around a death

Though grieving may seem acceptable behaviour in a widow or widower, you should accept as normal similar behaviour in close friends of the dead person, or anyone to whom the loss is significant – including you and your staff. Some deaths will be more upsetting than others; staff members may be particularly affected when an unresolved personal grief is reactivated. This can happen when the circumstances or the people involved resemble the carer's own family background, or simply when the loss is recent and feelings are still raw. You should monitor such a situation closely and be prepared to rearrange the duty rota if this would allow the staff member to withdraw from an unbearably painful situation.

Sometimes those looking after older people can seem to become inappropriately casual about their deaths. This is neither healthy nor useful. It is most likely to happen when staff are not allowed to express their feelings, so you should be able to prevent it by making opportunities for distressing events to be tackled and wept over. There is no need for you to hide your sorrow about a death in the Home from the other residents. They may be comforted by realising how much you value them.

## Giving support after the funeral

This may be especially necessary for the surviving partner of a long-established couple. However, older people are also much distressed if a younger relative such as a child or grandchild dies before them.

Support for bereaved people often dwindles as relatives and friends return to their homes after the funeral, though mourners badly need a listening ear. Do not blot out their need to express grief by making continual neutral conversation, or by jollying them along. Do not feel guilty if something you say stimulates tears, or if you start crying – shared tears may do a lot to reduce feelings of isolation.

Sorrow will not be the only emotion a mourner experiences and needs to talk about; anger is very common. Carers and relatives may be 'blamed' for the death, and the mourner may also be angry with the dead person themselves, especially if the death was sudden and the deceased's affairs were not in order.

Feelings of guilt are also common. Mourners may feel guilty about real, imagined or magnified faults in the relationship that has ended, especially if there were disagreements during a long illness and the bereaved person felt irritated or now feels angry. Try to reassure mourners that they did all that was humanly possible in the circumstances, if this is true; if not, maintain a tactful silence.

Sometimes dead people are spoken about almost as saints, and 'shrines' are set up in their honour with photographs, flowers and candles. Resist the temptation to point out how far this rosy picture is from the truth; these feelings too must be allowed to run their course. Just occasionally, idealisation is used to cover anger that the mourner is unable to express; when you suspect this, try introducing a little reality into the situation.

It often seems to comfort the survivors if another person somewhere has benefited from their loss. The fact that someone else has received a transplanted organ, or that useful medical information has been gained from a post-mortem examination can help the bereaved person. Even the amount of memorial donations to a favourite charity provides comfort.

Well-intentioned friends often urge bereaved people to attend doctors' surgeries asking for 'something for their nerves'. In general this is unwise, as the suppressed grief will emerge later in one form or another, and may then be even more difficult to endure. Occasionally a mourner becomes exhausted, and then an occasional hypnotic to provide a restful night may be useful and harmless. If you are worried about the mourner's mental or physical health, consider getting in touch with the GP; if suicide is mentioned, do this without delay.

Some mourners benefit from bereavement counselling, and the local Age Concern or hospice will know what is available in your area. Organisations such as Cruse – Bereavement Care, the Lesbian and Gay Bereavement Project and the National Association of Widows may also be useful contacts.

# Bereaved people who are mentally frail

Grieving is difficult for people with dementia. They cannot remember the fact of the loss for more than a few minutes, they do not understand why the dead person is missing, but they know something is badly wrong. Staff distress is inevitable here: it can be unbearably poignant to see a puzzled older person endlessly watching or searching for someone they will never meet again.

The way to cope is to use the principles summarised on page 160. Never, ever, be tempted to tell the confused resident that the dead person is staying with friends, on holiday or will come round after tea. If they are clear-minded enough to absorb the information, remind them about the fact of the death, perhaps talking about the funeral or the large number of letters of sympathy that arrived. However, there is no need to confront someone who is too agitated and upset to absorb the information with the bald fact of the death. It is sensible then to assure the confused mourner that the dead person is 'quite all right now', try to calm them with a distracting cup of tea and save the reality orientation for a more lucid time.

Do allow the confused resident to talk about their loss, and help their memory with photographs and similar mementoes. It may help to remember with them the achievements of the dead person's life. Words are not always necessary, or adequate: it may be more helpful to respond to strong feelings silently. If you find the resident in tears, there may be no need to explore the situation: just sit beside them, squeeze their hand briefly and, if they seem to want to, let them hold on.

---

This chapter has been about the loss of another human being, but the other losses common in old age will be grieved for in the same way – when a pet dies, for instance, or when a part of the body is 'lost' following a stroke, a mastectomy or an amputation. Do not forget that everyone coming into residential care has been bereaved of a previous home, with all the memories it holds.

Grief is the price we have to pay for loving, committed relationships; mourning is sad, but it would be even sadder to have nothing and no one to mourn.

**KEY POINTS**

■ Dying people may pass back and forth between stages of denial, anger, withdrawal, regression and acceptance; staff who know to expect such feelings will find them easier to cope with.

■ You and the GP may wish to call on skilled help to relieve pain and other symptoms in a dying person. A hospice outreach team or specialist cancer nurses may be useful contacts.

■ Support your staff in talking honestly and humanely with dying residents.

■ Someone who is dying should not be left alone. Try to make them as comfortable as possible – physically, mentally and spiritually.

■ Take care to follow religious or ethnic customs; ask advice from appropriate religious or community leaders if necessary.

■ Deaths in the Home should not be hidden from other residents. Allow them to decide each time the extent to which they want to be involved.

■ It is natural for you, your staff and other residents to be affected by a death; arrange for outside support if necessary.

# 11 Getting Help from Other Agencies

The services provided by statutory and voluntary agencies can help to improve the quality of life of your residents. Remember that both the amount and type of help available may vary considerably around the country.

## CO-ORDINATING LOCAL SERVICES

As you will be dealing with a variety of people, it will help to brush up on your interpersonal skills. Make as many personal contacts as you can in your local health and social services, and find out and use the names of people you come across regularly. When others have been especially helpful, send a card at Christmas, or an invitation to a social event: people are more likely to put themselves to extra trouble when they feel their efforts are valued.

Try to remain polite and pleasant in your dealings with people providing services, even when they seem unhelpful and your problems are over-whelming. Though difficult, this is the best way to ensure that the vulnerable residents who depend on you receive the help they require.

# USING THE HEALTH SERVICE

## Primary health care team

This consists of a general practitioner, district nurses and perhaps a health visitor, community psychiatric nurse or others of the health workers described below.

## General practitioner

Residents of Homes, like everyone else, are entitled to choose their own GPs.

Make sure that residents are registered with a GP when they enter the Home. It may be possible for a newcomer to keep the GP they have already, but check with the resident that the doctor is aware of the change of address, and that it is within the practice catchment area. If this is not done, difficulties may arise if the resident needs to call the doctor out for a home visit. Allowing choice in this way obviously increases the number of doctors you and your staff have to work with, but you should not press residents to change doctors when they do not want to. When a new GP has to be found, the choice of doctor is of course up to the resident; you may, however, be asked for advice, and should be prepared with suggestions. If you need to, you can obtain a list of GPs from main post offices, public libraries, the local telephone book or directly from the Family Health Services Authority (FHSA), formerly the Family Practitioner Committee (FPC). The Community Health Council (CHC) (see below) can also help with addresses and with the administrative procedures used to find or change a GP.

Some family doctors are especially interested in older people and their medical problems; you could find out whether any GPs nearby have this special interest. It helps if the GP works as part of a primary health care team, at a health centre that offers a range of resources. The surgery premises should be easy for residents to get to independently, and the practice staff helpful.

Apart from attending to a resident's day-to-day health needs, the GP provides access to other medical services such as hospital specialists and can also refer patients for help from other members of the primary health care team.

## The GP's relationship with the residents

Encourage residents to deal directly with their doctors; if confidential information comes your way, be careful to keep it private. You may sometimes feel it would help if you knew more about a resident's medical condition, but if they wish to keep this information private, they have every right to do so. You may wonder whether you should confide your worries about a resident's health to a doctor, nurse or other health care professional without the resident's consent. This can be very difficult to decide. Mentally intact people have a right not to consult the doctor if they do not wish to do so. In such cases, you may try to persuade the sick resident to seek help, but have no right to over-ride their decision to manage unaided. At other times you may fear that the resident's judgement is so clouded by illness that they are unable to make sensible decisions. The best course then is to notify the doctor and explain the situation. The doctor can then decide what to do next, usually visiting the sick resident to make a skilled assessment of their health, especially the mental state.

It is best for residents who are able to do so to go to the surgery or health centre to see the doctor. Visiting doctors should usually see residents alone in the privacy of their own rooms. There are a few exceptions to this rule: for instance, the resident might ask you to stay to act as advocate or interpreter, or the doctor might need a chaperon. It may also be wise for someone – a relative, advocate or staff member – to stay with a mentally frail resident. However, this should not be done without giving the matter careful thought, and the confused resident should still be given the chance to talk to the doctor directly him- or herself.

When a number of frail residents are on one GP's list, the doctor may make regular visits at a pre-arranged time. This will enable you to explain how someone's health and independence are being maintained from day to day, and the doctor can alert you to warning signs or allay your unnecessary fears. Any decline in a resident's condition is more likely to be spotted early, and repeat prescriptions for drugs properly reassessed. Regular attendance at a Home helps the doctor too, as any non-urgent problems can often be held over until the next visit. You may be able to work with the doctor and avoid an upset for a resident by spotting a potential emergency; for instance, if a resident seems unwell before a long weekend or public holiday, you can make sure the doctor sees them beforehand rather than waiting to see what happens.

## The GP's duties

Patients have a right to see a doctor – not necessarily their own GP – at the surgery during surgery hours. People who have not made an appointment may be offered one at a later surgery. If they think their problem will not wait till then, they should say so, politely but firmly. Many practices keep a space in surgery appointment lists for genuine emergencies. However, to minimise disruption to other patients, those with urgent problems will have to see whichever doctor is available, and may have to wait to do so.

A GP is not obliged to make a home visit whenever asked to do so; the decision as to whether this is necessary is up to the doctor. If you think that a resident's condition warrants an early visit but the GP's receptionist seems reluctant to arrange this, ask when you can discuss the matter directly with the doctor. Be prepared to ring back at a time when the doctor is free to take such calls.

When telephoning the doctor in an emergency, try to have the reason for the call clear in your mind. There are three ways in which doctors help sick people: by working out what is wrong with them, by curing the illness or relieving its symptoms, and by telling patients and those around them what to expect to happen next. If the resident needs help in any of these ways, your call is justified.

Put out emergency calls between the hours of, say, midnight and 7.00am only if it is absolutely necessary to do so. Of course, illness, accident and mishap are no respecters of the clock or the calendar, and there is sometimes no alternative to asking for help in these unsocial hours. Doctors usually have to do a full day's work the day before and the day after a night on call. They will be more likely to respond quickly and cheerfully to an emergency call if they know that the person on the other end makes such calls only when absolutely necessary. While you should never take chances in a real emergency, you may be able to avoid the night hours. If someone seems unwell at 9.00pm, for instance, it is better to notify the doctor before he or she retires to bed rather than to wait and see what happens. In the same way it may be possible to keep a call until 7.00am rather than to put it out an hour or so earlier. Of course, you should always err on the side of caution: you are not expected to make medical decisions.

Make sure that you give adequate basic information as to who the patient is and where they are. At night it is a great help in finding an address if someone puts lights on at the front of the building.

No patient is automatically entitled to a second opinion from a hospital specialist unless the GP thinks it is necessary. There are two reasons for this: first, it is often difficult for a patient to understand on the basis of their symptoms which hospital doctor is required; without the GP's general medical knowledge, the patient may not be directed to the correct specialist, and treatment may be delayed. Secondly, a few people make repeated, unnecessary demands for referral. They may be suffering from depression, or have other social or psychological problems. The GP can make sure that they get appropriate help, rather than making a wearying and useless round of hospital specialists.

GPs now offer all patients over 75 years old an annual consultation, either at the surgery or at home (see p 61).

Practices now produce information leaflets describing the services they offer. You may like to collect these for you and your residents to refer to.

# Nurses

## District (or community) nurses

These visit residents in Homes to assess nursing needs, provide nursing care or give nursing guidance to staff. Homes should aim to look after sick residents in the same way that competent and caring relatives would do in their own homes. The responsibility for provision and oversight of nursing services rests with the district nurse, even if the head of the Home or another staff member holds a nursing qualification. However, the district nurse can delegate some aspects of care to a registered nurse employed in the Home and may also teach other staff how to undertake nursing procedures.

District nurses are usually attached to GP practices, so if several different doctors care for your residents, there are also likely to be a number of different district nurses in attendance on the Home.

## Practice nurses

Many doctors also employ practice nurses, who carry out a range of investigations and treatments. They often run preventative health care services such as screening clinics, and may help with weight control and stopping smoking. They may also monitor long-standing conditions such as high blood pressure and diabetes, dress wounds, give injections and syringe ears.

District and practice nurses will be likely to know which of the specialised nurses described below work in your area, and how you can reach them.

## Community psychiatric nurses (CPNs)

These have special qualifications in mental health nursing. They care for people of any age who have mental health problems, and also for confused older people. They are useful sources of advice on ways of coping with confused residents who wander, neglect themselves or show other sorts of challenging behaviour. If you have difficulty in getting medical help for someone who seems to have a psychiatric illness, it is sometimes useful to ask if a CPN can visit to assess the situation.

You may be able to get in touch with a CPN direct at the headquarters of a community mental health care team, or you may need to work through the GP. To find out what the arrangements are in your area, ask the GP's receptionist or practice manager, the district or practice nurse or the secretary of the local community health council.

## Continence advisers

These nurses are specially trained to help with faults of bladder or bowel function. They work in continence clinics in hospitals or health centres, but also visit patients.

The GP or practice nurse may know if there is a continence adviser working locally. You could also get in touch with the Continence Foundation, which has information about all services round the country.

Incontinence pads and pants may be available free or at low cost from the health authority, but sometimes the range is limited. The continence adviser or district nurse will be able to say whether something more suitable is available, or you could ask the Continence Foundation. The social services department may run an incontinence laundry service, and you may want to ask about this.

A Factsheet called 'Help with Incontinence' is available from Age Concern England (see p 282).

## Cancer nurses

These have special training in helping with symptom relief and also with the emotional needs of cancer sufferers and their families. The Macmillan Fund (National Society for Cancer Relief) and the Marie Curie Memorial Foundation both operate a district nursing service; the GP and district nurse have access to these. Also, your local hospice may have an out-reach team to look after people at home; the Hospice Information Service can provide further details.

## Stoma care nurses

These work in hospitals and in the community, helping patients to adjust to the change in their bodies and to cope with day-to-day care of the stoma. Residents who have had a colostomy or ileostomy for years may have lost contact with the stoma care nurse; the district nurse will know how to get in touch with one.

## Health visitors

These are nurses who have had an extra year's training in preventive medicine, psychology, public health and sociology. They will usually be part of the primary health care team based at the health centre or GP surgery.

'Geriatric health visitors', who specialise in the care of older people, are invaluable. They are trained to recognise the early signs of illness and the social circumstance that predispose to it, and are often involved in the Over-75 check. Health visitors should know the full range of health and social services available to your residents.

# Physiotherapists

Physiotherapists work in hospitals, including day hospitals, and increasingly in the community, often treating patients at home. Whether they will treat residents in your Home will depend on local policy. They specialise in movement and its disorders as well as helping people with chest disease or incontinence. Physiotherapists can help to strengthen weak muscles, loosen stiff joints and help people with disabling conditions such as stroke or Parkinson's disease to make the best use of their remaining abilities. They can also give carers practical advice on how to lift and handle a disabled person, and say which mobility aid will be most helpful (see pp 116–119).

NHS physiotherapy is sometimes in short supply. You can find out more about your local service by getting in touch with the local hospital or GP. It is possible to get treatment privately. It is wise for a resident considering this to ask the doctor if physiotherapy is likely to be helpful, and, if so, to write a referral letter. Suitable physiotherapists will be state registered and members of the Chartered Society of Physiotherapy, with the letters SRP, MCSP after their name.

# Dentists

Since October 1990, patients can register with a dentist for continuing care in the same way as with a GP. Dentists do not have to take on everyone who applies to them, and some older people have difficulty in finding a dentist who provides NHS care. They can ask for help from the Family Health Services Authority, the Community Health Council, the local branch of Age Concern or the district dental officers of the Community Dental Service, reached via the health authority.

If older people have difficulty in getting to the surgery, the dentist may visit them. The Community Dental Service may provide clinics and in some cases takes mobile caravans to rural areas. You can find out more from the Family Health Service Authority. Alternatively, it may be possible to arrange special transport to the surgery, for instance via Dial-a-Ride.

People who have registered with a dentist for continuing care will be able to get telephone advice in an emergency arising outside surgery hours, and if necessary will be given urgent treatment.

Further information can be found in the Factsheet 'Dental Care in Retirement' from Age Concern England.

## Chiropodists

These can diagnose and treat foot disorders, which are a common cause of mobility problems. It is especially important that people with diabetes get regular chiropody, preferably from someone with a special interest in this sort of work.

Chiropody is available on the NHS, and a doctor's referral letter is not always needed. The local authority may arrange through the health authority for a chiropodist to visit the Home, or your residents may be able to attend special chiropody clinics. In some areas, NHS chiropody is in short supply, and residents may decide to have private treatment; you may want to arrange for a private chiropodist to visit the Home. Health centre staff or the district nurse may be able to recommend someone suitable. (See also p 60.)

It is not always possible to see the chiropodist or foot care assistant often enough to keep the toenails properly cut, and your staff may have to perform some basic foot care. They should be shown how to do this by a qualified chiropodist, and such training may be available through the NHS chiropody service.

## Community Health Councils (CHCs)

Community Health Councils were introduced in the 1970s to bridge the gap between the organisations providing health services and the patients who used them. CHC members were supposed to keep the local NHS under review by visiting hospitals and clinics to see how services worked and then suggesting possible improvements. They were also expected to comment on how well health and social services worked together in 'grey areas', and to make sure that services corresponded to what was needed locally and roughly conformed to national norms.

Despite NHS changes that have affected their powers, CHCs remain an invaluable source of information as to what local health services are available and how best to use them. The Secretary and staff were in a good position to collate and pass on facts about unmet needs to organisations that could do something about them. They are still able to help with complaints about health services and the staff who operate them. This sort of work is often best done informally, but when a formal complaint is necessary, CHC staff can give it the best chance of success by making sure it passes through the proper channels in good time.

CHCs often have High Street premises and are usually open during office hours. Their meetings are open to the public, and the Secretary and staff are useful contacts.

Recent legislation has limited the role of CHCs to some extent. For instance, though a Regional Health Authority must consult the CHC on proposals to establish an NHS trust, once the trust has been set up it does not need to consult the CHC before altering service provision. The role of CHCs is now limited at meetings of health authorities and NHS trusts: members will not necessarily be supplied with the relevant papers beforehand, they may speak only if invited and may be excluded from non-public parts of meetings. These changes seem likely to make it more difficult for CHCs to fulfil their previous role in the long run, and health services are likely to become less responsive to those who use them.

# USING SOCIAL SERVICES

## Effects of community care legislation

The way in which social services departments work has always varied from one local authority to another. These differences have increased since recent legislation has been enacted. You will need to do your own research into local conditions, but you can find out more about the new legislation from Age Concern's publication *The Community Care Handbook* (see p 278); your local library or Town Hall will have information about the social services department.

The people and services described below usually come under the jurisdiction of the social services department, though the department may have arranged for some services to be provided by independent organisations. Some of your residents will have had their places purchased for them by the local authority. These local authorities will monitor the contract with your Home; you should let them know if the resident's needs change.

# Occupational therapists (OTs)

Occupational therapists help people to maintain independence and daily living skills. They visit people with an illness or disability to find out whether equipment such as walking aids or modified cutlery would help them, and, if so, to arrange for it to be provided. The OT can also suggest useful adaptations such as ramps for wheelchair access or extra hand-rails.

Unfortunately, in some areas there are very long waiting lists both for the OT's original assessment visit and, after it, for equipment to be provided or work to be done. Faced with these problems, you may need to help your residents to obtain what they need more quickly from another source. Disabled Living Centres can advise about what is available, and residents can make appointments to try out equipment. This is not on sale at centres, but can be ordered from the manufacturers. The Disabled Living Foundation in London can direct you to your nearest Disabled Living Centre.

Alternatively, some equipment can be bought at large pharmacists or by mail order.

In some areas OTs also visit Homes to help organise activities. You can find out about this and other aspects of the OT's work from the social services department.

# Speech and language therapists

Speech and language therapists assess, treat and advise people with difficulties in speaking, understanding and communicating. They will also help with swallowing problems. Although they may not be able to visit residents regularly, they will be able to help staff and relatives to help the resident to eat and communicate as well as possible. They will also know about any local support services and voluntary organisations for people with speech problems and their families; Action for Dysphasic Adults is one of these.

# Social workers

These can be reached at the area or team office of the social services department. Social workers may be available to advise and counsel residents, and to help with advocacy in difficult situations. A social worker will often help a prospective resident to decide to move into your Home, so you will need to liaise closely with him or her to ensure the move goes smoothly.

Residents who are admitted to hospital and who need help after discharge should have an assessment of their future care needs. This may be carried out by a hospital social worker.

# VOLUNTARY SOCIAL SERVICES

These vary in different areas, but where available give useful back-up to the services arranged by the local authority. They may include voluntary visiting services, a transport service such as Dial-a-Ride, recreational activities and holidays for older people.

Organisations for people with particular diseases (eg stroke, Parkinson's, Alzheimer's) or disabilities (eg deafness) may provide social contact for sufferers and practical help of various kinds. You can find out where they are from the local telephone book, or by getting in touch with the head office listed in the Useful Addresses section.

Voluntary organisations are now playing a more prominent role than ever before. Many are planning to provide service through contracts with local authorities under NHS and community care legislation. Your local branch of Age Concern, Citizens Advice Bureau or Council for Voluntary Service should be able to tell you about all the voluntary organisations in your area.

# HELP FROM RELIGIOUS ORGANISATIONS

Many people who have attended a place of worship regularly will want to go on being part of the congregation as they grow older. Try to help any resident who so wishes to continue attending their place of worship; it is often possible to find a member of the congregation who will provide transport there and back. Others return in old age to beliefs and practices that they may have abandoned for a while. Some have never joined any organised religion, or may continue to hold humanist or atheist beliefs.

Meeting the religious needs of these different groups while respecting the wishes of people with no interest in religion may be a difficult job. You may also have beliefs of your own, and it hardly needs saying that you must avoid imposing these on your residents. Whenever necessary, ask advice from community or religious leaders from ethnic or religious groups other than your own.

Clergy are as variable in their personalities and talents as any other group of people, and the enthusiasm of their congregations will also be unpredictable. What you can expect in terms of spiritual support and pastoral care for your residents will vary widely from place to place. It is a good idea for clergy to become sufficiently 'part of the scenery' around the Home so as not to be regarded with alarm as heralds of approaching death. House-bound people who are unable to attend their old place of worship may welcome a service being held in the Home, whatever the denomination.

Clergy and church officials may be reluctant to intrude on a Home if they fear that their visit will be unwelcome, and they may be unaware of the special needs of someone who has fallen sick or has been bereaved. It is therefore important for you to make tactful enquiries if you think a resident would like to see a minister of religion. You may also wish to try to involve a local church, synagogue, mosque or other religious organisations in the life of the Home by inviting a congregation to a social evening.

# Useful Addresses

**Action for Dysphasic Adults**
1 Royal Street
London SE1 7LL
Tel: 0171-261 9572

**Age Concern London**
54 Knatchbull Road
London SE5 9QY
Tel: 0171-737 3456

**Age Exchange Reminiscence Centre**
11 Blackheath Village
London SE3 9LA
Tel: 0181-318 9105/3504

**Alcohol Concern**
305 Gray's Inn Road
London W1X 8QF
Tel: 0171-833 3471

**Alcoholics Anonymous**
PO Box 1
Stonebow House
Stonebow
York YO1 2NJ
Tel: 01904 644026

**Alzheimer's Disease Society**
Gordon House
10 Greencoat Place
London SW1P 1PH
Tel: 0171-306 0606

**Arthritis and Rheumatism Council for Research**
PO Box 177
Chesterfield S41 7TQ
Tel: 01246 558033

**ASH (Action on Smoking and Health)**
109 Gloucester Place
London W1H 3PH
Tel: 0171-935 3519

**Association of Community Health Councils for England and Wales**
30 Drayton Park
London N5 1PB
Tel: 0171-609 8405

**Association of Teachers of Lipreading to Adults**
c/o S Gaston
3 Halons Road
Eltham
London SE9 5BS
Tel: 0181-850 4066

**BACUP**
3 Bath Place
Rivington Street
London EC2A 3JR
Tel: 0171-696 9003

**Breast Care and Mastectomy Association**
15–19 Britten Street
London SW3 3TZ
Tel: 0171-867 1103

**British Association for the Hard of Hearing**
7–11 Armstrong Road
London W3 7JL
Tel: 0181-743 1110

**British Association for Service to the Elderly (BASE)**
119 Hassell Street
Newcastle
Staffordshire ST5 1AX

**British Colostomy Association**
15 Station Road
Reading
Berkshire RG1 1LG
Tel: 01734 391537

**British Diabetic Association**
10 Queen Anne Street
London W1M 0BD
Tel: 0171-323 1531

**British Heart Foundation**
14 Fitzhardinge Street
London W1H 4DH
Tel: 0171-935 0185

**British Lung Foundation**
8 Peterborough Mews
London SW6 3BL
Tel: 0171-371 7704

**British Tinnitus Association**
105 Gower Street
London WC1E 6AH
Tel: 0171-387 8033

**British Wireless for the Blind Fund**
34 New Road
Chatham
Kent ME4 4QR
Tel: 01634 832501

**Broadcasting Support Services**
252 Western Avenue
London W3 6XJ
Tel: 0181-992 5522

**Cancerlink**
17 Britannia Street
London WC1X 9JN
Tel: 0171-833 2451

**Carers National Association**
20–25 Glasshouse Yard
London EC1A 4JS
Tel: 0171-490 8818

**Centre for Policy on Ageing**
25–31 Ironmonger Row
London EC1V 3QP
Tel: 0171-253 1787

**Centre for Sheltered Housing Studies**
Dog Lane Mews
Dog Lane
Bewdley
Worcs DY12 2EF
Tel: 01299 402722

**Continence Foundation**
2 Doughty Street
London WC1N 2PH
Tel: 0171-404 6875
Helpline: 0191-213 0050

**Counsel and Care**
Twyman House
16 Bonny Street
London NW1 9PG
Tel: 0171-485 1566

**Cruse – Bereavement Care**
Cruse House
126 Sheen Road
Richmond
Surrey TW9 1UR
Tel: 0181-940 4818

**Disabled Living Foundation**
380 Harrow Road
London W9 2HU
Tel: 0171-289 6111

**DSS Leaflets Unit**
PO Box 21
Stanmore
Middlesex HA7 1AY

**Elderly Accommodation Counsel**
46A Chiswick High Road
London W4 1SZ
Tel: 0181-742 1182
    0181-995 8320

**EXTEND (Exercise Training for the Elderly and Disabled)**
1A North Street
Sheringham
Norfolk NR26 8LG
Tel: 01263 822479/824355

**Health Education Authority**
Hamilton House
Mabledon Place
London WC1H 9TX
Tel: 0171-383 3833

**Help the Aged**
16–18 St James's Walk
London EC1R 0BE
Tel: 0171-253 0253

**Hospice Information Service**
St Christopher's Hospice
51 Lawrie Park Road
London SE26 6DZ
Tel: 0181-778 9252

**Keep Fit Association**
Francis House
Francis Street
London SW1P 1DE
Tel: 0171-233 8898

**Lesbian and Gay Bereavement Project**
Vaughan M Williams Centre
Colindale Hospital
Colindale Avenue
London NW9 5GH
Tel: 0181-200 0511

**Marie Curie Memorial Foundation**
28 Belgrave Square
London SW1X 8QG
Tel: 0171-235 3325

**Medic Alert Foundation**
12 Bridge Wharf
156 Caledonian Road
London N1 9UU
Tel: 0171-833 3034

**National Association of Widows**
54–57 Allison Street
Digbeth
Bimingham B5 5TH

Tel: 0121-643 8348

**National Council for Hospice and Specialist Palliative Care Services**
59 Bryanston Street
Digbeth
London W1A 2AZ

Tel: 0171-611 1153/1216/1225

**National Library for the Blind**
Cromwell Road
Bredbury
Stockport SK6 2SG

Tel: 0161-494 0217

**National Society for Cancer Relief (Macmillan Fund)**
Anchor House
15 Britten Street
London SW3 3TZ

Tel: 0171-351 7811

**Parkinson's Disease Society**
22 Upper Woburn Place
London WC1H 0RA

Tel: 0171-383 3513

**Partially Sighted Society**
Low Vision Adviser
62 Salusbury Road
London NW6 6NS

Tel: 0171-372 1551

**Relatives Association**
5 Tavistock Place
London WC1H 9SS

Tel: 0171-916 6055

**Royal College of Psychiatrists**
17 Belgrave Square
London SW1X 8PG

Tel: 0171-235 2351

**Royal National Institute for the Blind (RNIB)**
224 Great Portland Street
London W1N 6AA

Tel: 0171-388 1266

**Royal National Institute for Deaf People (RNID)**
105 Gower Street
London WC1E 6AH

Tel: 0171-387 8033

**SPOD (Association to Aid the Sexual and Personal Relationships of People with a Disability)**
286 Camden Road
London N7 0BJ

Tel: 0171-607 8851

**Stroke Association**
CHSA House
123–127 Whitecross Street
London EC1Y 8JJ

Tel: 0171-289 6111

**Talking Book Library**
*see* Royal National Institute for the Blind

**Talking Newspaper Association**
National Recording Centre
Heathfield
East Sussex TN21 8DB

Tel: 01435 866102

**Terrence Higgins Trust**
52–54 Gray's Inn Road
London WC1X 8JU
Tel: 0171-831 0330
Helpline: 0171-242 1010
12.00 noon–10.00 pm

**Winslow**
Telford Road
Bicester
Oxon OX6 0TS
Tel: 01869 244733

**Women's Nationwide Cancer Control Campaign**
128–130 Curtain Road
London EC2A 3AR
Tel: 0171-729 1735
Helpline: 0171-729 2229

# Further Reading

You can ask for books produced by commercial publishers at your local bookshop or library. Books or leaflets produced by national organisations can be obtained from the addresses on pages 267–271. When a leaflet is free, it is wise to send a large sae or label with your request.

## Good health in later life

*Keeping Well – A guide to health in retirement* (1991) Anne Roberts. Faber & Faber, London. Obtainable from Centre for Sheltered Housing Studies.

## Good eating

*Eat Well, Stay Well – Healthy eating for people over 60* and *Eat Well, Stay Well for Afro-Caribbean Pensioners.* Available from Age Concern Greater London.

## Sensible drinking

*Alcohol and Older People – Safer drinking for the over-60s.* Available from Alcohol Concern or Age Concern England.

## Smoking

'Give Up' – free from ASH; for a publications list, write to the address on page 267.

*Stopping Smoking Made Easier.* Free from Health Education Authority.

# Exercise

*The Magic of Movement – A tonic for older people* (1988) Laura Mitchell, Age Concern England.

# Sex, loving and relationships

*Living, Loving and Ageing – Sexual and personal relationships in later life* (1989) Wendy Greengross and Sally Greengross, Age Concern England.

Various SPOD publications, including *Sexuality and the Physically Disabled – An introduction for counsellors.* Write to the address on p 270 for a publications list.

*Loneliness – How to overcome it* (1988) Val Marriot and Terry Timblick, Age Concern England.

# Body maintenance

*The Foot Care Book – an A–Z of fitter feet* (1988) Judith Kemp, Age Concern England.

Leaflets, including 'Cervical Smear Test: when did you have your last test?' and 'Everyone's Having the Smear Test' from Women's Nationwide Cancer Control Campaign.

# Common illnesses in later life

Various books and leaflets by appropriate organisations, such as Stroke Association, Parkinson's Disease Society, BACUP, etc. Write for publications list to appropriate addresses on pages 267–271.

# The eyes and sight problems

'All about Glaucoma'; 'All about Macular Degeneration'; 'All about Diabetic Retinopathy'; 'All about Cataracts'. Free leaflets from RNIB: write for a publications list.

*In Touch Handbook 1994–95.* From Broadcasting Support Services.

*Learning to Live with It – Ageing maculopathy* and *Coping with Sight Loss at 80 plus.* Among other 'In Touch' Care Guides, from Broadcasting Support Services.

## The ears and hearing impairment

'Understanding Hearing Aids'; 'Installation Guidelines for Induction Loops in Public Places'; 'Questions about Tinnitus'; 'A Layman's Guide to Tinnitus and How to Live with It'. All available from RNID.

## Difficulties with continence

*In Control – Help with incontinence* (1990) Penny Mares, Age Concern England

Factsheet 23 'Help with Incontinence'. From Age Concern England.

## Depression

'Depression in the Elderly' and other literature in the Defeat Depression campaign. From Royal College of Psychiatrists.

## Confusion and dementia

'Caring for the Person with Dementia'; 'Advice Sheets' and 'Information Sheets'. Available from the Alzheimer's Disease Society: write for a publications list.

*Aggression; Wandering; Screaming and Shouting; Inappropriate Urination.* All by Graham Stoke, Winslow Press, London.

*Dementia and Mental Illness in Older People*, 2nd edition (1993) Elaine Murphy, Papermac, London.

*The 36-hour Day – A family guide to caring at home for people with Alzheimer's disease and other confusional illnesses* (1993) Nancy L Mace and Peter V Rabins, Age Concern England.

*Failure-free Activities for the Alzheimer's Patient – A guidebook for care givers and families* (1992) Carmel Sheridan, Macmillan, Basingstoke and London.

*Let's Go Wheelies! Ill conceived behaviour among staff caring for people with dementia* (1992) Brian Lodge, British Association for Service to the Elderly.

*Standards for the Residential Care of Older People with Mental Disorders* (1993) Social Services Inspectorate, HMSO, London

# Medicines

*Administration and Control of Medicines in Residential and Children's Homes* (1994) Royal Pharmaceutical Society of Great Britain.

*Code of Practice for the Safe Use and Disposal of Sharps*, British Medical Association, London.

*Infection Control: A community perspective* (1994) Infection Control Nurses Association. Available from Daniels Publishing, Cambridge.

*Joint Guidelines for the Use of Medicines in Residential Homes*, Royal Pharmaceutical Society of Great Britain and Age Concern England.

*Know Your Medicines* (1991) Pat Blair, Age Concern England.

# Looking after dying people

*I Don't Know What to Say – How to help and support someone who is dying* (1988) Dr Rob Buckman, Papermac, London.

*Caring for Dying People of Different Faiths* (1987) Julia Neuberger, Austen Cornish. From bookshops and libraries.

# Ethnic elders

*Multicultural Health Care and Rehabilitation of Older People* (1991) Amanda Squires (ed), Edward Arnold, London.

# Rights and Risk-taking

*Your Rights* (published annually) Sally West, Age Concern England.

*Rights and Risk*, Alison J Norman. A discussion document on Civil Liberty in Old Age. From Centre for Policy on Ageing.

*Living Dangerously – Risk taking, safety and older people*, Deirdre Wynne-Harley. From Centre for Policy on Ageing.

*Speak Up for Yourself – Putting advocacy into practice.* A guide available from Age Concern England.

*The Law and Vulnerable Elderly People* (1986) Sally Greengross (ed), Age Concern England.

*The Right to Take Risks.* Available from Counsel and Care.

## General

*Home Life – A code of practice for residential care*, Centre for Policy on Ageing. Available from Bailey Bros and Swinfen Ltd, Warner House, Folkestone, Kent CT19 6PH.

*Homework: Meeting the needs of elderly people in residential homes* (1988) Judith Hodgkinson, Centre for Policy on Ageing.

# About Age Concern

*Health Care in Residential Homes* is one of a wide range of publications produced by Age Concern England, the National Council on Ageing. Age Concern England is actively engaged in training, information provision, fundraising and campaigning for retired people and those who work with them, and also in the provision of products and services such as insurance for older people.

A network of over 1,400 local Age Concern groups, with the support of around 250,000 volunteers, aims to improve the quality of life for older people and develop services appropriate to local needs and resources. These include advice and information, day care, visiting services, transport schemes, clubs, and specialist facilities for older people who are physically and mentally frail.

Age Concern England is a registered charity dependent on public support for the continuation and development of its work.

**Age Concern England**
1268 London Road
London SW16 4ER
Tel: 0181-679 8000

**Age Concern Scotland**
113 Rose Street
Edinburgh EH2 3DT
Tel: 0131-220 3345

**Age Concern Cymru**
4th Floor
1 Cathedral Road
Cardiff CF1 9SD
Tel: 01222 371566

**Age Concern Northern Ireland**
3 Lower Crescent
Belfast BT7 1NR
Tel: 01232 245729

# Publications from ◆A◆C◆E◆ Books

A wide range of titles is published by Age Concern England under the ACE Books imprint.

## Health and care

### Taking Good Care: A handbook for care assistants
*Jenyth Worsley*
Written for all those concerned with caring for older people, this book covers such vital issues as communication skills, the medical and social problems encountered by carers, the role of the assistant, the resident's viewpoint, and activities and group work.
**£6.95    0–86242–072–5**

### Good Care Management: A guide to setting up and managing a residential home
*Jenyth Worsley*
This companion volume to *Taking Good Care* has been written for care home proprietors and managers, present and prospective. Topics covered include setting up a home, contracts, budgetary planning, staff management and training, the management of care and quality control.
**£9.95    0–86242–104–7**

### The Community Care Handbook – New edition
*Barbara Meredith*
The delivery of care in the community has changed dramatically as a result of recent legislation, and continues to evolve. Written by one of the country's foremost experts, this book explains in practical terms why the reforms were necessary, what they are, how they operate and whom they affect.
**£12.95    0–86242–171–3**

## Expanding Care: A practical guide to diversification for care homes
*Jenyth Worsley*

The business repercussions resulting from the introduction of the new community care system have led many care homes to examine the opportunities to diversify their activities. This handbook outlines some of the options – including the provision of domiciliary, day and respite care – and offers advice on assessing local needs and marketing and tendering, and explores the practical arrangements surrounding implementation.

£14.95   0–86242–154–3

## CareFully: A guide for home care assistants
*Lesley Bell*

Recent legislation places increasing emphasis on the delivery of care to older people in their own homes, thereby underlining the crucial role of home care assistants. This accessible guide provides practical advice on the day-to-day tasks assistants encounter and addresses such issues as legal responsibilities and emotional involvement.

£9.95   0–86242–129–2

## Caring in a Crisis: Caring for Someone Who is Dying
*Penny Mares*

Confronting the knowledge that a loved one is going to die soon is always a moment of crisis. And the pain of the news can be compounded by the need to take responsibility for the care and support given in the last months and weeks. This book attempts to help readers cope with their emotions, identify the needs which the situation creates and make the practical arrangements necessary to ensure that the passage through the period is as smooth as possible.

£6.95   0–86242–158–6

## Reminiscence and Recall: A guide to good practice
*Faith Gibson*

Reminiscence work is acknowledged as a successful way of improving communication with older people. This new guide provides practical advice on planning and running reminiscence activity in a residential or day care setting and examines suitable approaches for people with particular conditions.

£9.95   0–86242–142–X

### Dementia Care: A handbook for residential and day care
*Alan Chapman, Alan Jacques and Mary Marshall*
The number of dementia sufferers requiring care is increasing continuously. Written to complement *Taking Good Care*, this practical guide for professional carers offers an understanding of the condition and provides advice on such issues as daily care, health maintenance, home design and staffing strategies.

£9.95    0–86242–128–4

## Money matters

### Your Rights
*Sally West*
A highly acclaimed annual guide to the State benefits available to older people. Contains current information on Income Support, Housing Benefit and retirement pensions, among other matters, and provides advice on how to claim them.

Further information on application

### Managing Other People's Money
*Penny Letts*
The management of money and property is usually a personal and private matter. However, there may come a time when someone else has to take over on either a temporary or a permanent basis. This book looks at the circumstances in which such a need could arise and provides a step-by-step guide to the arrangements that have to be made.

£5.95    0–86242–090–3

## Policy

### Age: The unrecognised discrimination
*Edited by Evelyn McEwen*
Comprising a series of discursive essays by leading specialists on evidence of age discrimination in British society today, including the fields of employment, health care, leisure and the voluntary sector, this book is an important contribution to the growing debate.

£9.95    0–86242–094–6

### The Law and Vulnerable Elderly People
*Edited by Sally Greengross*

This report raises fundamental questions about the way society views and treats older people. The proposals put forward seek to enhance the self-determination and autonomy of vulnerable old people while ensuring that those who are physically or mentally frail are better protected in the future.

£6.50    0–86242–050–4

---

If you would like to order any of these titles, please write to the address below, enclosing a cheque or money order for the appropriate amount made payable to Age Concern England. Credit card orders may be made on 0181-679 8000.

**Publications Unit**
Age Concern England
PO Box 9
London SW16 4EX

# Factsheets from Age Concern

Age Concern England produces over 30 factsheets on a variety of subjects. Among these the following titles may be of interest to readers of this book:

**Factsheet 5** *Dental care in retirement*

**Factsheet 23** *Help with incontinence*

**Factsheet 32** *Disability and ageing: your rights to social services*

## To order factsheets

Single copies are available free on receipt of a 9″ × 6″ sae. If you require a selection of factsheets or multiple copies totalling more than five, charges will be given on request.

A complete set of factsheets is available in a ring binder at the current cost of £34, which includes the first year's subscription. The current cost for annual subscription for subsequent years is £14. There are different rates of subscription for people living outside the UK.

---

For further information, or to order factsheets, write to:

**Information and Policy Department**
Age Concern England
1268 London Road
London SW16 4ER

---

# Index